EVERYMAN'S LIBRARY

481

PHILOSOPHY & THEOLOGY

Everyman, I will go with thee, and be thy guide,
In thy most need to go by thy side

SPINOZA, BARUCH, born at Amsterdam in 1632 of an Iberian-Jewish family and naturalized as a Dutchman. Excommunicated for heresy on expressing sympathy with Descartes in 1656, and changed his name to Benedictus de Spinoza. Earned his living grinding optical lenses. Died at Amsterdam in 1677.

SPINOZA'S ETHICS

AND DE INTELLECTUS EMENDATIONE

TRANSLATED BY
ANDREW BOYLE

INTRODUCTION BY
T. S. GREGORY, M.A.

LONDON J. M. DENT & SONS LTD
NEW YORK E. P. DUTTON & CO INC

INTRODUCTION

'THE popular philosophy starts from creatures: Descartes starts from mind: I start from God.' These were Spinoza's words reported to Leibniz. Baruch Spinoza was a Jew. His mother's name was Hannah Deborah. He was educated at the Jewish College in Amsterdam where he was born. Excommunicated from the synagogue, he settled among a sect of Anabaptist mystics, who like himself were victims of persecution and students of Descartes. A Jew, an exile, a mystic, and a philosopher, he ground and polished lenses for a living, refused a fortune, and declined a dignified appointment as professor of Heidelberg: he had some devoted friends and many distinguished correspondents and acquaintances. He died of consumption at the age of forty-four.

First and last and always he is a Jew. The Englishman's most accessible introduction to the *Ethics*, his confession of faith, is the Old Testament, in which it is written as follows:

> In the beginning, God created the heaven and the earth·
> And the earth was without form and void: and darkness was upon the face of the deep. And the spirit of God moved upon the face of the waters. And God said . . . and there was.
>
> . . . And Moses said unto God, Behold when I come unto the children of Israel and shall say unto them, the God of your fathers hath sent me unto you, and they shall say unto me, What is his name? What shall I say unto them?
>
> And God said unto Moses, I AM THAT I AM: and he said, Thus shalt thou say unto the children of Israel, I AM hath sent me unto you.
>
> . . . Hear, O Israel: the Lord our God, the Lord is One. And thou shalt love the Lord thy God with all thine heart, and with all thy soul, and with all thy might.
>
> . . . Thou hast beset me behind and before, and laid thine hand upon me. Such knowledge is too wonderful for me: it is high, I cannot attain unto it. Whither shall I go from

thy spirit? Or whither shall I flee from thy presence? If I ascend up into heaven, thou art there. If I make my bed in hell, behold thou art there. If I take the wings of the morning and dwell in the uttermost parts of the sea, even there shall thy hand lead me and thy right hand shall hold me.

This last is the song of an exile, such as Spinoza was, not only as excommunicate from the synagogue, but first as a member of it and a child of Abram whose vocation had been, Get thee out of thy country and from thy kindred and from thy father's house. Spinoza was a Marrano, born of a sect of Spanish Jews, who, forced into Christian baptism, had maintained their faith and practice in secret among the Gentiles. Exiled from his exiled people, Spinoza learned Gentile speech and expounded Descartes, but he was not a Cartesian. His reason for 'demonstrating ethics in geometric order' was profound and theological. It was also derived from his experience. He had pitched and struck his tent in many places and was not contained in any. He was not, like Leibniz, a local resident surveying the universe with domestic prudence. He had no domicile but God. The things he had to say were not idiomatic but universal, and universal by force not merely of logic and method, but of inheritance and circumstance. 'I affirm with Paul,' he said, 'that all things are in God, herein agreeing . . . with all the ancient philosophers and perhaps even with all the ancient Hebrews. Those who think that the argument of the Tractatus rests on the identification of God with nature, taking nature in the sense of a certain mass of corporeal matter, are entirely wrong.'

Yes, indeed! Yet this was the common sense of the word nature, as an anthropomorphic image was a common interpretation of the word God. Even now, so clear an exponent as Mr Hampshire may be confused by Spinoza's simplicity. 'The notion of a Creator distinct from his creation,' says Mr Hampshire, 'contains an evident contradiction, involving as it must the conception of two substances, one the cause of the other.' And so it must if by Creator and creation we mean what these words meant in the 'vulgus philosophicum' and at the same time adopt Spinoza's definition of substance. But in the scholastic philosophy which spoke of a transcendent creator there was no limit to the number of substances, and in Spinoza's doctrine where there is but one Substance the distinction between Substance and mode is as absolute as the distinction between God and creatures in Jewish or Christian orthodoxy. The 'evident contradiction' comes like most contradictions of confusing different languages.

Again it is by no means safe to translate Spinoza's doctrine as Professor Roth does into such forthright English as the following: 'Divine and natural forces are one. It follows that the order of nature of which man is a part is the order of God, and that its fixed and eternal decrees are the decrees of God. It is no use turning to God by way of appeal against Nature. God *is* Nature.' Amos or the author of the Book of Job would have understood these words, but in modern English their *prima facie* meaning is pantheism or atheism. Pantheism, to be sure, is a mere term of abuse, for a language trained like English in the service of the God of the Hebrews for a thousand years cannot find or make sense in the proposition that God is everything. But atheism, one of the most severe and subtle of world religions, has often used such language. 'A rumour gained currency,' wrote Spinoza, 'that I had in the press a book on God in which I was trying to prove that God does not exist. The story was generally believed.' The belief endured. 'The fundamental principle of the atheism of Spinoza,' said David Hume, 'is the doctrine of the simplicity of the universe and the unity of that substance in which he supposes both thought and matter to inhere.' Hume then summarizes what he takes to be Spinoza's one-substance theory as if Spinoza thought in eighteenth-century English of what an English empiricist would mean by such words as 'substance' and 'universe.' And indeed—*Deus sive Natura*—if God is Nature why not forget the tremendous word so often, so cruelly mishandled, and deal henceforth with Nature in which Homer and Aristotle, Shakespeare and Newton, and for that matter all our appetites and misfortunes have made us at home.

In fact, however, Spinoza's *Ethics* is the voice of a mystical devotion so relentless, a sanctity so pure, that such misconception of it serves only to reveal the scope of its *amor intellectualis Dei,* as if one should complain that the sky was empty because it was cloudless. Most Gentiles demand some concession to the ancient gods, some particular eidolon or image. Their mixed and disillusioned humanity needs impressions and ideas of great variety and strength. They must be able to accuse their faith and to be accused by it, to feel that it is something odd and alien inciting them to conversion and reform. But to understand the *Ethics* it is necessary first to realize that Spinoza believed in God and loved God in unperturbed singleness of life, and that this book was written not as instruction or apology but as prayer. *Nihil in sensu quod non prius in Deo.* That is why the book is or seeks to be tautological. It is Spinoza's apprehension of the simple and simultaneous.

The key to his language is the formula, esse = agere, to be is to act. God is Pure Act. The actual is divine. Whereas in common speech, the word God ranks as a noun so that theologians will make Him the subject or object of quite ordinary predicates with astonishing facility, Spinoza thinks of God rather as a verb and of all existent things as modes of this activity. The world is not a collection of things but a conflagration of Act whose innumerable flames are but one fire. With this Actual theology we shall avoid the more persistent misjudgments of his ethical doctrine. To begin with, we shall recognize that it is ethics not metaphysics. We shall see that this ethical doctrine is religious, that it is concerned with purification and with what it means to be pure in heart. It is of the essence of such a work not to describe this purity but to be pure: its method and matter are one and the same. Spinoza's doctrine of God and ethical intention imply his 'geometric order' and equally refuse empirical description. They give no hostages to what St Paul called the 'mind of the flesh'; they abhor nouns and nominal thinking. The strength of an ethical geometry lies not in its cogency of reason but in the integrity of its liturgical pattern. Spinoza does not set himself like Aquinas to meet and answer objections; he expresses without distraction a whole insight, an absolute certainty, so whole and absolute that they are not his own or any man's. We must begin at the beginning. In the beginning is God.

Normally we think with names, for a name is the eldest form of abstraction. It reduces thinking to a routine of classification and distinguishes one thing from another on the basis of a pre-established harmony. Thus a nominal philosophy beholds a world of monads, of wholly objective objects, and as Leibniz says: 'C'est justement par ces Monades que le Spinozisme est détruit.' But there is no Spinozism. Spinoza refuses abstraction. It was his paradox. All meaning is what God means and God is actual. Now, the cosmic liturgy would be well enough as a spectacle to be watched at a distance, and the name-language of ordinary speech makes us spectators rather than players. It gives us 'extrinsic denominations, relations, and circumstances which are far removed from the inmost essences of things.' We can see from our enclosure without sharing the action. Thus in a mood of curious expectancy the spectator may picture his mind as a blank sheet of paper, or perhaps even as an empty warehouse waiting to be 'furnished,' as Locke puts it, with experience. 'The next thing to be considered,' says Locke, 'is how bodies produce ideas in us; and that is manifestly by impulse, the only way which we can conceive bodies to operate in,' and 'it is evident that some motion must be thence continued by our nerves or animal spirits, by some parts of our bodies, to the brain or the seat of sensation, there to produce in our minds the particular ideas we have of them.' Evident indeed! We watch the furniture carried into the warehouse. But what is evident? Why, that if you push things, they are pushed, that if you write on paper, there will be writing on it!

This naïve empiricism, however, served the purpose of its invention, to save the thinker's integrity by keeping him separate from his thoughts. It committed him to nothing, commanded him not at all, left him free to make such contract as he pleased, and gave him at least an illusion of being master of his soul and his property. He was greater than his thoughts, greater than the events that 'produced them in his mind.' Such was the profound conviction of liberal Calvinism which encouraged Locke to write his *Essay* and constrained Spinoza to withhold his *Ethics* from publication. And so, like the great houses of Amsterdam, God and the universe are built to the specification of my necessities, interests, and uses. Indeed the most significant name of Godhead is 'Author of my being.' 'From these premises it follows,' says Spinoza, 'that men think themselves free inasmuch as they are conscious of their volitions and desires and, as they are ignorant of the causes by which they are led to wish and desire, they do not even dream that these causes exist. It follows that men do all things with an end in view, that is they seek what is useful. . . . They are bound to conclude on the analogy of the means which they are in the habit of providing for themselves, that there exists some ruler or rulers of nature endowed with human liberty who provided everything for them and made all things for their especial benefit.'

This utilitarian structure Spinoza rejects as the prophets denounced idolatry. We are not names but acts, not spectators but part of the game, and we exist as we play it. We do not think from noun to noun forging a chain of logical or mechanical connections between each. Nor are we blank entities waiting to be furnished, nor self-contained objects that collide with one another. We are acts of God or modes of an eternal intellection whose activity knows no limit. We start from *Causa sui* whose definition is its existence— I AM THAT I AM—from Substance which is in itself and is conceived through itself from Free Being which exists because it exists and acts as it acts because it is what it is. Such definitions are obviously not the datum of a philosophical inquiry, but the terminus of a religious search. They mean God or nothing, and nothing but God. No philosopher can begin from the postulate that the matter of his inquiry cannot be conceived except through itself. If Spinoza does not start from creatures, neither does he start from mind. This is the language of the *via remotionis* travelled by mystics in faith which is 'darkness of the understanding,' for the absolute good, as Plotinus reminds us, cannot be spoken or written. 'Thou shalt not make unto thyself the likeness of any form,' says the God of Sinai.

Like the tribes in the wilderness or exiles by the rivers of Babylon, like Job listening to the whirlwind or Elijah to the stillness or Jacob wrestling with the Unseen, Spinoza reached the quietus of empirical reason after experience had convinced him that common occurrences are vain and futile. 'I at length determined to search out whether there were not something truly good and communicable to man by which his spirit might be affected to the exclusion of all other things.'

A strange search it seems until we recognize that it is the aspiration of a religious:

> Whom have I in heaven but thee?
> And there is none upon earth that I desire beside thee.

This 'exclusion of all else' is the definition of his people's exodus and exile, for their God is a jealous God. 'Ye have seen what I did to the Egyptians and how I bare you on eagles' wings and brought you unto myself.' Experience of the Hebrew, vigil of the 'patient eremite,' but also grace of the martyr, and from his childhood Spinoza remembered how 'Juda, surnamed the Believer, in the midst of the flames, when he was thought already to be dead, began to sing the psalm, To thee O God, do I lift up my soul.'

Exile, martyrdom, oppression, the external circumstance of sacred history were also the present and aggressive condition of contemporary Europe. The Scriptures, as Spinoza translated them, commented on the visible world as present not past. 'Hear ye indeed but understand not. . . . Until the cities be wasted without inhabitant and the houses without man.' Prophetic denunciations of human stupidity are never out of date; they were never more apposite than in Spinoza's Europe, wasted as no civilization had ever been wasted by perverse and 'inadequate ideas.' Such remedies as found favour with the prudent appeared rather to fix a norm of war than to propose reconciliation. God had become a name of carnage, theology a permanent controversy, glory was arrogance, and faith persecution. Where every formulary was a *casus belli*, every cause was a contention and every reform an injustice. The industrious optimism with which Leibniz prescribed for this state of things reads like the prattle of Job's friends. There is a bland and virtuous frivolity about his endeavour to turn this world into a conversation of enlightened and princely souls, the more frivolous as he was by no means unaware of the disorder. 'They love the present confusion,' he wrote of his countrymen, 'in which everyone is free to create factions, to impede his opponent, to elude judgment and the law, to fasten himself upon his friends, and to live irresponsibly in whatever manner he likes best. Common people fear oppression; the mighty fear curtailment of their limitless power, for in fact they recognize no sovereign.' A description without a diagnosis. The fault, as Spinoza recognized, lay not in events or creatures, but in the mind, that is in the way people think or fail to think, and in their notion of what thinking is, when, for example, like Descartes, they separate will from intellect, and look at things as external causes. The whole perplexity of religious hate and dynastic ambition springs from this nominal trick of looking as spectators at things from the outside and seeing therefore only a succession of casual and unnecessary pheno- mena. Passions are a reaction to this 'external' circum- stance; they are linked to the 'thought of some external cause' and supervene where judgment is suspended and 'necessity' and the 'mind which apprehends it' are obscured. We hate what we think need not happen; our wrath reacts to what seems a casual and contingent interruption of being. Disentangle emotion from this 'external cause' and 'unite it with other thoughts'; revive, in other words, the actual understanding and 'love and hatred towards the external cause as well as waverings of the mind which arise from these emotions are extinguished.'

This was an ancient wisdom. 'Wars, factions, and fight- ing,' said Socrates as he looked forward from his last hour, 'have no other origin than this same body and its lusts. . . . We must set the soul free from it; we must behold things as they are. And having thus got rid of the foolishness of the body, we shall be pure and hold converse with the pure, and shall in our own selves have complete knowledge of the In- corruptible which is, I take it, no other than very truth.' Spinoza's paradox, in the eyes of his fellows, was that we free the soul from the body, we get rid of the body's foolish- ness by accepting it, by understanding it. From the lowest level of awareness given by casual experience (*experientia vaga*) the active mind ascends to a rational understanding and then to intuitive science or insight not by despising and rejecting the casual experience but by integrating it and healing the casualty. 'Will is a general being or idea whereby we explain all individual volitions.' This doctrine chal- lenged the accepted 'correspondence theory of truth' which defined truth not as 'complete knowledge of the Incorrupt- ible,' or 'converse of the pure with the pure,' but as 'con- formity and correspondence of thing and intellect.' A picture not a definition, and not intended as an answer to any searching questions, this 'correspondence' merely stated the fact. It was a theory for painters like Vermeer, for poets and framers of poetic diction discovering 'obscured likenesses' and expressing human emotions in images and similitudes of an external world. It marked no difference, as Spinoza said, between experience of dreams and experience of reality. Granted the correspondence, the question is whether it merely happens to be so, to be described perceptually or has a reason inherent in the nature of things and in our awareness of them. And if there is a reason, it must be sought not in some *thing* called a 'universal,' accepted as objectively and externally as the things it purports to explain or defined as a mere abstraction from them, but in a lived and actual community or converse. Spinoza's universal is active: it involves the will in all ideation, idea in every volition. It recognizes that extension is inherent in the actual thinking which is God.

The 'correspondence' theory holds a 'mirror' up to nature without asking what the 'nature' or the mirror is. Its true setting was the absolute space and earth-centred cosmos such as natural philosophers in Spinoza's day no longer accepted. English vernacular grew up in this pictorial notion. English philosophers were slow to abandon it. English moralists like Butler believed in its educative virtue. Locke was unaware of its problems. Leibniz based his later philosophy upon it. Neither Berkeley nor Hume escaped its pervasive suggestion. Hume's individual is a monad bereft of 'pre-established harmony,' and the 'impressions' and 'ideas' of his *Treatise* present human understanding not as an act but in mechanical fashion, as a kind of camera facing the scene which is 'impressed' upon its sensitive plate and retained upon it as a memory or 'idea.' Hume indeed exposed the bankruptcy of the theory which he had inherited but retired from the consequence of his detection with the elegant excuse that philosophers ought to know when to stop. He was a historian and a librarian. Spinoza was not so happily confined.

More significant was the place of this naïve epistemology within the rational system in which Spinoza learned his rational art, significant because Descartes no less than the English philosophers accepted the 'mirror' theory though he had every reason to reject it. Cartesian 'ideas' are really precepts, 'clear' as they are given to the mind which makes them 'distinct' by thinking about them. The mind is the 'substance in which thought resides.' The intellect and vision are passive in Descartes as in Aristotle. The active principle is the will. Above all 'the actions of the soul are *desires*, since we find in experience that they proceed directly from our soul and appear to depend upon it alone.' And so the European tragedy was launched, not indeed by Descartes, but by these direct actions of the soul, desires released from intellect and bereft of vision, and the process as it gathered momentum seemed to discover the power which Hobbes likened to the fall of heavy bodies, a huge impotence resembling power only from the bigness of its catastrophe. The subject-object relation might serve almost as a name of the increasing systems of estrangement and enmity, religious, political, economic devised in the service of 'our desires.' It is the fruitful source of epistemological confusion down to our own time. No wonder the mirror theory prevailed. It looks self-evident, for we cannot choose but see, nor can we resist an Euclidean demonstration, whereas our wills feel as if they were and are commonly said to be our selves in action.

But evident or not, this nice differentiation of faculties is a nominal and misleading trick. Desires are not acts of the soul but dreams that haunt the sleep of thought. Pure percepts would be truly (*re vera*) suspensions of judgment. And there can be no free will *in vacuo*: we do not will the unconceived. Even to be aware of frustration we must have some idea of what we want, and it is only when we suffer a measure of frustration, some weakness, distance, or difficulty between conceiving and realizing a purpose that we recognize an act of will. Unimpeded will, which simultaneously achieves its end, and infinitely possesses its object, we call not will but love (*amor*) and then as the will suffers no frustration we feel as if we were not exerting it at all but rather were instruments of the beloved object or 'modes' of its activity. Such is the 'dereliction of the will' in which St John of the Cross or the 'abjection' in which St Francis of Sales discerns charity, and such the *necessity* which is freedom in Spinoza's language. This is the freedom 'which exists by the mere necessity of its own nature and is determined in its actions by itself alone.' 'He who loves God cannot endeavour to bring it about that God should love him in return.'

This 'marvellous saying' kindled Goethe's imagination, who seems, nevertheless, in his comment upon it to have understood but imperfectly what Spinoza was saying. 'To be unselfish in everything, most of all in love and friendship,' says Goethe, 'was my highest pleasure, my rule of life, my exercise.' That is much. But in the last part of the *Ethics* treating of 'the way which leads to liberty' Spinoza seems to have ascended beyond this village of affections to the level where *amor* and *intellectus* are one act. Here 'the human mind knows itself and its body under the species of eternity, and thus far necessarily has knowledge of God and knows that it exists in God and is conceived through God.' In that stupendous moment which other mystics have described, God is apprehended by love in such unanimity as leaves no spectator in the soul to discern or assess or even clearly remember what takes place, but that the lover is nothing but a flame of the eternal. But Spinoza does not describe an event. He states a necessity demonstrated in geometric order. There is no heat, there is only light and transparency. The philosopher is not a maker of mirrors but a grinder and polisher of lenses, and his business is not to catch and reflect an image but to transmit unimpeded vision. There is no refraction, no conflict between willing and thinking nor any conscious reconciliation between them. 'Intellect and will are the same.'

And so we are at the central question. Why did Spinoza set such store by 'the freedom of the mind we have in mathematics'? Why did he seek not experience but tautology? Why was his method all deduction so as to incur the charge, so plausible and so false, of determinism?

The most obvious answer is that Spinoza thinks in the present tense, and the present offers no alternative. It is necessary as it is real, the one because the other, and it is not an object or subject, but the moment of their identity. The self-evident fact is that there is no such thing as a 'might-have-been-present,' and it is not determinism but freedom to accept without reserve what only delusion could half refuse. When Spinoza says that 'substance is prior in its nature to its modifications' or that it is 'that which is in

itself and is conceived through itself' he defines the only
substantial reality, the inevitable present. The Christian's
locus classicus of this ethical realism is the sixth chapter of
St Matthew's Gospel. Spinoza's simple and secluded life,
his regular habits, and refusal of acquisitive distraction
extinguished the temptation to think prudentially or split
his attention between what was, what is, and what may be,
and the force of utilitarian morality trained upon future
happiness here or hereafter was nothing to him. He has no
doctrine of progress, and his lack of narrative sense gives his
ethics an appearance of ontology. He does not naturally
think of conduct in terms of doing, having, seeking, resisting,
and the rest, of praising or blaming or earning, but simply
of being. All thinking is where the thinker is. I AM, whatever those words may mean, is the primal and ultimate
expression of reality available in human speech. Though
they may refer only to Baruch Spinoza they are equally the
nearest verbal notation of 'that which is in itself and is
conceived through itself.' 'The idea or knowledge of the
human mind is granted in God.' Spinoza is a mode of the
divine act. 'The idea of an individual thing actually existing
has God for its cause.' 'The essence of man is constituted
by certain modes or attributes of God, that is by certain
modes of thinking.'

For, secondly, this present and actual thinking is all the
thinking there is. If I recall a proposition or system of
philosophy from the past, I do not revive an image but think
the proposition or system again as actively and critically as
at my first acquaintance with it. I cannot properly remember thinking as past, I can only think it as present. As
thinking in this sense has no history, so neither is it a possession. Men do not own thoughts; they think. They are not
furnished with sensations; they feel. The verb not the noun
signifies what really happens. The notion, therefore, that
we derive our thinking from some perceptual datum is
illusion. 'An idea is a concept of the mind which the mind
forms because it is a *res cogitans*. I say concept rather than
percept, because perception seems to indicate that the mind is
passive, but concept seems to express an *act* of the mind.'
But the mind itself is act. It is not the subject, possibility,
or continuum of thought but thinking-in-itself. Spinoza's

word for the object of thinking is 'ideatum,' the past and
passive participle of the verb 'to idea.' The idea which
constitutes the human mind has for its ideatum the human
body, and all the extended world which this ideatum implies.

Then instead of 'correspondence' (*adaequatio*) Spinoza
thinks of an act of 'coming together' (*convenire*), a companion-
ship of talkers who may never look *at* each other long enough
even to know the colour of their clothes, yet as they walk the
same road and face the same prospect are absorbed in the
same discourse. They may quarrel and will certainly differ;
yet the conceptual process unites them, requiring of them
not an agreement of opinion but the activity of thinking.
Only before they are properly started or when thinking flags
does either notice the other or the road or the scenery or
flight of time or ask the practical use of it all. Spinoza
himself belonged to such a 'convention' of thinkers who never
or seldom saw one another; he learned Latin for this community, and wrote letters which yield little for the narrative
of his biography, but contributed and still contribute to the
discourse. The truth in this conversation is not an 'object,'
nor an objective statement of subjective intention. It has
no litigious or diplomatic value, and indeed is not a statement
at all, nor a pattern or coherence of statements, for Spinoza
has no 'coherence theory of truth' in the manner of his late
Hegelian disciples. Nor is it a 'will to truth' as if somewhere
at the end of the road lay a final formulary. What then is
this conceptual process that carries the thinker in oblivion of
himself along its own road, the science that so takes possession
as to make the scientist an anonymous instrument? It is
thinking, actual, infinite, self-subsistent, self-defined. We
cannot describe it, we can only be it. 'It does not depend
upon any other thing.' 'It exists by the necessity of its
own nature.'

Spinoza's '*via remotionis*' has carried us far, as far as that
by which his medieval masters travelled to find the Ineffable.
The primal and absolute, present and actual intellection
hinted at in his experience and daily practice is apprehended
in a perfect transparency. The lens grinder may die of glass
powder, but the glass is perfect. The thinking thing has
ceased altogether to be a thing and is all thinking. This is
Spinoza's 'geometric order,' the self-evidence of deduction.

It would make no difference to this deduction though certain supposed 'necessities of thought' were shown to be paradox or delusion, though Euclid ceased to compel or the syllogism proved unseaworthy. The particular geometry may lose its cogency, or the logical discipline may vanish with its linguistic idiom and the world itself may vanish away like smoke, but Necessity remains. I am I; the end of the world is the end of the world. Purity gives no escape. Like charity it beareth all things and never faileth. In a sense Spinoza was an atheist as were Jews and Christians in a world of images when theism was an experience of things seen, an atheist in that he would not upon any persuasion use the word *Deus* of any term that could be held captive in any perceptual experience. You could not remember God or write any history of God or imagine him or put him in a context. God could not be glorified in the likeness of human approvals or disapprovals, loves or hates. Spinoza refused to say, Lo here! and Lo there! and as human piety clings to images, opinions, and localities of speech and emotion his *amor intellectualis* seemed impious and cold. But it was because his soul was not contaminated that being pure he held converse with the pure and attained to that 'third kind of knowledge,' *scientia intuiva*, 'the love of God with which God loves himself, not as he is infinite but as he can be expressed through the essence of the human mind considered under the species of eternity,' 'not contingent but necessary.' This is Spinoza's tautology. No experience is alien to it. It washed the intellectual firmament clean of contempts and prescriptions. It was a declaration of scientific independence and a profession of scientific faith. In the union of *amor* and *intellectus* Spinoza discovered that neither knows any frontier. All things are in God. 'For I am persuaded,' says another Jewish mystic in exile, 'that neither death nor life nor angels nor principalities nor powers nor things present nor things to come nor height nor depth nor any other creature shall be able to separate us from the love of God.'

T. S. GREGORY

SELECT BIBLIOGRAPHY

The two works published during Spinoza's lifetime were: *Renati des Cartesii principiorum philosophiæ, Mori geometrico demonstratæ*, 1663, *Tractatus theologico-politicus*, etc., 1670.

His works were published the year of his death; a complete definitive edition appeared under the editorship of Van Vloten and Land, 2 vols., 1882–3; 3 vols., 1895; it contains beyond the two works mentioned above: *Tractatus de Intellectus Emendatione; Ethica ordine geometrico demonstrata, Tractatus politicus; Annotationes in Tractatum Theologico Politicum post librum editum adscriptæ; Epistolæ doctorum quorundam virorum ad B. A. S. et Auctoris Responsiones; Epistolæ Johannis a Wullen, De Obitu Cartesii; Korte Verhandeling van God, de Mensch, en deszelfs Welstand* (a first sketch of the Ethics); Appendix, *Contens Cogitata Metaphysica; Stelkonstige Reeckening van den Refenboog; Reeckening van Kanssen; Compendium Grammatices Linguæ Hebræ*. The best edition is now that edited by C. Gebhardt, 4 vols., 1926.

ENGLISH TRANSLATIONS: *A Treatise, partly Theological, partly Political*, 1689; *A Treatise on Politics*, W. Maccall, 1854; *Ethics*, by D. D. S., 1876; W. Hale White, 1883 (English and Foreign Philological Library), 2nd and 3rd editions, revised by Amelia H. Stirling, 1894, 1899; *The Philosophy of Spinoza as contained in the 1st, 2nd, and 5th parts of Ethics*, G. S. Fullerton (series of Modern Philosophers), 1892; H. H. Joachim: *A Study of the Ethics*, 1901; J. A. Picton, *A Handbook to the Ethics*, 1907; *A Short Treatise on God, Man, and Human Welfare*, T. G. Robinson, 1907; *A Short Treatise on God, Man, and His Wellbeing*, 1910. A translation of the complete works was begun in 1928 by Abraham Wolf with a volume of Spinoza's correspondence.

LIFE, etc.: Sir F. Pollock: *Spinoza, His Life and Philosophy*, 1880, 1899, 1935; J. Martineau: *A Study of Spinoza*, 1882; W. Knight: *Spinoza, Four Essays*, etc., 1882; A. B. Moss: *Bruno and Spinoza*, 1885; M. H. Friedländer: *Spinoza, his Life and Philosophy*, 1887; W. J. Collins: *Spinoza, a Short Account of his Life and Philosophy* 1889; R. A. Duff: *Spinoza's Political and Ethical Philosophy*, 1903; J. Iverach: *Descartes, Spinoza, and the New Philosophy* (World's Epoch Makers), 1904; E. E. Powell: *Spinoza and Religion*, etc., 1906; J. M. Robertson: *Spinoza* (Pioneer Humanists), 1907. *The Oldest Biography of Spinoza*, edited and translated by A. Wolf, 1927; L. Roth: *Spinoza*, 1929 A. Wolfson: *Spinoza, A Life of Reason*, 1932; H. A. Wolfson: *The Philosophy of Spinoza*, 1934; A. Shanks: *An Introduction to Spinoza's Ethics*, 1938; D. Bidney: *The Psychology and Ethics of Spinoza*, 1940; H. A. Myers: *The Spinoza-Hegel Paradox*, 1944.

CONTENTS

	PAGE
Introduction by T. S. Gregory	v

PART I

CONCERNING GOD

DEFINITIONS—

I. Cause of Itself (*causa sui*)	I
II. Finite in its Kind (*in suo genere finita*) . . .	I
III. Substance (*substantia*)	I
IV. Attribute (*attributum*)	I
V. Mode (*modus*)	I
VI. God (*Deus*)	I
VII. The thing is said to be Free (*libera*), Necessary (*necessaria*), or Compelled (*coacta*)	2
VIII. Eternity (*æternitas*)	2

AXIOMS I.-VII. . . . . | 2 |

PROPOSITIONS—

I. A substance is prior in its nature to its modifications .	3
II. Two substances, having different attributes, have nothing in common between them	3
III. Of two things having nothing in common between them, one cannot be the cause of the other . .	3
IV. Two or three distinct things are distinguished one from the other either by the difference of the attributes of the substances or by the difference of their modifications .	3
V. In the nature of things, two or more things may not be granted having the same nature or attribute . .	3
VI. One substance cannot be produced by another . .	4
Corollary	4
VII. Existence appertains to the nature of substance . .	4
VIII. All substance is necessarily infinite	4
Notes	5
IX. The more reality or being a thing has, the more attributes will it have	7
X. Each attribute of the one substance must be concieved through itself	7
Note	7

xxi

PROPOSITIONS   PAGE

XI. God or a substance consisting of infinite attributes, each
    of which expresses eternal and infinite essence, neces-
    sarily exists   7
    Note   9

XII. No attribute of a substance can be truly conceived,
     from which it would follow that substance can be
     divided into parts   10

XIII. Substance absolutely infinite is indivisible   .   .   10
     Corollary   10
     Note   10

XIV. Except God no substance can be granted or conceived   11
     Corollaries   11

XV. Whatever is, is in God, and nothing can exist or be con-
    ceived without God   11
    Note   11

XVI. Infinite things in infinite modes (that is, all things
     which can fall under the heading of infinite intellect)
     must necessarily follow from the necessity of divine
     nature   15
     Corollaries   15

XVII. God acts merely according to his own laws, and is
      compelled by no one   15
     Corollaries   15
     Note   16

XVIII. God is the indwelling and not the transient cause of
       all things   18

XIX. God and all the attributes of God are eternal .   .   18
     Note   18

XX. God's existence and his essence are one and the same
    thing   19
    Corollaries   19

XXI. All things which follow from the absolute nature of
     any attribute of God must exist for ever and infinitely,
     or must exist eternally and infinitely through that same
     attribute   19

XXII. Whatever follows from an attribute of God, in so far
      as it is modified by such a modification as exists of
      necessity and infinitely through the same, must also
      exist of necessity and infinitely   20

XXIII. Every mode which of necessity and infinitely exists
       must of necessity have followed either from the absolute
       nature of some attribute of God, or from some attribute
       modified by a modification which exists of necessity
       and infinitely   20

XXIV. The essence of things produced by God does not
      involve existence   21
      Corollary   21

Contents

PROPOSITIONS   PAGE

XXV. God is not only the effecting cause of the existence of things, but also of their essence 21

Note 21

Corollary 21

XXVI. A thing which is determined for the performing of anything was so determined necessarily by God, and a thing which is not determined by God cannot determine of itself to do anything 21

XXVII. A thing which is determined by God for the performing of anything cannot render itself undetermined 22

XXVIII. Every individual thing, or whatever thing that is finite and has a determined existence, cannot exist nor be determined for action unless it is determined for action and existence by another cause which is also finite and has a determined existence; and again, this cause also cannot exist nor be determined for action unless it be determined for existence and action by another cause which also is finite and has a determined existence: and so on to infinity 22

Note 23

XXIX. In the nature of things nothing contingent (*contingens*) is granted, but all things are determined by the necessity of divine nature for existing and working in a certain way 23

Note 24

XXX. Intellect, finite or infinite in actuality (*actus*), must comprehend the attributes of God and the modifications of God and nothing else 24

XXXI. The intellect in action, whether it be finite or infinite, as will, desire, love, etc., must be referred not to active but passive nature 24

Note 25

XXXII. Will can only be called a necessary cause, not a free one 25

Corollaries 25

XXXIII. Things could not have been produced by God in any other manner or order than that in which they were produced. 26

Notes 26

XXXIV. The power of God is the same as his essence . 29

XXXV. Whatever we conceive to be in the power of God necessarily exists 29

XXXVI. Nothing exists from whose nature some effect does not follow 29

APPENDIX 30

PART II

CONCERNING THE NATURE AND ORIGIN OF THE MIND

PAGE

PREFACE 37

DEFINITIONS—

I. Body (*corpus*) 37

II. That which appertains to the essence of a thing . . 37

III. Idea (*idea*) 37

IV. Adequate Idea (*idea adæquata*) 37

V. Duration (*duratio*) 38

VI. Reality and Perfection (*realitas et perfectio*) . . 38

VII. Individual Things (*res singulares*) 38

AXIOMS I.-V. 38

PROPOSITIONS—

I. Thought (*cogitatio*) is an attribute of God, or God is a thinking thing 38

Note 39

II. Extension (*extensio*) is an attribute of God, or God is an extended thing 39

III. In God there is granted not only the idea of his essence, but also the idea of all the things which follow necessarily from his essence 39

Note 39

IV. The idea of God from which infinite things in infinite modes follow can only be one 40

V. The formal being of ideas acknowledges God as its cause only in so far as he is considered as a thinking thing, and not in so far as he is revealed in some other attribute: that is, the ideas, not only of the attributes of God, but also of individual things, do not acknowledge their ideals or the objects perceived as their effecting cause, but God himself in so far as he is a thinking thing . 40

VI. The modes of any attribute of God have God for their cause only in so far as he is considered through that attribute, and not in so far as he is considered through any other attribute 41

Corollary 41

VII. The order and connection of ideas is the same as the order and connection of things 41

Corollary 41

Note 41

VIII. The ideas of individual things or modes which do not exist must be comprehended in the infinite idea of God in the same way as the formal essences of individual things or modes are contained in the attributes of God . 42

Contents XXV

PROPOSITIONS   PAGE

Corollary 42

Note 43

IX. The idea of an individual thing actually existing has God for its cause, not in so far as he is infinite, but in so far as he is considered as affected by the idea of another individual thing actually existing of which also God is the cause, in so far as he is affected by another third idea, and so on to infinity. 43

Corollary 44

X. The being of substance does not appertain to the essence of man, or, again, substance does not constitute the form (*forma*) of man 44

Notes 44

Corollary 44

XI. The first part which constitutes the actual being of the human mind is nothing else than the idea of an individual thing actually existing 45

Corollary 46

Note 46

XII. Whatever happens in the object of the idea constituting the human mind must be perceived by the human mind, or the idea of that thing must necessarily be found in the human mind: that is, if the object of the idea constituting the human mind be the body, nothing can happen in that body which is not perceived by the mind 46

Note 47

XIII. The object of the idea constituting the human mind is the body, or a certain mode of extension actually existing and nothing else 47

Corollary 47

Note 47

Axioms I., II. 48

Lemmas I.-III. 48

Corollary 49

Axioms I.-III. 50

Lemmas IV.-VII. 50

Note 51

Postulates I.-VI. 52

XIV. The human mind is apt to perceive many things, and more so according as its body can be disposed in more ways 52

XV. The idea which constitutes the formal being of the human mind is not simple, but composed of many ideas 53

XVI. The idea of every mode in which the human body is affected by external bodies must involve the nature of the human body and at the same time the nature of the external body 53

Corollaries 53

PROPOSITIONS   PAGE

XVII. If the human body is affected in a mode which involves the nature of any external body, the human mind
regards that external body as actually existing, or as
present to itself until the body is affected by a modification which cuts off the existence or presence of that body   53

Corollary   54

Note   54

XVIII. If the human body has once been affected at the
same time by two or more bodies, when the mind afterwards remembers any one of them it will straightway
remember the others   55

Note   55

XIX. The human mind has no knowledge of the human
body, nor does it know it to exist save through ideas of
modifications by which the body is affected   .   .   56

XX. The idea or knowledge of the human mind is granted in
God and follows in God in the same manner, and is referred to God in the same manner as the idea or knowledge of the human body   57

XXI. This idea of the mind is united to the mind in the same
manner as the mind is united to the body .   .   .   57

Note   58

XXII. The human mind perceives not only the modifications
of the body, but also the ideas of these modifications .   58

XXIII. The mind has no knowledge of itself save in so far as
it perceives the ideas of the modifications of the body .   58

XXIV. The human mind does not involve an adequate
knowledge of the component parts of the human body   59

XXV. The idea of each modification of the human body does
not involve an adequate knowledge of the external body   60

XXVI. The human mind perceives no external body as
actually existing save through ideas of modifications of
its body   60

Corollary   60

XXVII. The idea of each modification of the human body
does not involve adequate knowledge of the human body
itself   60

XXVIII. The ideas of the modifications of the human body,
in so far as they are referred to the human mind alone,
are not clear and distinct but confused   .   .   .   61

Note   61

XXIX. The idea of the idea of each modification of the
human mind does not involve adequate knowledge of
the human mind   61

Corollary   62

Note   62

XXX. We can have only a very inadequate knowledge of the
duration of our body   62

PROPOSITIONS   PAGE

XXXI. We can only have a very inadequate knowledge of individual things which are outside us . . . 63

Corollary 63

XXXII. All ideas, in so far as they have reference to God, are true 63

XXXIII. There is nothing positive in ideas, wherefore they could be called false 63

XXXIV. Every idea in us which is absolute, or adequate and perfect, is true 63

XXXV. Falsity consists in privation of knowledge which is involved by inadequate or mutilated and confused ideas 64

Note 64

XXXVI. Inadequate and confused ideas follow from the same necessity as adequate or clear and distinct ideas . 64

XXXVII. That which is common to all, and that which is equally in a part and in the whole, do not constitute the essence of an individual thing 65

XXXVIII. Those things which are common to all, and which are equally in a part and in the whole, can only be conceived as adequate 65

Corollary 65

XXXIX. That which is common to and a property of the human body, and certain external bodies by which the human body is used to be affected, and which is equally in the part and whole of these, has an adequate idea in the mind 66

Corollary 66

XL. Whatever ideas follow in the mind from ideas which are adequate in the mind, are also adequate . . . 66

Notes 66

XLI. Knowledge of the first kind is the only cause of falsity; knowledge of the second and third kinds is necessarily true 69

XLII. Knowledge of the second and third kinds and not of the first kind teaches us to distinguish the true from the false 69

XLIII. He who has a true idea, knows at that same time that he has a true idea, nor can he doubt concerning the truth of the thing 69

Note 70

XLIV. It is not the nature of reason to regard things as contingent but necessary 71

Corollaries 71

Note 71

XLV. Every idea of every body or individual thing actually existing necessarily involves the eternal and infinite essence of God 72

Note 73

PROPOSITIONS   PAGE

XLVI. The knowledge of the eternal and infinite essence of
God which each idea involves is adequate and perfect   .   73

XLVII. The human mind has an adequate knowledge of the
eternal and infinite essence of God   73

Note   74

XLVIII. There is in no mind absolute or free will, but the
mind is determined for willing this or that by a cause
which is determined in its turn by another cause, and
this one again by another, and so on to infinity .   .   74

Note   75

XLIX. There is in the mind no volition or affirmation and
negation save that which the idea, in so far as it is an
idea, involves   75

Corollary   76

Note   76

PART III

CONCERNING THE ORIGIN AND NATURE OF THE EMOTIONS

DEFINITIONS—

I. Adequate Cause (*adæquata causa*); Inadequate or Partial
(*inadæquata seu partialis*)   84

II. Action and Passion   84

III. Emotion (*affectus*)   84

POSTULATES I., II.   85

PROPOSITIONS—

I. Our mind acts certain things and suffers others: namely,
in so far as it has adequate ideas, thus far it necessarily
acts certain things, and in so far as it has inadequate
ideas, thus far it necessarily suffers certain things   .   85

Corollary   86

II. The body cannot determine the mind to think, nor the
mind the body to remain in motion, or at rest, or in any
other state (if there be any other)   86

Note   86

III. The actions of the mind arise from adequate ideas alone,
but passions depend on inadequate ideas alone   .   .   90

Note   90

IV. Nothing can be destroyed save by an external cause   .   90

V. Things are contrary by nature, that is, they cannot exist
in the same subject in so far as one can destroy the other   90

VI. Everything in so far as it is in itself endeavours to persist in its own being   91

Contents

PROPOSITIONS   PAGE

VII. The endeavour wherewith a thing endeavours to persist in its being is nothing else than the actual essence of that thing   91

VIII. The endeavour wherewith a thing endeavours to persist in its own being involves no finite time but an indefinite time   91

IX. The mind, in so far as it has both clear and distinct and confused ideas, endeavours to persist in its being for an indefinite period, and is conscious of this its endeavour   92
Note   92

X. The idea which cuts off the existence of our body cannot be given in our mind, but is contrary thereto . .   92

XI. Whatever increases or diminishes, helps or hinders the power of action of our body, the idea thereof increases or diminishes, helps or hinders the power of thinking of our mind   93
Note   93

XII. The mind, as much as it can, endeavours to imagine those things which increase or help its power of acting.   94

XIII. When the mind imagines things which diminish or hinder the power of acting of the body, it endeavours as much as it can to remember things which will cut off their existence   94
Corollary   95
Note   95

XIV. If the mind were once affected at the same time by two emotions, when afterwards it is affected by one of them it will be also affected by the other . . .   95

XV. Anything can accidentally be the cause of pleasure, pain, or desire   95
Corollary   96
Note   96

XVI. From the fact alone that we imagine anything which has something similar to an object which is wont to affect the mind with pleasure or pain, although that in which the thing is similar to the object be not the effecting cause of those emotions, nevertheless we shall hate or love it accordingly   96

XVII. If we imagine a thing which is wont to affect us with the emotion of sadness to have something similar to another thing which equally affects us with the emotion of pleasure, we will hate and love that thing at the same time   96
Note   97

XVIII. A man is affected with the same emotion of pleasure or pain from the image of a thing past or future as from the image of a thing present   97
Notes   98

PROPOSITIONS   PAGE

XIX. He will be saddened who imagines that which he
loves to be destroyed: if he imagines it to be preserved
he is rejoiced   98

XX. He will be rejoiced who imagines what he hates to be
destroyed   99

XXI. He who imagines that which he loves to be affected
by pleasure or pain, will also be affected by pleasure or
pain: and these will be greater or less in the lover according as they are greater or less in the thing loved .   99

XXII. If we imagine anything to affect with pleasure what
we love, we are affected with love towards it: and, on
the other hand, if we imagine anything to affect it with
pain, we are affected with hatred towards it   .   .   100
    Note   100

XXIII. He will be rejoiced who imagines that which he
hates to be affected with pain; if, on the other hand, he
imagines it to be affected with pleasure, he will be
saddened: and these emotions will be greater or less
according as the contrary emotions were greater or less
in the things hated   100
    Note   101

XXIV. If we imagine any one to affect a thing we hate with
pleasure, we are affected with hatred towards that
person. If, on the other hand, we imagine him to
affect it with pain, we are affected with love towards
him   101
    Note   101

XXV. We endeavour to affirm, concerning ourselves or
what we love, everything that we imagine to affect
what we love or ourselves with pleasure; and, on the
other hand, we endeavour to deny, concerning ourselves
and the object loved, everything that we imagine to
affect us or the object loved with pain   .   .   .   101

XXVI. We endeavour to affirm, concerning a thing that
we hate, that which we imagine will affect it with pain,
and, on the contrary, to deny all that which we imagine
will affect it with pleasure   102
    Note   102

XXVII. By the fact that we imagine a thing which is like
ourselves, and which we have not regarded with any
emotion to be affected with any emotion, we also are
affected with a like emotion   102
    Notes   103
    Corollaries   103

XXVIII. We endeavour to promote the being of everything
that we imagine conducive to pleasure; but what we
find repugnant or conducive to pain we endeavour to
remove or destroy   103

Contents

PROPOSITIONS   PAGE

XXIX. We also shall endeavour to do everything which we imagine men to regard with pleasure, and, on the other hand, we shall be averse to doing what we imagine men to turn away from 104

Note 104

XXX. If any one has done anything which he imagines to affect others with pleasure, he will be affected with pleasure accompanied by the idea of himself as the cause, or he will regard himself with pleasure. On the other hand, if he has done anything which he imagines to affect the others with pain, he regards himself then with pain 105

Note 105

XXXI. If we imagine any one to love, desire, or hate anything which we ourselves love, hate, or desire, by that very fact we shall love, hate, or desire it the more. But, on the other hand, if we imagine that what we love is avoided by some one, then we undergo a wavering of the mind 105

Corollary 106

Note 106

XXXII. If we imagine any one to enjoy anything which only one can possess, we shall endeavour to bring it to pass that he does not possess it 106

Note 106

XXXIII. When we love a thing similar to ourselves, we endeavour as much as possible to bring it about that it also should love us 107

XXXIV. The greater the emotion with which we imagine a thing loved to be affected towards us, the greater will be our vanity 107

XXXV. If any one imagines that the thing loved is joined to another than himself with the same or a faster bond of love than that which binds it to him, he will be affected with hatred towards the object loved, and envy towards the other 108

Note 108

XXXVI. He who recollects a thing which he once enjoyed, desires to possess it under the same circumstances as those with which he first enjoyed it 109

Corollary 109

Note 109

XXXVII. The desire which arises by reason of sadness, joy, hatred, or love, is greater according as the emotion is greater 109

XXXVIII. If any one begins to hate a thing loved so that his love for it is clearly laid aside, he will bear greater hatred towards it on that very account than if he had never loved it, and the more so according as his former love was greater 110

PROPOSITIONS   PAGE

XXXIX. He who hates any one will endeavour to do him
    harm unless he fears to receive a greater harm from him;
    and, on the other hand, he who loves some one will by
    the same law endeavour to do him good   .   .   .   110
        Note   111

XL. He who imagines himself to be hated by another, and
    believes that he has given the other no cause for hatred,
    will hate that person in return   111
        Notes   112
        Corollaries   112

XLI. If any one imagines himself to be loved by some one
    else, and does not believe that he has given any cause
    for this love, he shall love that person in return .   .   113
        Notes   113
        Corollary   113

XLII. He who confers a benefit on any one moved by love,
    or by the hope of honour, will be saddened if he sees that
    the benefit is received with ingratitude   .   .   .   113

XLIII. Hatred is increased by reciprocal hatred, and, on the
    other hand, can be destroyed by love   .   .   .   114

XLIV. Hatred which is entirely conquered by love passes
    into love, and love on that account is greater than if it
    had not been preceded by hatred   114
        Note   114

XLV. If one imagines that any one similar to himself is
    affected with hatred towards another thing similar to
    himself whom he himself loves, then he will hate the
    first of these two   115

XLVI. If any one has been affected with pleasure or pain
    by another person of a class or nation different to his
    own, and that accompanied by the idea of that person
    under the general name of that class or nation as the
    cause of the pleasure or pain, he will love or hate not
    only that person, but all of that class or nation .   .   115

XLVII. Joy which arises from the fact that we imagine a
    thing which we hate to be destroyed or affected by
    some evil never arises without some pain in us   .   .   115
        Note   115

XLVIII. Love and hatred, for example, towards Peter,
    are destroyed, if the pain which the latter involves, and
    the pleasure which the former involves, are connected to
    the idea of another thing as a cause; and each of them
    will be diminished in so far as we imagine Peter not to be
    the only cause of either   116

XLIX. Love or hatred towards a thing which we imagine
    to be free must be greater than the love or hatred
    towards a necessary thing, provided both are subject
    to the same cause   116
        Note   117

L. Anything can be accidentally the cause of hope or fear .   117
        Note   117

PROPOSITIONS   PAGE

LI. Different men can be affected by one and the same object
in different manners, and one and the same man can be
affected by one and the same object in different ways at
different times 117

    Note 118

LII. We cannot regard an object which we have seen before
together with some others, or which we imagine to have
nothing that is not common to many, as long as one
which we imagine to have something singular about it . 119

    Note 119

LIII. When the mind regards itself and its power of acting
it is rejoiced, and the more so the more distinctly it
imagines itself and its power of acting . . . 120

    Corollary 120

LIV. The mind endeavours to imagine those things only
which impose its power of action on it . . . 121

LV. When the mind imagines its want of power it is saddened
by that fact 121

    Corollaries 121

    Notes 121

LVI. There are as many species of pleasure, pain, desire,
and consequently any emotion which is composed of
these, such as wavering of the mind, or which is derived
from these, such as love, fear, hope, hatred, etc., as there
are species of objects by which we are affected . . 123

    Note 124

LVII. Any emotion of every individual differs from the
emotion of another only in so far as the essence of one
differs from the essence of another 124

    Note 125

LVIII. Besides pleasure and desire which are passions,
there are other emotions of pleasure and pain which
refer to us in so far as we are active 125

LIX. Among all the emotions which have reference to the
mind, in so far as it is active, there are none which have
not reference to pleasure or desire 126

    Note 126

DEFINITIONS OF THE EMOTIONS—

I. Desire (*cupiditas*) 128

II. Pleasure (*lætitia*) 128

III. Pain (*tristitia*) 128

IV. Wonder (*admiratio*) 129

V. Contempt 130

VI. Love (*amor*) 130

VII. Hatred (*odium*) 130

VIII. Inclination (*propensio*) 130

IX. Aversion (*aversio*) 130

DEFINITIONS OF THE EMOTIONS   PAGE

    X. Devotion (*devotio*) 131
   XI. Derision (*irrisio*) 131
  XII. Hope (*spes*) 131
 XIII. Fear (*metus*) 131
 XIV. Confidence (*securitas*) 131
  XV. Despair (*desperatio*) 131
 XVI. Joy (*gaudium*) 132
XVII. Disappointment (*conscientiæ morsus*) . . . 132
XVIII. Pity (*commiseratio*) 132
 XIX. Favour (*favor*) 132
  XX. Indignation (*indignatio*) 132
 XXI. Partiality (*existimatio*) 133
 XXII. Disparagement (*despectus*) 133
XXIII. Envy (*invidia*) 133
XXIV. Compassion (*misericordia*) 133
 XXV. Self-complacency (*acquiescentia in seipso*) . . 133
XXVI. Humility (*humilitas*) 133
XXVII. Repentance (*pœnitentia*) 133
XXVIII. Pride (*superbia*) 134
XXIX. Self-despising or dejection (*abjectio*) . . 135
 XXX. Honour or glory (*gloria*) 135
XXXI. Shame (*pudor*) 135
XXXII. Regret (*desiderium*) . . . . , , 136
XXXIII. Emulation (*æmulatio*) 136
XXXIV. Gratefulness or gratitude (*gratia seu gratitudo*) . 137
XXXV. Benevolence (*benevolentia*) 137
XXXVI. Anger (*ira*) 137
XXXVII. Vengeance (*vindicta*) 137
XXXVIII. Cruelty or savageness (*crudelitas seu sævitas*) . 137
XXXIX. Timidity (*timor*) 137
  XL. Daring (*audacia*) 137
 XLI. Cowardice (*pusillanimitas*) 137
 XLII. Consternation (*consternatio*) 138
XLIII. Politeness or modesty (*humanitas seu modestia*) . 138
XLIV. Ambition (*ambitio*) 138
 XLV. Luxury (*luxuria*) 138
XLVI. Drunkenness (*ebrietas*) 138
XLVII. Avarice (*avaritia*) 138
XLVIII. Lust (*libido*) 138
GENERAL DEFINITION OF THE EMOTIONS 139

Contents

PART IV

ON HUMAN SERVITUDE, OR THE STRENGTH OF THE EMOTIONS

PAGE

PREFACE 141

DEFINITIONS—

    I. Good (*bonum*) 144

    II. Bad (*malum*) 144

    III. Contingent individual things (*contingentes*) . . 144

    IV. Possible individual things (*possibiles*) . . . 144

    V. Contrary Emotions (*affectus contrarii*) . . . 144

    VI. Emotion towards a thing future, present, or past . 144

    VII. End (*finis*) 145

    VIII. Virtue (*virtus*) 145

AXIOM 145

PROPOSITIONS—

    I. Nothing positive, which a false idea has, is removed from the presence of what is true in so far as it is true . 145

      Note 145

    II. We are passive in so far as we are a part of nature which cannot be conceived through itself without others . 146

    III. The force with which man persists in existing is limited, and is far surpassed by the power of external causes . 146

    IV. It cannot happen that a man should not be a part of nature, and that he should be able not to suffer changes, save those which can be understood through his nature alone, and of which he is the adequate cause . . 147

      Corollary 148

    V. The force and increase of any passion, and its persistence in existing, are not defined by the power whereby we endeavour to persist in existing, but by the power of an external cause compared with our own . . . 148

    VI. The force of any passion or emotion can so surpass the rest of the actions or the power of a man that the emotion adheres obstinately to him . . . 148

    VII. An emotion can neither be hindered nor removed save by a contrary emotion and one stronger in checking emotion 148

      Corollary 149

    VIII. The knowledge of good or evil is nothing else than the emotion of pleasure or pain, in so far as we are conscious of it 149

PROPOSITIONS   PAGE

IX. An emotion whose cause we imagine to be with us at the
    present is stronger than if we did not imagine it to be
    present   149
    Note   150
    Corollary   150

X. Towards a future thing which we imagine to be close at
   hand we are more intensely affected than if we imagine
   the time of its existing to be further distant from the
   present; and by the recollection of a thing which we
   imagine to have passed not long ago we are more intensely affected also than if we imagine it to have
   passed long ago   150
   Note   151

XI. The emotion towards a thing which we imagine to be
    necessary is more intense, *cæteris paribus*, than towards
    a thing possible, contingent, or not necessary . .   151

XII. The emotion towards a thing which we know to be non-
     existent at the present time, and which we imagine
     possible, is more intense, *cæteris paribus*, than that
     towards a thing contingent   151
     Corollary   151

XIII. Emotion towards a thing contingent, which we know
      does not exist in the present, is far more mild, *cæteris
      paribus*, than emotion towards a thing past . .   152

XIV. A true knowledge of good and evil cannot restrain any
     emotion in so far as the knowledge is true, but only in so
     far as it is considered as an emotion . . .   152

XV. Desire which arises from a true knowledge of good and
    evil can be destroyed or checked by many other desires
    which arise from emotions by which we are assailed .   152

XVI. The desire which arises from the knowledge of good
     and evil, in so far as this knowledge has reference to the
     future, can more easily be checked or destroyed than
     the desire of things which are pleasing in the present . 153

XVII. Desire which arises from true knowledge of good and
      evil, in so far as this concerns things contingent, can be
      far more easily restrained than the desire for things which
      are present   153
      Note   153

XVIII. Desire which arises from pleasure is stronger, *cæteris
       paribus*, than the desire which arises from pain . .   154
       Note   154

XIX. Each one necessarily desires or turns from, by the
     laws of his nature, what he thinks to be good or evil .   156

XX. The more each one seeks what is useful to him, that is,
    the more he endeavours and can preserve his being, the
    more he is endowed with virtue; and, on the contrary,
    the more one neglects to preserve what is useful, or his
    being, he is thus far impotent or powerless . .   156
    Note   156

Contents xxxvii

PROPOSITIONS   PAGE

XXI. No one can desire to be blessed, to act well, or live well,
who at the same time does not desire to be, to act, and
to live, that is, actually to exist 157

XXII. No virtue can be conceived as prior to this virtue of
endeavouring to preserve oneself 157
Corollary 157

XXIII. Man, in so far as he is determined to do anything,
by the fact that he has inadequate ideas cannot absolutely be said to act from virtue, but only in so far as he
is determined by the fact that he understands . . 157

XXIV. To act absolutely according to virtue is nothing else
in us than to act under the guidance of reason, to live so,
and to preserve one's being (these three have the same
meaning) on the basis of seeking what is useful to oneself 158

XXV. No one endeavours to preserve his being for the sake
of anything else 158

XXVI. Whatever we endeavour to do under the guidance of
reason is nothing else than to understand; nor does the
mind, in so far as it uses reason, judge anything useful
to itself save what is conducive to understanding . . 158

XXVII. We know nothing to be certainly good or evil save
what is truly conducive to understanding or what prevents us from understanding 159

XXVIII. The greatest good of the mind is the knowledge of
God, and the greatest virtue of the mind is to know God 159

XXIX. Any individual thing whose nature is altogether
different to ours can aid or hinder our power of understanding, and absolutely nothing can be either good or
bad save if it have something in common with us . 160

XXX. Nothing can be bad through that which it has in
common with our nature; but in so far as it is bad, thus
far it is contrary to us 160

XXXI. In so far as anything agrees with our nature, thus
far it is necessarily good 161
Corollary 161

XXXII. In so far as men are liable to passions they cannot
thus far be said to agree in nature 161
Note 161

XXXIII. Men can differ in nature in so far as they are
assailed by emotions which are passions, and thus far
one and the same man is variable and inconstant . 162

XXXIV. Men, in so far as they are assailed by emotions
which are passions, can be contrary one to the other . 162
Note 162

XXXV. In so far as men live under the guidance of reason,
thus far only they always necessarily agree in nature . 163
Corollaries 164
Note 164

PROPOSITIONS   PAGE

XXXVI. The greatest good of those who follow virtue is
common to all, and all can equally enjoy it   .   .   165
  Note   165

XXXVII. The good which each one who follows virtue
desires for himself, he also desires for other men, and
the more so the more knowledge he has of God .   .   165
  Notes   166

XXXVIII. That is useful to man which so disposes the
human body that it can be affected in many modes, or
which renders it capable of affecting external bodies in
many modes, and the more so according as it renders
the body more apt to be affected in many modes or to
affect other bodies so; and, on the contrary, that is
harmful (noxius) to man which renders the body less
apt for this   169

XXXIX. Whatever brings it to pass that the proportion
of motion and rest which the parts of the human body
hold one to the other is preserved, is good; and contrariwise, that is bad which brings it about that the
parts of the human body have another proportion
mutually of motion and rest   169
  Note   170

XL. Whatever is conducive of the common society of men,
or whatever brings it about that men live together in
peace and agreement, is useful, and, on the contrary,
that is bad which induces discord in the state .   .   171

XLI. Pleasure clearly is not evil but good; but pain, on the
contrary, is clearly evil   171

XLII. There cannot be too much merriment, but it is always
good; but, on the other hand, melancholy is always
bad   171

XLIII. Titillation can be excessive and be bad; but grief
may be good in so far as titillation or pleasure is bad . 171

XLIV. Love and desire can be excessive   .   .   .   172
  Note   172

XLV. Hatred can never be good   173
  Notes   173
  Corollaries   173

XLVI. He who lives under the guidance of reason endeavours as much as possible to repay his fellow's
hatred, rage, contempt, etc., with love and nobleness . 174
  Note   174

XLVII. The emotions of hope and fear cannot be in themselves good   175
  Note   175

XLVIII. The emotions of partiality and disparagement are
always bad   175

XLIX. Partiality easily renders the man who is over-estimated, proud   175

Contents **xxxix**

PROPOSITIONS PAGE

L. Pity in a man who lives under the guidance of reason is in itself bad and useless 175

    Corollary 176

    Note 176

LI. Favour is not opposed to reason, but can agree with it and arise from it 176

    Note 176

LII. Self-complacency can arise from reason, and that self-complacency which arises from reason alone is the greatest 177

    Note 177

LIII. Humility is not a virtue if it does not arise from reason 177

LIV. Repentance is not a virtue, or, in other words, it does not arise from reason, but he who repents of an action is twice as unhappy or as weak as before . . . 178

    Note 178

LV. The greatest pride or dejection is the greatest ignorance of self 178

LVI. The greatest pride or dejection indicates the greatest weakness of mind 178

    Corollary 179

    Note 179

LVII. A proud man loves the presence of parasites or flatterers, but the presence of noble people he hates . 179

    Note 179

LVIII. Honour is not opposed to reason, but can arise from it 180

    Note 180

LIX. For all actions for which we are determined by an emotion which is a passion we can be determined without that emotion by reason alone 181

    Note 182

LX. Desire which arises from pleasure or pain which has reference to one or certain parts of the body has no advantage to man as a whole 183

    Note 183

LXI. Desire which arises from reason can have no excess . 183

LXII. In so far as the mind conceives a thing according to the dictate of reason, it will be equally affected whether the idea be of a thing present, past, or future . . 184

    Note 184

LXIII. He that is led by fear to do good in order to avoid evil is not led by reason 184

    Notes 185

    Corollary 185

LXIV. The knowledge of evil is inadequate knowledge . 185

    Corollary 186

PROPOSITIONS   PAGE

LXV. Under the guidance of reason we follow the greater
of two things which are good and the lesser of two
things which are evil   186

Corollary   186

LXVI. Under the guidance of reason we desire a greater
future good before a lesser present one, and a lesser evil
in the present " before a greater in the future " (Van
Vloten's version)   186

Corollary   186

Note   186

LXVII. A free man thinks of nothing less than of death,
and his wisdom is a meditation not of death but of life   187

LXVIII. If men were born free they would form no conception of good and evil as long as they were free .   187

Note   187

LXIX. The virtue of a free man appears equally great in
refusing to face difficulties as in overcoming them .   188

Corollary   188

Note   188

LXX. A free man who lives among ignorant people tries as
much as he can to refuse their benefits .   .   .   188

Note   189

LXXI. Only free men are truly grateful one to the other .   189

Note   189

LXXII. A free man never acts by fraud, but always with
good faith   189

Note   190

LXXIII. A man who is guided by reason is more free in a
state where he lives according to common law than in
solitude where he is subject to no law .   .   .   190

Note   190

APPENDIX   191

PART V

CONCERNING THE POWER OF THE INTELLECT
OR HUMAN FREEDOM

PREFACE   199

AXIOMS I., II.   202

PROPOSITIONS—

I. Just as thoughts and the ideas of the mind are arranged
and connected in the mind, so in the body its modifications or the modifications of things are arranged and
connected according to their order   202

Contents

PROPOSITIONS   PAGE

II. If we remove disturbance of the mind or emotion from
the thought of an external cause and unite it to other
thoughts, then love or hatred towards the external
cause, as well as waverings of the mind which arise from
these emotions, are destroyed   202

III. An emotion which is a passion ceases to be a passion as
soon as we form a clear and distinct idea of it   .   .   203
Corollary   203

IV. There is no modification of the body of which we cannot
form some clear and distinct conception   .   .   .   203
Corollary   203
Note   203

V. Emotion towards a thing which we imagine simply and
not as necessary nor possible nor contingent is, *cæteris
paribus*, the greatest of all   204

VI. In so far as the mind understands all things as necessary
it has more power over the emotions or is less passive to
them   205
Note   205

VII. Emotions which arise or are excited by reason, if we
regard time, are greater than those which are referred to
individual things which we regard as absent   .   .   205

VIII. The more an emotion is excited by many emotions concurring at the same time, the greater it will be   .   206
Note   206

IX. Emotion which has reference to many different causes
which the mind regards at the same time as the emotion
itself is less harmful, and we are less passive to it and
less affected toward each cause than another emotion
equally great which has reference to one alone or fewer
causes   206

X. As long as we are not assailed by emotions which are contrary to our nature we are able to arrange and connect
the modifications of the body according to their intellectual order   206
Note   207

XI. The more any image has reference to many things, the
more frequent it is, the more often it flourishes, and the
more it occupies the mind   209

XII. The images of things are more easily joined to images
which have reference to things which we understand
clearly and distinctly than to others   .   .   .   209

XIII. The more an image is associated with many other
things, the more often it flourishes   .   .   .   209

XIV. The mind can bring it to pass that all the modifications
of the body or images of things have reference to the
idea of God   209

XV. He who understands himself and his emotions loves
God, and the more so the more he understands himself
and his emotions   209

PROPOSITIONS   PAGE

XVI. This love towards God must occupy the mind chiefly .   210

XVII. God is free from passions, nor is he affected with any
emotion of pleasure or pain   210
Corollary   210

XVIII. No one can hate God   210
Corollary   210
Note   210

XIX. He who loves God cannot endeavour to bring it about
that God should love him in return   .   .   .   211

XX. This love towards God cannot be polluted by an
emotion either of envy or jealousy, but it is cherished
the more, the more we imagine men to be bound to God
by this bond of love   211
Note   211

XXI. The mind can imagine nothing nor recollect past
things save while in the body   213

XXII. In God, however, there is necessarily granted the
idea which expresses the essence of this or that human
body under the species of eternity   .   .   .   213

XXIII. The human mind cannot be absolutely destroyed
with the human body, but there is some part of it that
remains eternal   213
Note   214

XXIV. The more we understand individual things, the more
we understand God   214

XXV. The greatest endeavour of the mind and its greatest
virtue is to understand things by the third class of
knowledge   214

XXVI. The more apt the mind is to understand things by
the third class of knowledge, the more it desires to
understand things by this class of knowledge   .   .   215

XXVII. From this third class of knowledge the greatest
possible mental satisfaction arises   215

XXVIII. The endeavour or desire of knowing things according to the third class of knowledge cannot arise from
the first but the second class of knowledge .   .   .   215

XXIX. Whatever the mind understands under the species
of eternity, it does not understand owing to the fact that
it conceives the actual present existence of the body,
but owing to the fact that it conceives the essence of the
body under the species of eternity   216
Note   216

XXX. The human mind in so far as it knows itself and its
body under the species of eternity, thus far it necessarily
has knowledge of God, and knows that it exists in God
and is conceived through God   216

XXXI. The third kind of knowledge depends on the mind
as its formal cause in so far as the mind is eternal   .   217
Note   217

Contents

PROPOSITIONS   PAGE

XXXII. Whatever we understand according to the third
class of knowledge we are pleased with, and that accompanied with the idea of God as the cause . . . 217
Corollary 218

XXXIII. The intellectual love towards God which arises
from the third kind of knowledge is eternal . . 218
Note 218

XXXIV. The mind is only liable to emotions which are
referred to passions while the body lasts . . . 218
Corollary 218
Note 218

XXXV. God loves himself with infinite intellectual love . 219

XXXVI. The mental intellectual love towards God is the
very love of God with which God loves himself, not in so
far as he is infinite, but in so far as he can be expressed
through the essence of the human mind considered
under the species of eternity, that is, mental intellectual
love towards God is part of the infinite love with which
God loves himself 219
Corollary 219
Note 219

XXXVII. There is nothing in nature which is contrary to
this intellectual love or which can remove it . . 220
Note 220

XXXVIII. The more the mind understands things by the
second and third kinds of knowledge, the less it will be
passive to emotions which are evil, and the less it will
fear death 220
Note 221

XXXIX. He who has a body capable of many things, has a
mind of which the greater part is eternal . . . 221
Note 221

XL. The more perfection anything has, the more active and
the less passive it is; and contrariwise, the more active
it is, the more perfect it becomes 222
Corollary 222
Note 222

XLI. Although we did not know that our mind is eternal,
we would hold before all things piety and religion, and
absolutely all things which we have shown in Part IV.
to have reference to courage and nobility . . . 223
Note 223

XLII. Blessedness is not the reward of virtue, but virtue
itself: nor should we rejoice in it for that we restrain
our lusts, but, on the contrary, because we rejoice
therein we can restrain our lusts 223
Note 224

TREATISE ON THE CORRECTION OF THE UNDERSTANDING

PAGE

I. On the Good Things which Men desire for the most Part . 227

II. On the True and Supreme Good 229

III. Certain Rules of Life 231

IV. On the Four Modes of Perception 232

V. On the Best Mode of Perception 234

VI. On the Instruments of the Understanding, True Ideas . 235

VII. On the Right Method of Knowing 237

VIII. First Part of the Method—On Fictitious Ideas . . 241

IX. On the False Idea 248

X. On the Doubtful Idea 252

XI. On Memory and Forgetfulness—Conclusion . . . 253

XII. Second Part of the Method—On Double Perception . 256

XIII. On the Conditions of Definition 258

XIV. Of the Means by which Eternal Things are known . 259

XV. On the Power of the Understanding and its Properties . 261

BENEDICT DE SPINOZA

ETHICS

PROVED IN GEOMETRICAL ORDER

(ordine geometrico demonstrata)

DIVIDED INTO FIVE PARTS

SPINOZA'S ETHICS

FIRST PART

CONCERNING GOD

DEFINITIONS

I. I UNDERSTAND that to be CAUSE OF ITSELF (*causa sui*) whose essence involves existence and whose nature cannot be conceived unless existing.

II. That thing is said to be FINITE IN ITS KIND (*in suo genere finita*) which can be limited by another thing of the same kind. *E.g.*, a body is said to be finite because we can conceive another larger than it. Thus a thought is limited by another thought. But a body cannot be limited by a thought, nor a thought by a body.

III. I understand SUBSTANCE (*substantia*) to be that which is in itself and is conceived through itself: I mean that, the conception of which does not depend on the conception of another thing from which it must be formed.

IV. An ATTRIBUTE (*attributum*) I understand to be that which the intellect perceives as constituting the essence of a substance.

V. By MODE (*modus*) I understand the Modifications (*affectiones*) of a substance or that which is in something else through which it may be conceived.

VI. GOD (*Deus*) I understand to be a being absolutely infinite, that is, a substance consisting of infinite attributes, each of which expresses eternal and infinite essence.

Explanation.—I say absolutely infinite, but not in its kind. For of whatever is infinite only in its kind, we may deny the attributes to be infinite; but to what is absolutely infinite there appertains whatever expresses essence and involves no negation.

VII. That thing is said to be FREE (*libera*) which exists by the mere necessity of its own nature and is determined in its actions by itself alone. That thing is said to be NECESSARY (*necessaria*), or rather COMPELLED (*coacta*), when it is determined in its existence and actions by something else in a certain fixed ratio.

VIII. I understand ETERNITY (*æternitas*) to be existence itself, in so far as it is conceived to follow necessarily from the definition of an eternal thing.

Explanation.—For such existence is conceived as an eternal truth, just as is the essence of a thing, and therefore cannot be explained by duration or time, although duration can be conceived as wanting beginning and end.

AXIOMS

I. All things which are, are in themselves or in other things.

II. That which cannot be conceived through another thing must be conceived through itself.

III. From a given determined cause an effect follows of necessity, and on the other hand, if no determined cause is granted, it is impossible that an effect should follow.

IV. The knowledge of effect depends on the knowledge of cause, and involves the same.

V. Things which have nothing in common reciprocally cannot be comprehended reciprocally through each other, or, the conception of the one does not involve the conception of the other.

VI. A true idea should agree with its ideal (*ideatum*), *i.e.*, what it conceives.

VII. The essence of that which can be conceived as not existing does not involve existence.

PROPOSITIONS

PROP. I. A substance is prior in its nature to its modifications.

Proof.—This is obvious from Def. 3 and 5.

PROP. II. Two substances, having different attributes, have nothing in common between them.

Proof.—This also is obvious from Def. 3. For each of them must be in itself and through itself be conceived, or the conception of one of them does not involve the conception of the other.

PROP. III. Of two things having nothing in common between them, one cannot be the cause of the other.

Proof.—If they have nothing in common reciprocally, therefore (Ax. 5) they cannot be known through each other, and therefore (Ax. 4) one cannot be the cause of the other. *Q.e.d.*

PROP. IV. Two or three distinct things are distinguished one from the other either by the difference of the attributes of the substances or by the difference of their modifications.

Proof.—All things that are, are either in themselves or in other things (Ax. 1), that is (Def. 3 and 5), beyond the intellect nothing is granted save substances and their modifications. Nothing therefore is granted beyond the intellect, through which several things may be distinguished one from the other except substances, or, what is the same thing (Def. 4), their attributes and modifications. *Q.e.d.*

PROP. V. In the nature of things, two or more substances may not be granted having the same nature or attribute.

Proof.—If several distinct substances are given, they must be distinguished one from the other either by the difference of their attributes or their modifications (prev. Prop.). If, then, they are to be distinguished by the difference of their attributes, two or more cannot be granted having the same attribute. But if they are to be distinguished by the difference of their modifications, since a substance is prior in its nature to its modifications (Prop. 1), therefore let the modifications be laid aside and let the substance itself be considered in itself, that is (Def. 3 and 6), truly considered, and it could not then be distinguished from another, that is (prev. Prop.), two or more substances cannot have the same nature or attribute. *Q.e.d.*

PROP. VI. One substance cannot be produced by another.

Proof.—In the nature of things two substances cannot be granted with the same attribute (prev. Prop.), that is (Prop. 2), which have anything in common, and accordingly (Prop. 3) one of them cannot be the cause of the other or one cannot be produced by the other. *Q.e.d.*

Corollary.—Hence it follows that a substance cannot be produced from anything else. For in the nature of things nothing is given save substances and their modifications, as is obvious from Ax. 1 and Def. 3 and 5: and it cannot be produced from another substance (prev. Prop.). Therefore a substance cannot in any way be produced from anything else. *Q.e.d.*

Another Proof.—This can be more easily shown by the method of proving the contrary to be absurd. For if a substance can be produced from anything else, the knowledge of it should depend on the knowledge of its cause (Ax. 4), and consequently (Def. 3) it would not be a substance.

PROP. VII. Existence appertains to the nature of substance.

Proof.—A substance cannot be produced from anything else (prev. Prop., Coroll.): it will therefore be its own cause, that is (Def. 1), its essence necessarily involves existence, or existence appertains to the nature of it. *Q.e.d.*

PROP. VIII. All substance is necessarily infinite.

Proof.—No two or more substances can have the same attribute (Prop. 5), and it appertains to the nature of substance that it should exist (Prop. 7). It must therefore exist either finitely or infinitely. But not finitely. For (Def. 2) it would then be limited by some other substance of the same nature which also of necessity must exist (Prop. 7): and then two substances would be granted having the same attribute, which is absurd (Prop. 5). It will exist, therefore, infinitely. *Q.e.d.*

Note I.—As to call anything finite is, in reality, a denial in part, and to call it infinite is the absolute assertion of the existence of its nature, it follows, therefore (from Prop. 7 alone), that all substance must be infinite.

Note II.—I make no doubt but that to all those who form injudicious opinions of things and are not wont to see things through their first causes, it may be difficult to conceive the proof of the seventh Proposition; doubtless because they do not distinguish between the modifications of substances and the substances themselves, nor know they in what manner things are produced. Hence it comes to pass that they apply the principle which they see in common things to substances. For those who do not know the real causes of things confuse everything, and without the least mental repugnance they picture trees no less than men as speaking, and imagine men to be formed from stones no less than from seed, and any forms to be changed into any other forms whatsoever. Thus those who confuse divine with human nature easily attribute human passions to God, more especially if they do not know how passions are produced in the mind. But if men would give heed to the nature of substance they would doubt less concerning Prop. 7: rather they would reckon it an axiom above all others, and hold it among common opinions. For then by substance they would understand that which is in itself, and through itself is conceived, or rather that whose knowledge does not depend on the knowledge of any other thing; but by modification that which is in something else, and whose conception is formed from the conception of whatever it is in. Wherefore we may have true ideas of modifications which do not exist: since although they do not really exist outside the mind, yet their essence is comprehended in something else, and through that they may be conceived. The truth of true substances does not exist outside the mind unless it exists in themselves, because through themselves they are conceived. If any one should say, then, that he has a clear and distinct, that is a true, idea of substance, and should nevertheless doubt whether such substance existed, he would indeed be like one who should say that he had a true idea and yet should doubt whether it were false (as will be manifest to any one who regards it carefully); or if any one should say that substance was created, he would state at the same time that a false idea might be made true, than which it is difficult to conceive anything more absurd. And therefore it must necessarily be acknowledged that the existence of substance, like its essence, is an eternal truth. And hence we may conclude in another manner that there cannot be two substances of the same nature: which it is now perhaps worth while to show.   But let me arrange this in its proper order, therefore note: (1) the true definition of each thing involves nothing and expresses nothing but the nature of the thing defined.   From which it follows (2) that clearly no definition involves any certain number of individuals nor expresses it, since the definition expresses nothing else than the nature of a definite thing.   E.g., the definition of a triangle expresses nothing else than the simple nature of a triangle, but not a certain number of triangles.   Let it be noted again (3) that for each existing thing a cause must be given by reason of which it exists.   Note, moreover, that this cause, by reason of which anything exists, should either be contained in the very nature and definition of an existing thing (clearly because it appertains to its nature to exist), or should be given outside itself.   It follows from these positions that if a certain number of individuals exist in nature that a cause must necessarily be given why those individuals, and why not, more or less exist.   E.g., if in the nature of things twenty men were to exist (whom for the sake of better explanation I will say to have existed at the same time, and that none existed before them), it would not be enough when giving a reason why twenty men existed, to show the cause of human nature in kind, but it would be necessary also to show the cause why not more nor less than twenty existed: since (Note 3) a reason or cause should be given why each thing existed.   But this cause cannot be contained in human nature itself (Notes 2 and 3), since the true definition of man does not involve the number twenty.   Hence (Note 4) the reason why these twenty men exist, and consequently why each of them exists, must necessarily be given outside each one of them: and therefore it may be absolutely concluded that everything whose nature involves the existence of a certain number of individuals must of necessity have, since they exist, an external cause.   Now since, as has been shown already in this Note, existence appertains to the nature of substance, its definition must then of necessity involve existence, and therefore from its mere definition its existence can be concluded. But since, in Notes 2 and 3, we have shown that from its own definition the existence of several substances cannot follow, it follows necessarily therefore that two or more substances cannot have the same nature as was put forward.

PROP. IX. The more reality or being a thing has, the more attributes will it have.

Proof.—This is obvious from Def. 4.

PROP. X. Each attribute of the one substance must be conceived through itself.

Proof.—An attribute is that which the intellect perceives of a substance as constituting its essence (Def. 4), therefore (Def. 3) it must be conceived through itself. *Q.e.d.*

Note.—Hence it appears that, although two attributes are conceived really apart from each other, that is, one is conceived without the aid of the other, we cannot thence conclude that they form two entities or two different substances. For it follows from the nature of a substance that each of its attributes can be conceived through itself: since all the attributes it ever had were in it at the same time, nor could one of them be produced from another, but each of them expresses the reality or being of the substance. Therefore it is far from right to call it absurd to attribute several attributes to one substance; but on the other hand, nothing is more clear than that each entity should be conceived under the effects of some attribute, and the more reality or being it has, the more attributes expressing necessity or eternity and infinity belong to it; so that nothing can be clearer than that an entity must be defined as absolutely infinite (as we defined it in Def. 6), which consists of infinite attributes, each of which expresses a certain eternal and infinite essence. But if any one still asks by what sign we shall be able to know the difference of substances, let him read the following Propositions, which will show that in the nature of things only one substance exists, and that is absolutely infinite, wherefore he will ask for that sign in vain.

PROP. XI. God or a substance consisting of infinite attributes, each of which expresses eternal and infinite essence, necessarily exists.

Proof.—If you deny it, conceive, if it be possible, that God does not exist. Then (Ax. 7) his essence does not involve existence. But this (Prop. 7) is absurd. Therefore God necessarily exists. *Q.e.d.*

Another Proof.—A cause or reason ought to be assigned for each thing, why it exists or why it does not. *E.g.*, if a triangle exists, the reason or cause of its existence should be granted; but if it does not exist, the reason or cause should be granted which prevents it from existing or which takes its existence from it. Now this reason or cause must be contained in the nature of the thing or outside of it. *E.g.*, the reason why a square circle does not exist is shown by the very nature of the circle—clearly, for it involves a contradiction. On the other hand, the existence of substance follows from its nature alone, for that involves existence (*vide* Prop. 7). But the reason why a circle or triangle exists, or why it does not exist, does not follow from their nature, but from the order of universal corporeal nature. From this likewise it should follow either that a triangle necessarily exists or that it is impossible that it can now exist. But these are made manifest through themselves. From which it follows that that must of necessity exist concerning which no reason or cause is granted which could prevent its existence. If thus no reason or cause can be granted which could prevent the existence of God or take his existence from him, it must certainly be concluded that he does exist of necessity. But if such a reason or cause be granted, it must be granted either in the nature of God itself or outside of it, that is, in another substance of another nature. For if it were of the same nature, thereby it would be admitted that God is granted. But the substance of another nature has nothing in common with God (Prop. 2), and therefore can neither give him existence nor take it from him. And since the reason or cause which would take existence from God cannot be granted outside divine nature, *i.e.*, the nature of God, it must of necessity then be granted, if indeed God does not exist, in his own nature, and this would involve a contradiction. But to assert this of a being absolutely infinite and perfect in all things is absurd: therefore neither within God nor without him is any cause or reason granted which could take his existence from him, and consequently God must necessarily exist. *Q.e.d.*

Another Proof.—Inability to exist is want of power, and on the other hand, ability to exist is power (as is self-evident). If then that which now necessarily exists consists only of finite things, hence finite things are more powerful than a being absolutely infinite; and this, as is self-evident, is absurd. Therefore, either nothing exists, or a being absolutely infinite necessarily exists. But either in ourselves or in something else which exists of necessity, we also exist (*vide* Ax. 1, and Prop. 7). Therefore a being absolutely infinite, that is (Def. 6) God, necessarily exists. *Q.e.d.*

Note.—In this last proof, I wished to show the existence of God *a posteriori* so that it might the more easily be perceived, and not because the existence of God does not follow *a priori* from the same basis of argument. For since ability to exist is power, it follows that the more reality anything in nature has, the more power it will have to exist; and accordingly a being absolutely infinite, or God, has an absolutely infinite power of existence from itself, and on that account absolutely exists. Many, however, perhaps will not be able to see the truth of this proof easily, because they are accustomed to look at and consider things which flow from external causes and of these, those which are quickly made, that is, which exist easily, they see perish easily; and on the other hand, they judge those things to be harder to make, *i.e.*, not existing so easily, to which they find more attributes belong. But, in truth, to deliver them from these prejudices I need not show here in what manner or by what reason this statement, " that which is quickly made perishes speedily," is true, nor even, in considering the whole of nature, whether all things are equally difficult or not; but it suffices to note that I do not speak here of things which are made from external causes, but of substances alone which cannot be produced from any external cause. For those things which are made from external causes, whether they consist of many parts or few, whatever perfection or reality they have, it is all there by reason of their external cause, and therefore their existence arises merely from the perfection of some external cause and not their own. On the other hand, whatever perfection a substance may have is due to no external cause, wherefore its existence must follow from its nature alone, which is nothing else than its essence. Perfection, then, does not take existence from a thing, but on the contrary, gives it existence;

but imperfection, on the other hand, takes it away, and so we cannot be more certain of the existence of anything than of the existence of a being absolutely infinite or perfect, that is, God. Now since his essence excludes all imperfection and involves absolute perfection, by that very fact it removes all cause of doubt concerning his existence and makes it most certain: which will be manifest, I think, to such as pay it the least attention.

PROP. XII. No attribute of a substance can be truly conceived, from which it would follow that substance can be divided into parts.

Proof. — The parts into which substance so conceived may be divided will either retain the nature of substance or not. In the first case, then (Prop. 8), each part must be infinite and (Prop. 6) its own cause, and (Prop. 5) must possess different attributes; and so from one substance several can be made, which (Prop. 6) is absurd. Again, the parts would have nothing in common with the whole (Prop. 2), and the whole (Def. 4 and Prop. 10) could exist and be conceived without the parts which go to make it, which no one will doubt to be absurd. But in the second case, when the parts do not retain the nature of substance, then, when a substance is divided into equal parts, it will lose the nature of substance and will cease to be, which (Prop. 7) is absurd.

PROP. XIII. Substance absolutely infinite is indivisible.

Proof.—If it is divisible, the parts into which it is divided will either retain the nature of substance or will not. In the first case, several substances would be given having the same nature, which (Prop. 5) is absurd. In the second case, a substance absolutely infinite could cease to be (as above by Prop. 7), which is also absurd (Prop. 11).

Corollary.—From this it follows that no substance, and consequently no corporeal substance, in so far as it is substance, can be divided into parts.

Note.—That substance is indivisible can be seen more easily from this, that the nature of substance cannot be conceived except as infinite, and that by a part of a substance nothing else can be conceived than a finite substance, which (Prop. 8) involves an obvious contradiction.

PROP. XIV. Except God no substance can be granted or conceived.

Proof.—As God is a being absolutely infinite, to whom no attribute expressing the essence of substance can be denied (Def. 6), and as he necessarily exists (Prop. 11), if any other substance than God be given, it must be explained by means of some attribute of God, and thus two substances would exist possessing the same attribute, which (Prop. 5) is absurd; and so no other substance than God can be granted, and consequently not even be conceived. For if it can be conceived it must necessarily be conceived as existing, and this by the first part of this proof is absurd. Therefore except God no substance can be granted or conceived. *Q.e.d.*

Corollary I.—Hence it distinctly follows that (1) God is one alone, *i.e.*, there is none like him, or in the nature of things only one substance can be granted, and that is absolutely infinite, as we intimated in the Note of Prop. 10.

Corollary II.—It follows, in the second place, that extension and thought are either attributes of God or modifications of attributes of God.

PROP. XV. Whatever is, is in God, and nothing can exist or be conceived without God.

Proof.—Save God no substance is granted or can be conceived (Prop. 14), that is (Def. 3), a thing which is in itself and through itself is conceived. But modifications (Def. 5) cannot exist or be conceived without substance, wherefore these can only exist in divine nature, and through that alone be conceived. But nothing is granted save substances and their modifications (Ax. 1). Therefore nothing can exist or be conceived without God. *Q.e.d.*

Note.—There are some who think God to be like man in mind and body, and liable to all passions. Yet how far this is from a true conception of God must be seen already from what has already been proved. But I will pass by these people; for those who have considered divine nature in any manner have denied that God is corporeal; which they have excellently proved from the fact that by body we understand a certain quantity in length, breadth, and depth, with a certain shape, and what could be more absurd than to say this of God, a being absolutely infinite? However, from other arguments by which they try to prove this point, they show

clearly that they completely separate corporeal or extended
substance from divine nature and regard it as created by God.
But from what divine power it could have been created they
know not, which shows that they do not understand what they
themselves are saying. But I at least have proved with
sufficient clearness, I think, that no substance can be produced or created from another (*vide* Coroll., Prop. 6, and Note
2, Prop. 8). Moreover (in Prop. 14), we have shown that
save God no substance can be granted or conceived. Hence
we conclude that extended substance is one of the infinite
attributes of God. But for the better and fuller explanation of this I shall refute the arguments of my opponents
for all these arguments seem to return to this point. In the
first place, that corporeal substance, as far as it is substance
consists, they think, of parts: consequently they deny that
it can be infinite and consequently appertain to God. And
this they illustrate with many examples, from which I will
select one or two. If corporeal substance, they say, is infinite, let it be conceived as divided into two parts; each part
then will be either finite or infinite. If they are finite, then
the infinite is composed of two finite parts, which is absurd.
If they are infinite, then one thing is given as twice as
infinite as another, which also is absurd. Or again, if an

infinite distance is mea-
sured in equal feet, it
would consist of an in-
finite number of these,
or the same if it were
measured in inches; and
so one infinite number
would be twelve times
larger than another. And
then if you would con-
ceive an infinite quantity
from any point, let two
lines be drawn as AB
and AC, of a fixed length at first, but increasing to infinity; it is certain that the distance between B and C will
continue to increase, and from being a determined and finite
distance it will become immeasurable and infinite. They
consider then that these absurdities follow from the supposi-
tion of an infinite quantity, and thence conclude that corporeal substance must be finite, and consequently cannot

appertain to the essence of God. The second argument is
also drawn from the great perfection of God. For God, say
they, as a being perfect in all things, cannot be passive;
but corporeal substance, as it is divisible, can be passive.
It follows then that this cannot appertain to the essence of
God. These are the arguments which I find in the writings
of many who would endeavour to prove that corporeal substance is unworthy of divine nature and cannot appertain to
it. But in truth if any one carefully attends to this, he will
find that I have already answered these arguments, since
they are based on this: that they suppose corporeal substance to be composed of parts, which I have shown in Prop.
12 and the Coroll., Prop. 13, to be absurd. Thence if any
wish to consider the matter rightly, they will see that all
these absurdities (if indeed they are all absurdities, for I am
not disputing this now), from which they wish to conclude
that extended substance is finite, follow not from the fact
that an infinite quantity is supposed, but that they suppose
an infinite quantity to be measurable and composed of finite
parts; and from the absurdities which thence follow they
cannot conclude anything else than that an infinite quantity
is not measurable nor composed of finite parts. But this is
the same as we have already shown in Prop. 12, etc. And
so the arrow which they intended for us they now direct
against themselves. If, therefore, they nevertheless wish to
conclude from this absurdity of theirs that extended substance is finite, they do nothing else in truth than what he
would do who supposed a circle to have the properties of a
square, and thence concluded that a circle did not have a
centre from which all lines drawn to the circumference are
equal. For corporeal substance, which can only be conceived as infinite, without like and indivisible, they conceive,
in order to prove it finite, to be composed of finite parts, and
to be multiplex and divisible. Thus also others, having
pretended that a line is composed of points, can find many
arguments wherewith to show that a line cannot be infinitely
divided. And indeed it is no less absurd to suppose that
corporeal substance is composed of bodies or parts than to
suppose that a body is composed of surfaces, or surfaces
of lines, and lines of points. But this all must confess
who know clear reason to be infallible, and more especially
those who deny the possibility of a vacuum. For if corporeal substance could be thus divided so that its parts were

really distinct, why could not one part be annihilated while
the others remain united as before? and why should they all
be so adjusted lest a vacuum be made? For clearly of
things which in reality are reciprocally distinct from each
other, one can exist without the other and can remain in
the same condition. Since nature abhors a vacuum (of
which more is to be said), and all parts must so concur as to
prevent the formation of a vacuum, it follows that the parts
of a corporeal substance cannot be really distinguished one
from the other, that is, a corporeal substance, in so far as it
is substance, cannot be divided into parts. If any one
should still ask why we are so prone by nature to divide
quantities, I would make answer to him that quantity is
conceived by us in two manners, to wit, abstractly and super-
ficially, as an offspring of imagination or as a substance, which
is done by the intellect alone. If, then, we look at quantity
as it is in the imagination, which we often and very easily
do, it will be found to be finite, divisible, and composed of
parts; but if we look at it as it is in the intellect and conceive it, in so far as it is a substance, which is done with
great difficulty, then as we have already sufficiently shown,
it will be found to be infinite, without like, and indivisible.
This to all who know how to distinguish between the imagination and the intellect will be quite clear: more especially
if attention is paid to this, that matter is the same everywhere, and its parts cannot be distinguished one from the
other except in so far as we conceive matter to be modified in
different modes, whence its parts are distinguished one from
the other in mode but not in reality. *E.g.*, we can conceive
water, in so far as it is water, to be divided and its parts
separated one from the other: but not in so far as it is a corporeal substance, for then it is neither separated nor divided.
Again, water, in so far as it is water, can be made and destroyed, but in so far as it is substance it can neither be made
nor destroyed. And thus I think I have answered the second
argument, since it is also founded on this, that matter, in so
far as it is substance, is divisible and composed of parts. And
though this should not be so, I know not why substance
should be unworthy of the divine nature, for (Prop. 14)
beyond God no substance can be given by which it would
be affected. Everything, I say, is in God, and all things
which are made, are made by the laws of the infinite nature
of God, and necessarily follow from the necessity of his

essence (as I shall soon show). And therefore no reason can
be given by which it can be said that God is passive to anything else than himself, or that extended substance is unworthy of divine nature, though it be supposed divisible, as
long as it is granted to be eternal and infinite. But I have
said enough of this at present.

PROP. XVI. Infinite things in infinite modes (that is, all
things which can fall under the heading of infinite intellect)
must necessarily follow from the necessity of divine nature.

Proof.—This proposition must be manifest to every one
who will but consider this, that from a given definition of
everything the intellect gathers certain properties, which in
truth necessarily follow from the definition (that is, the very
essence of the thing), and so the more reality the definition
of a thing expresses, *i.e.*, the more reality the essence of a
definite thing involves, the more properties the intellect
will gather. But as divine nature has absolutely infinite
attributes, each of which expresses infinite essence in its kind,
infinite things in infinite modes (that is, all things that fall
under the heading of infinite intellect) must necessarily follow
its necessity. *Q.e.d.*

Corollary I.—Hence it follows that God is the effecting
cause of all things which can be perceived by infinite intellect.

Corollary II.—Hence it follows that God is the cause
through himself, and not indeed by accident.

Corollary III.—Hence it follows that God is absolutely
the first cause.

PROP. XVII. God acts merely according to his own laws,
and is compelled by no one.

Proof.—That infinite things must follow from the mere
necessity of divine nature, or what is the same thing, by the
mere laws of divine nature, we have just shown (Prop. 16),
and (Prop. 15) we have shown that nothing can be conceived without God, but that everything exists in God.
Therefore nothing outside God can exist by which he could
be determined or compelled in his actions; and therefore
God acts merely according to the laws of his nature, and is
compelled by no one. *Q.e.d.*

Corollary I.—Hence it follows that no cause can be given
except the perfection of God's nature which extrinsically or
intrinsically incites him to action.

Corollary II.—Hence it follows that God alone is a free cause. For God alone exists from the mere necessity of his own nature (Prop. 11, and Coroll. 1, Prop. 14), and by the mere necessity of his nature he acts (prev. Prop.). And therefore (Def. 7) he is the only free cause. *Q.e.d.*

Note.—Others think that God is a free cause because they think he can bring it to pass that those things which we say follow from his nature, that is, which are in his power, should not be made, or that they should not be produced by him. But this is the same as if they said that God can bring it to pass that it should not follow from the nature of a triangle that its three angles are equal to two right angles, or that from a given cause no effect should follow, which is absurd. For further on, without the aid of this proposition, I shall show that intellect and will do not appertain to the nature of God. I am well aware that there are many who say they can show that the greatest intellect and free will appertain to the nature of God: for they say they know nothing more perfect to attribute to God than that which among us is the greatest perfection. Further, although they conceive God's intellect as having the greatest perception of things in action, yet they do not believe that he can bring about the existence of everything which his intellect perceives in action: for they think they would thus destroy the power of God. They say that if he were to create everything that his intellect perceives, he would then not be able to create anything more, which they think opposed to the omnipotence of God; and accordingly they prefer to state that God is indifferent to all things, and creates nothing else than that which he determines to create by his own free will. But I think I have sufficiently shown (*vide* Prop. 16) that from God's supreme power or infinite nature, infinite things in infinite modes, that is, all things, necessarily flow, or always follow from the same necessity; in the same manner it also follows from the nature of a triangle from eternity to eternity that the three angles will be equal to two right angles. Wherefore God's omnipotence was in action from eternity, and will remain in the same state of action through all eternity. And in this manner, in my opinion, the perfection of God's omnipotence is asserted to be far greater. Indeed, the opponents of this view seem to deny (to speak freely) the omnipotence of God. For they are obliged to confess

that God's intellect perceives many things that could be
created which nevertheless he cannot ever create. Because
otherwise, if he created all that his intellect perceived, he
would, according to them, exhaust his omnipotence and
render himself imperfect. As, therefore, they say that God
is perfect, they are reduced to state at the same time that
he cannot complete all those things to which his power extends; and anything more absurd than this or more opposed
to the omnipotence of God I cannot imagine could be conceived. Moreover (as I would like to say something concerning the intellect and will which we commonly attribute to
God), if intellect and will appertain to the eternal essence of
God, something far else must be understood by these two
attributes than what is commonly understood by men. For
intellect and will, which would constitute the essence of God,
must differ *toto cælo* from our will and intellect, nor can
they agree in anything save name, nor any more than the
dog, as a heavenly body, and the dog, as a barking animal,
agree. This I shall show in the following manner. If intellect appertains to divine nature, it cannot, as with our
intellect, be posterior (as many would have it) or even simultaneous in nature with the things conceived by the intellect
since (Coroll. 1, Prop. 16) God is prior in cause alike to
all things; but on the other hand, truth and the formal
essence of things are such, because they so exist objectively
in God's intellect. Wherefore the intellect of God, as far as
it can be conceived to form his essence, is in truth the cause
of things, both of their essence and their existence: which
seems to have been noticed by those who have asserted that
God's intellect, will, and power are one and the same thing.
Now as God's intellect is the only cause of things, *i.e.*, the
cause both of their essence and their existence, it must therefore necessarily differ from them in respect to its essence
and in respect to its existence. For that which is caused
differs from its cause precisely in that which it has from its
cause. *E.g.*, a man is the cause of existence but not the
cause of essence of another man (for the latter is an eternal
truth): and so they can certainly agree in essence, but in
existence they must differ, and on that account if the existence of one of them perish, that of the other does not consequently perish; but if the essence of one of them could be
destroyed or be made false, the essence of the other must

also be destroyed. On this account a thing that is the cause of the essence and existence of any effect must differ from that effect both in respect to its essence and in respect to its existence. Now the intellect of God is the cause of the essence and existence of our intellect: and therefore God's intellect, in so far as it can be conceived to form part of his essence, differs from our intellect both in respect to its essence and in respect to its existence, nor in any other thing save name can agree with it, which we wished to prove. And the argument concerning will would proceed in the same manner, as can easily be seen.

Prop. XVIII. God is the indwelling and not the transient cause of all things.

Proof.—All things that are, are in God, and through God must be conceived (Prop. 15), and therefore (Prop. 16, Coroll. 1) God is the cause of all things which are in him: which is the first point. Again, beyond God no substance, that is (Def. 3), a thing which outside God is in itself, can be granted (Prop. 14): which was the second point. Therefore God is the indwelling and not the transient cause of all things. *Q.e.d.*

Prop. XIX. God and all the attributes of God are eternal.

Proof.—God (Def. 6) is a substance, which (Prop. 11) necessarily exists, that is (Prop. 7), to whose nature existence appertains, or (what is the same thing) from whose definition existence itself follows: accordingly (Def. 8) it is eternal. Again, by the attributes of God must be understood that which (Def. 4) expresses the essence of divine substance, that is, that which appertains to substance; that itself, I say, the attributes must involve. But eternity (as I have shown from Prop. 7) appertains to the nature of substance. Therefore each of the attributes must involve eternity, and therefore, they are all eternal. *Q.e.d.*

Note.—This proposition is also most clearly shown from the proof which I used to prove the existence of God. From that proof, I say, it is certain that the existence of God, that is, his essence, is an eternal truth. Again, in the principles of Cartesian philosophy (Part I. Prop. 19) I proved the eternity of God in another way, but it is not necessary to repeat it here.

Prop. XX. God's existence and his essence are one and the same thing.

Proof.—God (prev. Prop.) and all his attributes are eternal, that is (Def. 8), each of his attributes expresses existence. Therefore the same attributes of God, which (Def. 4) explain the eternal essence of God, explain at the same time his existence, that is, whatever forms the essence of God, forms also his existence: therefore the essence and existence of God are one and the same thing. *Q.e.d.*

Corollary I.—Hence it follows that the existence of God, like his essence, is an eternal truth.

Corollary II.—Hence it follows that God and all his attributes are immutable. For if they were changed with regard to existence, they must also (prev. Prop.) be changed with regard to essence, that is (as is self-evident), falsehood would be made from truth, which is absurd.

Prop. XXI. All things which follow from the absolute nature of any attribute of God must exist for ever and infinitely, or must exist eternally and infinitely through that same attribute.

Proof.—Conceive, if it can happen (if indeed you deny it), that anything in any attribute of God following from its absolute nature is finite and has a fixed existence or duration, *e.g.*, the idea of God in thought. But thought, since it is supposed an attribute of God, is necessarily (Prop. 11) infinite in its nature. In so far as it has the idea of God, it is supposed to be finite. But (Def. 2) it cannot be conceived finite unless it is limited by thought itself; but it cannot be limited by thought in so far as it forms the idea of God, for then it would be finite: so it must be limited by thought in so far as it does not form the idea of God, and this idea nevertheless (Prop. 11) must exist necessarily. A thought is therefore granted which does not form an idea of God, and therefore from its nature, in so far as it is an absolute thought, the idea of God does not necessarily follow: thought is then conceived as forming and not forming the idea of God, which is contrary to the hypothesis. So if the idea of God in thought or anything (whatever is assumed, for the proof is universal) in any attribute of God follows from the necessity of the absolute nature of that attribute, it must of necessity be infinite: which is the first point.

Again, that which follows from the necessity of the nature of any attribute cannot have a fixed duration. If you deny this, let something which follows from the necessity of the nature of any attribute be supposed to be granted in any attribute of God, *e.g.*, the idea of God in thought, and let it be supposed either not to have existed at some past time, or to cease to exist in some future time. But since thought is supposed to be an attribute of God, it must of necessity exist, and that immutably (Prop. 11, and Coroll. 2, Prop. 20). Thence it follows that outside the limits of the duration of the idea of God (for we suppose it once not to have existed, or not to exist at some future time), thought must exist without the idea of God: and this is contrary to the hypothesis, for it is supposed that the idea of God necessarily follows from the given thought. Therefore the idea of God in thought or anything that follows of necessity from the absolute nature of any attribute of God cannot have a fixed duration, but through the attribute itself is eternal: which was the second point. Note that this can be asserted of anything which in any attribute of God follows of necessity from the absolute nature of God.

PROP. XXII. Whatever follows from an attribute of God, in so far as it is modified by such a modification as exists of necessity and infinitely through the same, must also exist of necessity and infinitely.

Proofs.—The proof of this proposition proceeds in the same manner as the proof of the last proposition.

PROP. XXIII. Every mode which of necessity and infinitely exists must of necessity have followed either from the absolute nature of some attribute of God, or from some attribute modified by a modification which exists of necessity and infinitely.

Proof.—Now mode is in something else through which it must be conceived (Def. 5), that is (Prop. 15), it is in God alone, and can only be conceived through God. If, therefore, mode be conceived to exist of necessity and to be infinite, its existence and infinity must be concluded or perceived through some attribute of God, in so far as this attribute is conceived to express infinity and necessity of existence, or (Def. 8) eternity, that is (Def. 6 and Prop.

19), as far as it is considered absolutely. Mode, therefore, which of necessity and infinitely exists, must have followed from the absolute nature of some attribute of God, and that either immediately (concerning which see Prop. 21) or by means of some modification which follows from the absolute nature of the attribute, that is (prev. Prop.), which necessarily and infinitely exists. *Q.e.d.*

PROP. XXIV. The essence of things produced by God does not involve existence.

Proof.—This is clear from Def. 1. For that whose nature (considered in itself) involves existence is its own cause, and exists merely by the necessity of its own nature.

Corollary.—Hence it follows that God is not only the cause that all things begin to exist, but also that they continue to exist, or (to use a scholastic term) God is the cause of the being (*causa essendi*) of things. For whether things exist or whether they do not, however often we consider their essence, we will find it to involve neither existence nor duration; and their essence cannot be the cause either of their existence or their duration, but only God, to whose nature alone existence appertains (Coroll. 1, Prop. 14).

PROP. XXV. God is not only the effecting cause of the existence of things, but also of their essence.

Proof.—If you deny it, then let God be not the cause of the essence of things: therefore (Ax. 4) the essence of things can be conceived without God. But this (Prop. 15) is absurd. Therefore God is the cause of the essence of things. *Q.e.d.*

Note.—This proposition follows more clearly from Prop. 16. For it follows from this, that from a given divine nature, the essence, as well as the existence of things, must of necessity be concluded; and to express it shortly, in that sense in which God is said to be his own cause, he must also be said to be the cause of all things, which will be seen still more clearly from the following corollary.

Corollary.—Particular things are nothing else than modifications of attributes of God, or modes by which attributes of God are expressed in a certain and determined manner. The proof of this is clear from Prop. 15 and Def. 5.

PROP. XXVI. A thing which is determined for the performing of anything was so determined necessarily by God, and a thing which is not determined by God cannot determine of itself to do anything.

Proof.—That through which things are said to be determined for performing anything must necessarily be something positive (as is self-evident): and therefore God, by the necessity of his nature, is the effecting cause of the essence and existence of this (Prop. 25 and 16): which was the first point. From which clearly follows that which was proposed in the second place. For if a thing which is not determined by God could determine itself, the first part of this proof would be false: which is absurd, as we have shown.

PROP. XXVII. A thing which is determined by God for the performing of anything cannot render itself undetermined.

Proof.—This is obvious from the third axiom.

PROP. XXVIII. Every individual thing, or whatever thing that is finite and has a determined existence, cannot exist nor be determined for action unless it is determined for action and existence by another cause which is also finite and has a determined existence; and again, this cause also cannot exist nor be determined for action unless it be determined for existence and action by another cause which also is finite and has a determined existence: and so on to infinity.

Proof.—Whatever is determined for existence or action is so determined by God (Prop. 26, and Coroll., Prop. 24). But that which is finite and has a determined existence cannot be produced from the absolute nature of any attribute of God: for anything that follows from the absolute nature of any attribute of God must be infinite and eternal (Prop. 21). It must have followed, therefore, from God or from some attribute of his, in so far as it is considered as modified in some mode: for save substance and modes nothing is granted (Ax. 1, and Def. 3 and 5), and modes (Coroll., Prop. 25) are nothing else than modifications of attributes of God. But it also cannot have followed from God or any attribute of his, in so far as it is modified by some modification which is eternal and infinite (Prop. 22). It follows, then, that it must have been determined for existence or action by God or some attribute of his, in so far as it is modified by a modifica-

Concerning God

was the first point. Then again, this cause or mode (by the
same reason by which we have proved the first part) must
also have been determined by another cause which also is
finite and has a determined existence; and again, the latter
(by the same reason) must have been determined by another:
and so on to infinity. *Q.e.d.*

Note.—As certain things must have been produced immediately by God, for example, those things which necessarily
follow from his absolute nature, by means of these first
causes, which nevertheless cannot exist nor even be conceived without God, it follows that God is the proximate
cause of those things immediately produced by him, absolutely, not, as some would have it, in his kind. For the
effects of God cannot exist or be conceived without their
cause (Prop. 15, and Coroll., Prop. 24). It follows, again,
that God cannot be said in truth to be the remote cause
of individual things unless we would thus distinguish these
from the things which are immediately produced by God,
or rather which follow from his absolute nature. For we
understand by a remote cause one which is in no wise connected with its effect. But all things which are, are in God,
and so depend on God that without him they can neither
exist nor be conceived.

Prop. XXIX. In the nature of things nothing contingent
(*contingens*) is granted, but all things are determined by the
necessity of divine nature for existing and working in a certain
way.

Proof.—Whatever is, is in God (Prop. 15). But God
cannot be called a contingent thing: for (by Prop. 11) he
exists of necessity and not contingently. Again, the modes
of divine nature do not follow from it contingently, but of
necessity (Prop. 16), and that either in so far as divine nature
be considered absolutely or as determined for certain action
(Prop. 27). Now God is the cause of these modes, not only
in so far as they simply exist (Coroll., Prop. 24), but also in so
far as they are considered as determined for the working of
anything (Prop. 26). For if they are not determined by God,
it is impossible, not contingent indeed, that they should
determine themselves; and on the other hand, if they are
determined by God, it is impossible and in no wise contingent

for them to render themselves undetermined. Wherefore all things are determined by the necessity of divine nature, not only for existing, but also for existing and working after a certain manner, and nothing contingent is granted. *Q.e.d.*

Note.—Before proceeding, I would wish to explain, or rather to remind you, what we must understand by active and passive nature (*natura naturans* and *natura naturata*), for I think that from the past propositions we shall be agreed that by nature active we must understand that which is in itself and through itself is conceived, or such attributes of substance as express eternal and infinite essence, that is (Coroll. 1, Prop. 14, and Coroll. 2, Prop. 17), God, in so far as he is considered as a free cause. But by nature passive I understand all that follows from the necessity of the nature of God, or of any one of his attributes, that is, all the modes of the attributes of God, in so far as they are considered as things which are in God, and which cannot exist or be conceived without God.

PROP. XXX. Intellect, finite or infinite in actuality (*actus*), must comprehend the attributes of God and the modifications of God and nothing else.

Proof.—A true idea must agree with its ideal (Ax. 6), that is (as is self-evident), that which is contained in the intellect objectively must of necessity be granted in nature. But in nature (Coroll. 1, Prop. 14), only one substance can be granted, and that is God, and only such modifications can be granted (Prop. 15) as are in God and (same Prop.) cannot exist or be conceived without God. Therefore, intellect finite or infinite in actuality must comprehend the attributes and modifications of God and nothing else. *Q.e.d.*

PROP. XXXI. The intellect in actuality, whether it be finite or infinite, as also will, desire, love, etc., must be referred not to active, but passive nature.

Proof.—Now by intellect (as is self-evident) we do not understand absolute thought, but only a certain mode of thinking which differs from other modes, such as desire and love, etc., and therefore must (Def. 5) be conceived through absolute thought: moreover (Prop. 15 and Def. 6), it must be so conceived through some attribute of God which expresses eternal and infinite essence of thought, that

Concerning God25

without it, it can neither exist nor be conceived. On this
account (Note, Prop. 29), like the other modes of thinking,
the intellect must be referred not to active but passive
nature. *Q.e.d.*

Note.—The reason why I speak here of intellect in actuality
is not that I concede that intellect in potentiality can be
granted, but that I wish to avoid all confusion, and would
not speak of anything save that so easily perceived by us,
that is, understanding itself, for nothing is so clearly perceived
by us as this. For we can perceive nothing which does not
lead to a greater comprehension of understanding.

PROP. XXXII. Will can only be called a necessary cause,
not a free one.

Proof.—Will, like intellect, is only a certain mode of
thinking, and therefore (Prop. 28) any single volition
cannot exist or be determined for performing anything unless
it be determined by some other cause, and this one again
by another, and so on to infinity. Now if will be supposed
infinite, it must then be determined for existence and action
by God, in so far, not as he is an infinite substance, but as
he has an attribute expressing infinite and eternal essence of
thought (Prop. 23). So in whatever way it be conceived,
whether as finite or infinite, it requires a cause by which it
is determined for existence or action: and therefore (Def. 7)
it cannot be said to be a free cause, but only a necessary
one. *Q.e.d.*

Corollary I.—Hence it follows that God does not act from
freedom of will.

Corollary II.—Hence it follows again that will and intellect hold the same place in the nature of God as motion
and rest, and that, absolutely, as with all natural things which
(Prop. 29) must be determined by God in a certain way
for existence and action. For will, like all other things,
needs a cause by which it is determined in a certain way for
existence or action. And although from a given will or
intellect infinite things follow, yet it cannot be said on that
account that God acts from freedom of will any more than it
can be said that, as infinite things follow from motion and
rest (for infinite things follow from these too), God acts
from freedom of motion and rest. Wherefore will does not
appertain to the nature of God any more than the rest of

the things of nature, but holds the same place in God's nature as motion and rest, and all other things which we have shown to follow from the necessity of divine nature, and to be determined by it for existence and action in a certain way.

Prop. XXXIII. Things could not have been produced by God in any other manner or order than that in which they were produced.

Proof.—All things must have followed of necessity from a given nature of God (Prop. 16), and they were determined for existence or action in a certain way by the necessity of divine nature (Prop. 29). And so if things could have been of another nature or determined in another manner for action so that the order of nature were different, therefore, also, the nature of God could be different than it is now: then (Prop. 11) another nature of God must exist, and consequently two or more Gods could be granted, and this (Coroll. 1, Prop. 14) is absurd. Wherefore things could not have been produced in any other way or order, etc. *Q.e.d.*

Note I.—Although I have shown more clearly than the sun at noonday that there is absolutely nothing in things by which we can call them contingent, yet I would wish to explain here in a few words what is the signification of contingent (*contingens*); but first that of necessary (*necessarium*) and impossible (*impossibile*). Anything is said to be necessary either by reason of its essence or its cause. For the existence of anything necessarily follows either from its very essence or definition, or from a given effecting cause. A thing is said to be impossible by reason of these same causes: clearly for that its essence or definition involves a contradiction, or that no external cause can be given determined for the production of such a thing. But anything can in no wise be said to be contingent save in respect to the imperfection of our knowledge. For when we are not aware that the essence of a thing involves a contradiction, or when we are quite certain that it does not involve a contradiction, and yet can affirm nothing with certainty concerning its existence, as the order of causes has escaped us, such a thing can seem neither necessary nor impossible to us: and therefore we call it either contingent or possible.

Note II.—It clearly follows from the preceding remarks

that things were produced by the consummate perfection of
God, since they followed necessarily from a given most
perfect nature. Nor does this argue any imperfection in
God, for his perfection has forced us to assert this. And
from the contrary of this proposition it would have followed
(as I have just shown) that God was not consummately
perfect, inasmuch as if things were produced in any other
way there must have been attributed to God a nature
different to that which we are forced to attribute to him
from the consideration of a perfect being. I make no doubt,
however, but that many will deride this opinion as absurd,
nor will they agree to give up their minds to the contemplation of it: and on no other account than that they are wont
to ascribe to God a freedom far different to that which has
been propounded by us (Def. 6). They attribute to him
absolute will. Yet I make no doubt but that, if they wish
rightly to consider the matter and follow our series of propositions, weighing well each of them, they will reject that
freedom which they now attribute to God, not only as futile,
but also clearly as an obstacle to knowledge. Nor is there
any need for me here to repeat what was said in the note
on Prop. 17. But for their benefit I shall show this much,
that although it be conceded that will appertains to the
essence of God, yet it nevertheless follows that things could
not have been created in any other manner or order than
that in which they were created; and this will be easy to
show if first we consider the very thing which they themselves grant, namely, that it depends solely on the decree
and will of God that each thing is what it is, for otherwise
God would not be the cause of all things. They grant
further, that all the decrees of God have been appointed by
him through and from all eternity: for otherwise it would
argue mutability and imperfection in God. But as in
eternity there are no such things given as *when, before,* or
after, hence it follows merely from the perfection of God that
he never can or could decree anything else than what is
decreed, or that God did not exist before his decrees, nor
without them could he exist. But they say that although
we suppose that God had made the nature of things different
or had decreed otherwise concerning nature and her order
from all eternity, it would not thence follow that God was
imperfect. Now if they say this, they must also admit that

God can change his decrees.   For had God decreed otherwise
than he has concerning nature and her order, that is, had he
willed and conceived anything else concerning nature, he
must necessarily have some other intellect and will than those
which he now has.   And if it is permitted to attribute to
God another will and intellect than those which he now has,
without any change in his essence or perfection, what would
there be to prevent him from changing his decrees concerning
things created, and yet remaining perfect?   For his intellect
and will concerning things created and their order is the
same in respect to his essence and perfection, in whatever
manner they may be conceived.   Furthermore, all the
philosophers, I have seen, concede that no such thing as
potential intellect in God can be granted, but only actual.
But as they make no distinction between his intellect and
will and his essence, being all agreed in this, it follows then
that if God had another actual intellect and will, he must
necessarily also have another essence; and thence, as I
concluded in the beginning, that, were things produced in
any other way than that in which they were, God's intellect
and will, that is, as has been granted, his essence, also must
have been other than it is, which is absurd.

Now since things could not have been produced in any other
manner or order than that in which they were, and since this
follows from the consummate perfection of God, there is no
rational argument to persuade us to believe that God did
not wish to create all the things which are in his intellect,
and that in the same perfection in which his intellect conceived them.   But they say that in things there is no such
a thing as perfection or imperfection, but that which causes
us to call a thing perfect or imperfect, good or bad, depends
solely on the will of God; moreover that if God, had willed
it he could have brought to pass that what is now perfection
might have been the greatest imperfection, and *vice versâ*.
But what else is this than to openly assert that God who
necessarily understands what he wishes, could bring to pass
by his own will that his intelligence should conceive things
in another manner than they now do?   This (as I have just
shown) is the height of absurdity.   Wherefore I can turn
their argument against them in the following manner.   All
things depend on the power of God.   That things should be
different from what they are would involve a change in the

will of God, and the will of God cannot change (as we have most clearly shown from the perfection of God): therefore things could not be otherwise than as they are. I confess that the theory which subjects all things to the will of an indifferent God and makes them dependent on his good will is far nearer the truth than that which states that God acts in all things for the furthering of good. For these seem to place something beyond God which does not depend on God, and to which God looks in his actions as to an example or strives after as an ultimate end. Now this is nothing else than subjecting God to fate, a greater absurdity than which it is difficult to assert of God, whom we have shown to be the first and only free cause of the essence of all things and their existence. Wherefore let me not waste more time in refuting such idle arguments.

PROP. XXXIV. The power of God is the same as his essence.

Proof.—It follows from the mere necessity of the essence of God that God is his own cause (Prop. 11), and (Prop. 16 and its Coroll.) the cause of all things. Therefore the power of God, by which he and all things are and act, is the same as his essence. *Q.e.d.*

PROP. XXXV. Whatever we conceive to be in the power of God necessarily exists.

Proof.—Now whatever is in the power of God must (prev. Prop.) be so comprehended in his essence that it follows necessarily from it, and so it necessarily exists. *Q.e.d.*

PROP. XXXVI. Nothing exists from whose nature some effect does not follow.

Proof.—Whatever exists expresses in a certain and determined manner (Coroll., Prop. 25) the nature or essence of God, that is (Prop. 34), whatever exists expresses in a certain and determined way the power of God, which is the cause of all things, and therefore (Prop. 16) from it some effect must follow. *Q.e.d.*

Appendix

In these propositions I have explained the nature and
properties of God: that he necessarily exists: that he is one
alone: that he exists and acts merely from the necessity of
his nature: that he is the free cause of all things and in what
manner: that all things are in God, and so depend upon him
that without him they could neither exist nor be conceived:
and finally, that all things were predetermined by God, not
through his free or good will, but through his absolute
nature or infinite power. I have endeavoured, moreover,
whenever occasion prompted, to remove any misunderstandings which might impede the good understanding of my
propositions. Yet as many misunderstandings still remain
which, to a very large extent, have prevented and do prevent
men from embracing the concatenation of things in the
manner in which I have explained it, I have thought it
worth while to call these into the scrutiny of reason. Now
since all these misunderstandings which I am undertaking
to point out depend upon this one point, that men commonly
suppose that all natural things act like themselves with an end
in view, and since they assert with assurance that God directs
all things to a certain end (for they say that God made all
things for man, and man that he might worship God), I
shall therefore consider this one thing first, inquiring in the
first place why so many fall into this error, and why all are
by nature so prone to embrace it; then I shall show its falsity,
and finally, how these misunderstandings have arisen concerning good and evil, virtue and sin, praise and blame, order and
confusion, beauty and ugliness, and other things of this kind.
But this is not the place to deduce these things from the
nature of the human mind. It will suffice here for me to
take as a basis of argument what must be admitted by all:
that is, that all men are born ignorant of the causes of things,
and that all have a desire of acquiring what is useful; that
they are conscious, moreover, of this. From these premisses
it follows then, in the first place, that men think themselves
free inasmuch as they are conscious of their volitions and
desires, and as they are ignorant of the causes by which they
are led to wish and desire, they do not even dream of their
existence. It follows, in the second place, that men do all

things with an end in view, that is, they seek what is useful. Whence it comes to pass that they always seek out only the final causes of things performed, and when they have divined these they cease, for clearly then they have no cause of further doubt. If they are unable to learn these causes from some one, nothing remains for them but to turn to themselves and reflect what could induce them personally to bring about such a thing, and thus they necessarily estimate other natures by their own. Furthermore, as they find in themselves and without themselves many things which aid them not a little in their quest of things useful to themselves, as, for example, eyes for seeing, teeth for mastication, vegetables and animals for food, the sun for giving light, the sea for breeding fish, they consider these things like all natural things to be made for their use; and as they know that they found these things as they were, and did not make them themselves, herein they have cause for believing that some one else prepared these things for their use. Now having considered things as means, they cannot believe them to be self-created; but they must conclude from the means which they are wont to prepare for themselves, that there is some governor or governors, endowed with human freedom, who take care of all things for them and make all things for their use. They must naturally form an estimate of the nature of these governors from their own, for they receive no information as regards them: and hence they come to say that the Gods direct all things for the use of men, that men may be bound down to them and do them the highest honour. Whence it has come about that each individual has devised a different manner in his own mind for the worship of God, that God may love him above the rest and direct the whole of nature for the gratification of his blind cupidity and insatiable avarice. Thus this misconception became a superstition, and fixed its roots deeply in the mind, and this was the reason why all diligently endeavoured to understand and explain the final causes of all things. But while they have sought to show that nature does nothing in vain (that is, nothing which is not of use to man), they appear to have shown nothing else than nature, the Gods and men are all mad. Behold now, I pray you, what this thing has become. Among so many conveniences of nature they were bound to find some inconveniences—storms, earthquakes, and diseases.

etc.—and they said these happened by reason of the anger of the Gods aroused against men through some misdeed or omission in worship; and although experience daily belied this, and showed with infinite examples that conveniences and their contraries happen promiscuously to the pious and impious, yet not even then did they turn from their inveterate prejudice. For it was easier for them to place this among other unknown things whose use they knew not, and thus retain their present and innate condition of ignorance, than to destroy the whole fabric of their philosophy and re-construct it. So it came to pass that they stated with the greatest certainty that the judgments of God far surpassed human comprehension: and this was the only cause that truth might have lain hidden from the human race through all eternity, had not mathematics, which deals not in the final causes, but the essence and properties of things, offered to men another standard of truth. And besides mathematics there are other causes (which need not be enumerated here) which enabled men to take notice of these general prejudices and to be led to the true knowledge of things.

Thus I have explained what I undertook in the first place. It is scarcely necessary that I should show that nature has no fixed aim in view, and that all final causes are merely fabrications of men. For I think this is sufficiently clear from the bases and causes from which I have traced the origin of this prejudice, from Prop. 16, and the corollaries of Prop. 32, and above all, from all those propositions in which I have shown that all things in nature proceed eternally from a certain necessity and with the utmost perfection. I should add, however, this further point, that the doctrine of final causes overthrows nature entirely. For that which in truth is a cause it considers as an effect, and *vice versâ*, and so it makes that which is first by nature to be last, and again, that which is highest and most perfect it renders imperfect. As these two questions are obvious, let us pass them over. It follows from Prop. 21, 22, and 23, that the effect which is produced immediately from God is the most perfect, and that one is more imperfect according as it requires more intermediating causes. But if those things which are immediately produced by God are made by him for the attaining of some end, then it necessarily follows that the ultimate things for whose sake these first were made must transcend all others. Hence this doctrine destroys the perfection of God: for if God seeks an end, he necessarily desires something which he lacks. And although theologians and metaphysicians make a distinction between the end that is want and that which is assimilation, they confess that God acts on his own account, and not for the sake of creating things; for before the creation they can assign nothing save God on whose account God acted, and so necessarily they are obliged to confess that God lacked and desired those things for the attainment of which he wished to prepare means, as is clear of itself. Nor must I pass by at this point that some of the adherents of this doctrine who have wished to show their ingenuity in assigning final causes to things have discovered a new manner of argument for the proving of their doctrine, to wit, not a reduction to the impossible, but a reduction to ignorance, which shows that they have no other mode of arguing their doctrine. For example, if a stone falls from a roof on the head of a passer-by and kills him, they will show by their method of argument that the stone was sent to fall and kill the man; for if it had not fallen on him by God's will, how could so many circumstances (for often very many circumstances concur at the same time) concur by chance? You will reply, perhaps: "That the wind was blowing, and that the man had to pass that way, and hence it happened." But they will retort: "Why was the wind blowing at that time? and why was the man going that way at that time?" If again you reply: "That the wind had then arisen on account of the agitation of the sea the day before, and the previous weather had been calm, and that the man was going that way at the invitation of a friend," they will again retort, for there is no end to their questioning: "Why was the sea agitated, and why was the man invited at that time?" And thus they will pursue you from cause to cause until you are glad to take refuge in the will of God, that is, the asylum of ignorance. Thus again, when they see the human body they are amazed, and as they know not the cause of so much art, they conclude that it was made not by mechanical art, but divine or supernatural art, and constructed in such a manner that one part may not injure another. And hence it comes about that those who wish to seek out the causes of miracles, and who wish to understand the things of nature as learned men, and not stare at them in amazement like fools, are soon deemed heretical and impious, and proclaimed such by those whom the mob adore as the interpreters of nature and the Gods. For these know that once ignorance is laid aside, that wonderment which is the only means of preserving their authority would be taken away from them. But I now leave this point and proceed to what I determined to discuss in the third place.

As soon as men had persuaded themselves that all things which were made, were made for their sakes, they were bound to consider as the best quality in everything that which was the most useful to them, and to esteem that above all things which brought them the most good. Hence they must have formed these notions by which they explain the things of nature, to wit, good, evil, order, confusion, hot, cold, beauty, and ugliness, etc.; and as they deemed themselves free agents, the notions of praise and blame, sin and merit, arose. The latter notions I will discuss when I deal with human nature later on, but the former are to be discussed now. They call all that which is conducive of health and the worship of God good, and all which is conducive of the contrary, evil. And forasmuch as those who do not understand the things of nature are certain of nothing concerning those things, but only imagine them and mistake their imagination for intellect, they firmly believe there is order in things, and are ignorant of them and their own nature. Now when things are so disposed that when they are represented to us through our senses we can easily imagine and consequently easily remember them, we call them well-ordered; and on the other hand, when we cannot do so, we call them ill-ordered or confused. Now forasmuch as those things, above all others, are pleasing to us which we can easily imagine, men accordingly prefer order to confusion, as if order were anything in nature save in respect to our imagination; and they say that God has created all things in order, and thus unwittingly they attribute imagination to God, unless indeed they would have that God providing for human imagination disposed all things in such a manner as would be most easy for our imagination; nor would they then find it perhaps a stumbling-block to their theory that infinite things are found which are far beyond the reach of our imagination, and many which confuse it through its weakness. But of this I have said

enough. The other notions also are nothing other than modes
of imagining in which the imagination is affected in diverse
manners, and yet they are considered by the ignorant as
very important attributes of things: for as we have said, they
think all things were made for them, and call their natures
good or bad, healthy or rotten, and corrupt, according as they
are affected by them. *E.g.*, if motion, which the nerves
receive by means of the eyes from objects before us, is conducive of health, those objects by which it is caused are called
beautiful; if it is not, then the objects are called ugly. Such
things as affect the nerves by means of the nose are thus
styled fragrant or evil-smelling; or when by means of the
mouth, sweet or bitter, tasty or insipid; when by means of
touch, hard or soft, rough or smooth, etc. And such things
as affect the ear are called noises, and form discord or
harmony, the last of which has delighted men to madness,
so that they have believed that harmony delights God. Nor
have there been wanting philosophers who assert that the
movements of the heavenly spheres compose harmony. All
of which sufficiently show that each one judges concerning
things according to the disposition of his own mind, or rather
takes for things that which is really the modifications of his
imagination. Wherefore it is not remarkable (as we may inci-
dentally remark) that so many controversies as we find have
arisen among men, and at last Scepticism. For although
human bodies agree in many points, yet in many others they
differ, and that which seems to one good may yet to another
seem evil; to one order, yet to another confusion; to one
pleasing, yet to another displeasing, and so on, for I need not
treat further of these, as this is not the place to discuss them
in detail, and indeed they must be sufficiently obvious to all.
For it is in every one's mouth: " As many minds as men,"
" Each is wise in his own manner," " As tastes differ, so do
minds "—all of which proverbs show clearly enough that men
judge things according to the disposition of their minds, and
had rather imagine things than understand them. For if
they understood things, my arguments would convince them
at least, just as mathematics, although they might not attract
them.

We have thus seen that all the arguments by which the
vulgar are wont to explain nature are nothing else than modes
of imagination, and indicate the nature of nothing whatever,

but only the constitution of the imagination; and although they have names as if they were entities existing outside the imagination, I call them entities, not of reality, but of the imagination: and so all arguments directed against us from such notions can easily be returned. For many are wont thus to argue: If all things have followed from the necessity of the most perfect nature of God, whence have so many imperfections in nature arisen? For example, the corruption of things even to rottenness, the ugliness of things which often nauseate, confusion, evil, sin, etc. But as I have just said, these are easily confuted. For the perfection of things is estimated solely from their nature and power; nor are things more or less perfect according as they delight or disgust human senses, or according as they are useful or useless to men. But to those who ask, " Why did not God create all men in such a manner that they might be governed by reason alone? " I make no answer but this: because material was not wanting to him for the creating of all things from the highest grade to the lowest; or speaking more accurately, because the laws of his nature were so comprehensive as to suffice for the creation of everything that infinite intellect can conceive, as I have shown in Prop. 16. These are the misunderstandings which I stopped here to point out. If any of the same sort remain, they can be easily dispersed by means of a little reflection.

SECOND PART

CONCERNING THE NATURE AND ORIGIN OF THE MIND

PREFACE

I NOW pass on to explain such things as must follow from the essence of God or of a being eternal and infinite: not all of them indeed (for they must follow in infinite number and in infinite modes, as we have shown in Part I., Prop. 16), but only such as can lead us by the hand (so to speak) to the knowledge of the human mind and its consummate blessedness.

DEFINITIONS

I. By BODY (*corpus*) I understand that mode which expresses in a certain determined manner the essence of God in so far as he is considered as an extended thing (*vide* Part I., Prop. 25, Coroll.).

II. I say that appertains to the essence of a thing which, when granted, necessarily involves the granting of the thing, and which, when removed, necessarily involves the removal of the thing; or that without which the thing, or on the other hand, which without the thing can neither exist nor be conceived.

III. By IDEA (*idea*) I understand a conception of the mind which the mind forms by reason of its being a thinking thing.

Explanation.—I say conception rather than perception, for the name perception seems to point out that the mind is passive to the object, while conception seems to express an action of the mind.

IV. BY ADEQUATE IDEA (*idea adæquata*) I understand an idea which, if it is considered in itself without respect to

37

the object, has all the properties or intrinsic marks of a true idea.

Explanation.—I say intrinsic in order that I may exclude what is extrinsic, *i.e.*, the agreement between the idea and its ideal.

V. DURATION (*duratio*) is indefinite continuation of existing.

Explanation.—I say indefinite because it can in no wise be determined by means of the nature itself of an existing thing nor by an effecting cause, which necessarily imposes existence on a thing but cannot take it away.

VI. REALITY and PERFECTION (*realitas et perfectio*) I understand to be one and the same thing.

VII. BY INDIVIDUAL THINGS (*res singulares*) I understand things which are finite and have a determined existence; but if several of them so concur in one action that they all are at the same time the cause of one effect, I consider them all thus far as one individual thing.

AXIOMS

I. The essence of man does not involve necessary existence, that is, in the order of nature it can equally happen that this or that man exists as that he does not exist.

II. Man thinks.

III. The modes of thinking, such as love, desire, or any other name by which the emotions of the mind may be designated, are not granted unless an idea in the same individual is granted of the thing loved, desired, etc. But the idea can be granted although no other mode of thinking be granted.

IV. We feel that a certain body is affected in many ways.

V. We neither feel nor perceive any individual things save bodies and modes of thinking. For Postulates, see after Prop. 13.

PROPOSITIONS

PROP. I. Thought (*cogitatio*) is an attribute of God, or God is a thinking thing.

Proof.—Individual thoughts or this and that thought are

modes which express in a certain and determined manner the nature of God (Coroll., Prop. 25, Part I.). The attribute whose conception all individual thoughts involve and through which they are conceived, belongs to God (Def. 5, Part I.). Thought, therefore, is one of the infinite attributes of God which express the eternal and infinite essence of God (*vide* Def. 6, Part I.), or God is a thinking thing. *Q.e.d.*

Note.—This proposition is also clear from the fact that we can conceive an infinite thinking being. For the more a thinking being can think, the more reality or perfection we conceive it to have. Therefore a being which can think infinite things in infinite modes is necessarily, as regards thinking, infinite. Since, therefore, from the mere consideration of thought we can conceive an infinite being, therefore necessarily (Defs. 4 and 6, Part I.) thought is one of the infinite attributes of God, as we wished to prove.

PROP. II. Extension (*extensio*) is an attribute of God, or God is an extended thing.

Proof.—This proof proceeds in the same manner as that of the previous proposition.

PROP. III. In God there is granted not only the idea of his essence, but also the idea of all the things which follow necessarily from his essence.

Proof.—God can think infinite things in infinite modes (Prop. 1, Part II.), or (what is the same thing, by Prop. 16, Part I.) he can form an idea of his essence and of all things which follow from it. Now all that is in the power of God necessarily exists (Prop. 35, Part I.). Therefore such an idea is granted, and that only in God (Prop. 15, Part I.). *Q.e.d.*

Note.—The generality of people understand by the power of God the free will of God and his right over all things that are, and these accordingly are considered contingent. For they say that God has the power of destroying everything and reducing it to nothing. Moreover, they very often compare the power of God to that of kings. But this in Coroll. 1 and 2, Prop. 32, Part I., we have refuted; and in Prop. 16, Part I., we showed that God acts by the same necessity by which he understands himself: that is, it follows from the necessity of divine nature (as all will grant unani-

mously) that God understands himself, and from the same
necessity it follows that God performs infinite things in
infinite ways.   Again, in Prop. 34, Part I., we showed that
the power of God is nothing else than the active essence of
God: and accordingly it is as impossible for us to conceive
God inactive as to conceive him non-existent.   And if I may
pursue this subject further, I could furthermore point out
that the power which the generality attribute to God is not
only human power (showing that they conceive God to be a
man or like to one), but also involves want of power.   But
I do not wish to return to this subject so many times.   I
only ask the reader again and again to turn over in his mind
once and again what I have written on this subject in Part I.,
from Prop. 16 to the end.   For no one can rightly perceive
what I wish to point out unless he takes the greatest care
not to confound the Power of God with the human power or
right of kings.

PROP. IV. The idea of God from which infinite things in
infinite modes follow can only be one.
Proof.—Infinite intellect comprehends nothing save the
attributes and modifications of God (Prop. 30, Part I.).
God is one (Coroll. 1, Prop. 14, Part I.).   Therefore the idea
of God from which infinite things in infinite modes follow
can only be one.   *Q.e.d.*

PROP. V. The formal being of ideas acknowledges God as
its cause only in so far as he is considered as a thinking thing,
and not in so far as he is revealed in some other attribute:
that is, the ideas, not only of the attributes of God, but also
of individual things, do not acknowledge their ideals or the
objects perceived as their effecting cause, but God himself
in so far as he is a thinking thing.
Proof.—This is obvious from Prop. 3 of this part.   For
there we concluded that God can form an idea of his essence
and of all things which follow therefrom necessarily, and that
from this alone that he is a thinking thing, and not from the
fact that he is the object of his idea.   Wherefore the formal
being of ideas acknowledges God for its cause in so far as
he is a thinking thing.   But this can be shown in another
manner.   The formal being of ideas is a mode of thinking
(as is self-evident), that is (Coroll., Prop. 25, Part I.), a

mode which expresses in a certain manner the nature of God in so far as he is a thinking thing, and therefore (Prop. 10, Part I.) involves the conception of no other attribute of God, and consequently (Ax. 4, Part I.) is the effect of no other attribute but thought.   Therefore the formal being of ideas acknowledges God as its cause only in so far as he is a thinking thing, etc.   *Q.e.d.*

PROP. VI. The modes of any attribute of God have God for their cause only in so far as he is considered through that attribute, and not in so far as he is considered through any other attribute.

Proof.—Each attribute is conceived through itself without the aid of another (Prop. 10, Part I.).   Wherefore the modes of each attribute involve the conception of their attribute and not that of another; and so (Ax. 4, Part I.) the modes of any attribute of God have God for their causes only in so far as he is considered through that attribute, and not in so far as he is considered through any other attribute.   *Q.e.d.*

Corollary.—Hence it follows that the formal being of things which are not modes of thinking does not follow from divine nature because it has first known the things; but things conceived follow and are concluded from their attributes in the same manner and by the same necessity as we have shown ideas to follow from their attribute of thought.

PROP. VII. The order and connection of ideas is the same as the order and connection of things.

Proof.—This is clear from Ax. 4, Part I.   For the idea of everything that is caused depends on the knowledge of the cause of which it is an effect.

Corollary.—Hence it follows that God's power of thinking is equal to his actual power of acting: that is, whatever follows formally from the infinite nature of God, follows also invariably objectively from the idea of God in the same order and connection in God.

Note.—Before we proceed further, let us call to mind what we have already shown above: that whatever can be perceived by infinite intellect as constituting the essence of substance, invariably appertains to one substance alone; and consequently thinking substance and extended substance are one and the same thing, which is now comprehended through this and now through that attribute. Thus also a mode of extension and the idea of that mode are one and the same thing, but expressed in two manners, which certain of the Jews seem to have perceived but confusedly, for they said that God and his intellect and the things conceived by his intellect were one and the same thing. For example, a circle existing in nature and the idea of an existing circle which is also in God is one and the same thing, though explained through different attributes. And thus whether we consider nature under the attribute of extension or under the attribute of thought or under any other attribute, we shall find one and the same order and one and the same connection of causes: that is, the same things follow one another. Nor did I say that God is the cause of an idea of a circle only in so far as he is a thinking thing, and of a circle only in so far as he is an extended thing, with any other reason than that the formal being of the idea of a circle can only be perceived through some other mode of thought as its proximate cause, and that again through another, and so on to infinity: so that as long as things are considered as modes of thought we must explain by the mere attribute of thought the order or connection of causes of all nature; and in so far as things are considered as modes of extension, the order also of the whole of nature must be explained through the mere attribute of extension; and I understand the same of other attributes. Wherefore of things as they are in themselves, God is in truth the cause, forasmuch as he consists of infinite attributes; nor can I explain this more clearly at present.

Prop. VIII. The ideas of individual things or modes which do not exist must be comprehended in the infinite idea of God in the same way as the formal essences of individual things or modes are contained in the attributes of God.

Proof.—This proposition is clear from the preceding note.

Corollary.—Hence it follows that as long as individual things do not exist save in so far as they are comprehended in the attributes of God, their objective being or ideas do not exist save in so far as the infinite idea of God exists; and when individual things are said to exist not only in so far as they are comprehended in the attributes of God, but also in so far as they are said to last, their ideas also involve existence, through which they are said to last.

Note.—If any one should still ask for an example for the better explanation of this thing, I shall in truth not be able to give him one which will explain it adequately, for it is unique. I will endeavour, however, as far as possible to illustrate this. Now a circle is such by nature that if any number of straight lines intersect within it, the rectangles formed by their segments are equal to one another. Wherefore in a circle an infinite number of rectangles are contained equal to one another. Nevertheless none of these rectangles can be said to exist except in so far as the circle exists; nor even can the idea of any one of these rectangles be said to exist save in so far as it is comprehended in the idea of a circle. Let us conceive that out of these infinite lines two only exist, to wit, E and D. Now the ideas of these not only exist in so far as they are com-prehended in the idea of a

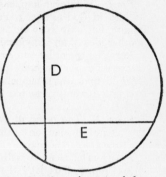

circle, but also in so far as they involve the existence of the rectangles: whence it comes about that they are distinguished from the remaining ideas of the remaining rectangles.

PROP. IX. The idea of an individual thing actually exist-ing has God for its cause, not in so far as he is infinite, but in so far as he is considered as affected by the idea of another individual thing actually existing of which also God is the cause, in so far as he is affected by another third idea, and so on to infinity.

Proof.—The idea of an individual thing actually existing is an individual mode of thinking and distinct from all others (Coroll. and Note, Prop. 8, Part II.); and therefore (Prop. 6, Part II.) has God, in so far only as he is a thinking thing, for its cause. But not (Prop. 28, Part I.) in so far as he is a thing thinking absolutely, but in so far as he is con-sidered as affected by another mode of thinking, and again he is the cause of this in so far as he is affected by a third, and so on to infinity. But the order and connection of ideas is the same (Prop. 7, Part II.) as the order and connection of causes. Therefore the cause of one individual idea is another idea of God in so far as he is considered as affected by the other idea: and of this idea God is the cause in so far as he is affected by another idea, and so on to infinity. *Q.e.d.*

Corollary.—The knowledge of whatever happens in the individual object of any idea is granted in God, but only in so far as he has the idea of the object.

Proof.—Whatever happens in the object of any idea has its idea in God (Prop. 3, Part II.), not in so far as he is infinite, but only in so far as he is considered as affected by another idea of an individual thing (prev. Prop.), but (Prop. 7, Part II.) the order and connection of ideas is the same as the order and connection of things. Therefore the knowledge of that which happens in any individual object is in God in so far only as he has the idea of the object. *Q.e.d.*

PROP. X. The being of substance does not appertain to the essence of man, or, again, substance does not constitute the form (*forma*) of man.

Proof.—The being of substance involves necessary existence (Prop. 7, Part I.). If therefore the being of substance appertains to the essence of man, substance being granted, man also must necessarily be granted (Def. 2, Part II.), and consequently man must necessarily exist, which (Ax. 1, Part II.) is absurd. Therefore, etc. *Q.e.d.*

Note.—This proposition may also be proved from Prop. 5, Part I., to wit, that two substances cannot be granted having the same nature. For as many men may exist, therefore that which constitutes the form of man is not the being of substance. Again, this proposition is manifest from the other properties of substance, to wit, that substance is in its nature infinite, immutable, indivisible, etc., as can easily be seen by all.

Corollary.—Hence it follows that the essence of man is constituted by certain modifications of attributes of God. For the being of substance (prev. Prop.) does not appertain to the essence of man. The latter is therefore something that is in God and which cannot exist or be conceived without God, whether it be a modification or a mode that expresses the nature of God in a certain determined manner.

Note.—All surely must admit that without God nothing

can exist or be conceived. For it must be agreed in the minds of all that God is the only cause of all things both of their essence and of their existence, that is, God is not only the cause of things with regard to their creation (*secundum fieri*), but also with regard to their being (*secundum esse*). But at the same time there are many who say that that appertains to the essence of anything without which the thing cannot either exist or be conceived: and therefore they believe either that the nature of God appertains to the essence of things created, or that things created can exist and be conceived without God, or, what is still more certain, they cannot properly satisfy themselves what is the cause. The cause of this I think has been that they have not observed the order of philosophical argument. For divine nature, which they ought to have considered before all things, for that it is prior in knowledge and nature, they have thought to be last in the order of knowledge, and things which are called the objects of the senses they have believed to be prior to all things. Hence it has come to pass that, while they considered the things of nature, they paid no attention to divine nature, and then when at last they directed their attention to divine nature they could have no regard for their first fabrications on which they had founded their knowledge of natural things, inasmuch as these things give no help to the knowledge of divine nature. No wonder, then, that they contradicted themselves at all points. But I will pass this by. For my intention here was only to give a reason why I did not say that that appertains to the essence of anything without which the thing can neither exist nor be conceived: clearly, for individual things cannot exist or be conceived without God, and yet God does not appertain to their essence. But I said that that necessarily constitutes the essence of anything which being granted the thing also is granted, which being removed, so also is the thing removed, or that without which the thing, or, on the other hand, that which without the thing, can neither exist or be conceived. Cf. Def. 2.

PROP. XI. The first thing which constitutes the actual being of the human mind is nothing else than the idea of an individual thing actually existing.

Proof.—The essence of man (Coroll., prev. Prop.) is constituted by certain modes of attributes of God; that is (Ax. 2, Part II.), by certain modes of thinking, of all which (Ax. 3, Part II.) the idea is prior in nature, and this idea being granted the remaining modes (to wit, those to which the idea is prior in nature) must be in the same individual (Ax. 4, Part II.). And therefore the idea is the first thing that constitutes the being of the human mind. But not the idea of a thing not existing: for then (Coroll., Prop. 8, Part II.) that very idea cannot be said to exist. It must therefore be the idea of a thing actually existing. But not of a thing infinite. For an infinite thing (Prop. 21 and 23, Part I.) must always necessarily exist. But this (Ax. 1, Part II.) is absurd. Therefore the first thing which constitutes the actual being of the human mind is the idea of an individual thing actually existing. *Q.e.d.*

Corollary.—Hence it follows that the human mind is a part of the infinite intellect of God, and thus when we say that the human mind perceives this or that, we say nothing else than that God, not in so far as he is infinite, but in so far as he is explained through the nature of the human mind, or in so far as he constitutes the essence of the human mind, has this or that idea: and when we say that God has this or that idea not only in so far as he constitutes the nature of the human mind, but also in so far simultaneously with the human mind as he has also the idea of another thing, then we say that the human mind perceives the thing only in part or inadequately.

Note.—Here doubtless the readers will become confused and will recollect many things which will bring them to a standstill: and therefore I pray them to proceed gently with me and form no judgment concerning these things until they have read all.

PROP. XII. Whatever happens in the object of the idea constituting the human mind must be perceived by the human mind, or the idea of that thing must necessarily be found in the human mind: that is, if the object of the idea constituting the human mind be the body, nothing can happen in that body which is not perceived by the mind.

Proof.—Now whatever happens in the object of any idea, the knowledge of it is necessarily granted in God (Coroll., Prop. 9, Part II.) in so far as he is considered as affected by the idea of that object, that is (Prop. 11, Part II.), in so far as he constitutes the mind of anything. Therefore whatever happens in the object of an idea constituting the human mind, knowledge of it must be granted in God in so far as he constitutes the nature of the human mind, that is (Coroll., Prop. 11, Part II.), the knowledge of this thing will be necessarily in the mind or the mind will perceive it. *Q.e.d.*

Note.—This proposition is obvious and is still more clearly understood from Note, Prop. 7, Part II., which see.

PROP. XIII. The object of the idea constituting the human mind is the body, or a certain mode of extension actually existing and nothing else.

Proof.—Now if the body is not the object of the human mind, the ideas of the modifications of the body would not be in God (Coroll., Prop. 9, Part II.) in so far as he constitutes our mind but the mind of some other thing, that is (Coroll., Prop. 11, Part II.), the ideas of the modifications of the body would not be in our mind. But (Ax. 4, Part II.) we have ideas of the modifications of the body. Therefore the object of the idea constituting the human mind is the body, and that (Prop. 11, Part II.) actually existing. Further, if there were still another object of the mind besides the body, then since (Prop. 36, Part I.) nothing can exist from which some effect does not follow, therefore (Prop. 11, Part II.) necessarily there would be in our mind an idea of some effect of that object. But (Ax. 5, Part II.) no idea of this is found. Therefore the object of our mind is the existing body and nothing else. *Q.e.d.*

Corollary.—Hence it follows that man consists of mind and body, and that the human body exists according as we feel it.

Note.—From these we understand not only that the human mind is united to the body, but also what must be understood by the union of the mind and body. But in truth no one will be able to understand this adequately or distinctly unless previously he is sufficiently acquainted with the nature of our body. For those things which we have so far propounded have been altogether general, and have not appertained more to man than to the other individual things which are all, though in various grades, animate (*animata*). For of all things there must necessarily be granted an idea in God, of which idea God is the cause, just as he is the cause of the idea of the human body; and so whatever we say concerning the idea of the human body must necessarily be said concerning the idea of any other thing. Nevertheless we cannot deny that, like objects, ideas differ one from another, one transcending another and having more reality, according as the object of one idea transcends the object of another or contains more reality than it. And so for the sake of determining in what the human mind differs from other things, and in what it excels other things, we must know the nature of its object, as we said, that is the human body. What this nature is, I am unable to explain here, but that is not necessary for what I am going to show. This, however, I will say in general, that according as a body is more apt than others for performing many actions at the same time, or receiving many actions performed at the same time, so is the mind more apt than others for perceiving many things at the same time: and according as the actions of a body depend more solely on itself, and according as fewer other bodies concur with its action, so the mind is more apt for distinct understanding. And thus we may recognise how one mind is superior to others, and likewise see the cause why we have only a very confused knowledge of our body, and many other things which I shall deduce from these. Wherefore I have thought it worth while to explain and prove more accurately these statements, for which purpose I must premise a few statements concerning the nature of bodies.

AXIOM I. All bodies are either moving or stationary.

AXIOM II. Each body is moved now slowly now more fast.

LEMMA I. Bodies are reciprocally distinguished with respect to motion or rest, quickness or slowness, and not with respect to substance.

Proof.—The first part of this proposition I suppose to be clear of itself. But that bodies should not be distinguished one from the other with respect to substance, is obvious both from Prop. 5 and Prop. 8, Part I., and still more clearly from what was said in the Note on Prop. 15, Part I.

LEMMA II. All bodies agree in certain respects.

Proof.—All bodies agree in this, that they involve the conception of one and the same attribute (Def. 1, Part II.): and again, that they may be moved more quickly or more slowly or be absolutely in motion or absolutely stationary.

LEMMA III. A body in motion or at rest must be determined for motion or rest by some other body, which, likewise, was determined for motion or rest by some other body, and this by a third, and so on to infinity.

Proof.—Bodies (Def. 1, Part II.) are individual things, which (Lemma 1) are distinguished reciprocally with respect to motion or rest: and, therefore (Prop. 28, Part I.), each must necessarily be determined for motion or rest by some other individual thing, that is (Prop. 6, Part II.), by another body, which (Ax. 1) also is either in motion or at rest. But this one also, by the same reason, cannot be in motion or at rest unless it was determined for motion or rest by another body, and that again (by the same reason) by another, and so on to infinity. *Q.e.d.*

Corollary.—Hence it follows that a moving body continues in motion until it is determined for rest by another body; and that a body at rest continues so until it is determined by another body for motion. This is self-evident. For if I suppose a given body A to be at rest and pay not attention to other moving bodies, I can say nothing concerning the body A save that it is at rest. And if it afterwards comes about that the body A moves, it clearly could not have been brought into motion by the fact that it was at rest: for from this it could only follow that it should remain at rest. If, on the other hand, the body A be supposed in motion, as long as we only have regard to the body A we can assert nothing concerning it save that it is in motion. And if it subsequently comes to pass that the body A comes to rest, it also clearly cannot have evolved from the motion which it had: for from this nothing else can follow than that A should be moved. It therefore comes to pass from something that was not in A, that is, from an external cause, that it was determined for rest.

AXIOM I. All modes in which any body is affected by another follow alike from the nature of the body affected and the body affecting: so that one and the same body may be moved in various ways according to the variety of the natures of the moving bodies, and, on the other hand, various bodies may be moved in various manners by one and the same body.

AXIOM II. When a moving body impinges another body at rest which cannot move, it recoils in order to continue to move: and the angle of the line of recoiling motion with the plane of the body at rest which it impinged will be equal to the angle which the line of the motion of incidence made with the same plane.

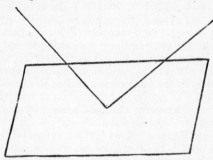

Thus far we have been speaking of the most simple bodies (*corpora simplicissima*), which are distinguished reciprocally merely by motion or rest, by swiftness or slowness: now we pass on to compound bodies (*corpora composita*).

Definition.—When a number of bodies of the same or different size are driven so together that they remain united one with the other, or if they are moved with the same or different rapidity so that they communicate their motions one to another in a certain ratio, those bodies are called reciprocally united bodies (*corpora invicem unita*), and we say that they all form one body or individual, which is distinguished from the rest by this union of the bodies.

AXIOM III. According as the parts of an individual or compound body are united on a greater or less surface so the greater is the difficulty or facility with which they are forced to change their position and, consequently, the greater the difficulty or facility with which it is brought about that the individual assumes another form. Hence bodies whose parts are united over a large surface I shall call hard (*dura*), and those whose parts are united over a small surface are called soft (*mollia*), and those whose parts are in motion among each other are called fluid (*fluida*).

LEMMA IV. If from a body or individual which is composed of several bodies certain ones are removed, and at the same time the same number of bodies of the same nature succeed to their place, the individual will retain its nature as before without any change of its form.

Proof.—Now bodies (Lemma 1) are not distinguished with respect to substance. But that which constitutes the form of an individual consists of a union of bodies (prev. Def.). But this union (by the hypothesis), although the change of bodies continue, is retained: the individual will therefore retain as before its nature both with respect to substance and mode. *Q.e.d.*

LEMMA V. If the parts composing an individual become larger or smaller, but in such proportion that they preserve between themselves with respect to motion and rest the same ratio as before, the individual will retain its nature as before without any change of form.

Proof.—This is the same as that of the previous lemma.

LEMMA VI. If certain bodies composing an individual are forced to change their motion which they had in one direction into another, but in such a manner that they can continue their motion and preserve one with the other the same ratio with respect to motion and rest as before, the individual will retain its nature without any change of form.

Proof.—This is self-evident. For it is supposed to retain all that which in its definition we said constituted its form.

LEMMA VII. Moreover, the individual thus composed retains its nature whether as a whole it be moved or remain at rest, whether it be moved in this or that direction, provided that each part retains its motion and communicates it as before to the other parts.

Proof.—This is clear from its definition (the definition of an individual), which see before, Lemma 4.

Note.—From these examples we thus see in what manner a composite individual can be affected in many ways and, despite this, preserve its nature. But thus far we have conceived an individual as composed only of bodies which are distinguished one from the other merely by motion or rest, rapidity or slowness, that is, as composed of the most simple bodies. But if we now conceive some other individual composed of many individuals of a different nature, we shall find that it can be affected in many other ways, preserving its nature notwithstanding. For since each part of it is composed of numerous bodies, each part will therefore (prev. Lemma) be able without any change in its nature to be moved now slower now faster, and consequently communicate its motions to the others with varying speeds. If we conceive a third class of individuals composed of these second ones, we shall find that this one can be affected in many other ways without any change of its form. And if thus still further we proceed to infinity, we can easily conceive that all nature is one individual whose parts, that is, all bodies, vary in infinite ways without any change of the individual as a whole. If it were my purpose to lecture on the body, I should explain and prove this in greater detail, but I have already said that this is not my intention, nor have I stayed at this point save that from these things I can more easily prove what I have before me.

Postulates

I. The human body (*corpus humanum*) is composed of many individuals (of different nature), each one of which is also composed of many parts.

II. The individuals of which the human body is composed are some fluid, some soft, and some hard.

III. The individuals composing the human body, and consequently the human body itself is affected in many ways by external bodies.

IV. The human body needs for its preservation many other bodies from which it is, so to speak, regenerated.

V. When the fluid part of the human body is so determined by an external body that it impinges frequently on another part which is soft, it changes its surface and imprints such marks on it as the traces of an external impelling body.

VI. The human body can move external bodies in many ways, and dispose them in many ways.

PROP. XIV. The human mind is apt to perceive many things, and more so according as its body can be disposed in more ways.

Proof.—Now the human body (Post. 3 and 6) is affected by external bodies in many ways and disposed to affect external bodies in many ways. But the human mind (Prop. 12, Part II.) must perceive all things which happen in the human body. Therefore the human mind is apt to perceive many things, and more so, etc. *Q.e.d.*

PROP. XV. The idea which constitutes the formal being of the human mind is not simple, but composed of many ideas.

Proof.—The idea which constitutes the formal being of the human mind is the idea of the body (Prop. 13, Part II.), which (Post. 1) is composed of many individuals, each composed of many parts. But the idea of each individual composing the body is necessarily granted in God (Coroll., Prop. 8, Part II.). Therefore (Prop. 7, Part II.) the idea of the human body is composed of the many ideas of the component parts. *Q.e.d.*

PROP. XVI. The idea of every mode in which the human body is affected by external bodies must involve the nature of the human body and at the same time the nature of the external body.

Proof.—All modes in which any body is affected follow from the nature of the body affected, and at the same time from the nature of the affecting body (Ax. 1, after Coroll., Lemma 3). Wherefore the idea of them (Ax. 4, Part I.) must involve necessarily the nature of each body. Therefore the idea of each mode in which the human body is affected by an external body involves the nature of the human body and that of the external body. *Q.e.d.*

Corollary I.—Hence it follows in the first place that the human mind can perceive the nature of many bodies at the same time as the nature of its own body.

Corollary II.—It follows in the second place that the ideas which we have of external bodies indicate rather the disposition of our body than the nature of the external bodies, which I explained in the appendix of Part I. with many examples.

PROP. XVII. If the human body is affected in a mode which involves the nature of any external body, the human mind regards that external body as actually existing, or as present to itself until the body is affected by a modification which cuts off the existence or presence of that body.

Proof.—This is clear. For as long as the human body is

thus affected, so long does the human mind regard this modification of the body (Prop. 12, Part II.); that is (prev. Prop.), it has the idea of the mode actually existing, and the idea involves the nature of the external body, that is, it has an idea which does not cut off the existence or presence of the nature of the external, but imposes it. Therefore the mind regards (Coroll. 1, prev. Prop.) the external body as actually existing or present, until it is affected, etc. *Q.e.d.*

Corollary.—The mind can regard external bodies by which the human body was once affected, although they do not exist, nor are present, as if they were present.

Proof.—When external bodies so determine the fluid parts of the human body that they often impinge the soft parts, they change the surface of them (Post. 5). Whence it comes about (Ax. 2, after Coroll., Lemma 3) that they are reflected thence in a different manner than before, and as afterwards they impinge on new surfaces by their spontaneous movement, they are reflected in the same manner as if they were driven towards those surfaces by external bodies, and consequently while they continue to be reflected they will affect the human body in the same manner, and the human mind will (Prop. 12, Part II.) again think of external bodies, that is (Prop. 17, Part II.), the human mind will regard the external body as present, and that as long as the fluid parts of the human body impinge the same surfaces by their spontaneous motion. Wherefore although the external bodies by which the human body was once affected no longer exist, the mind nevertheless regards them as present as often as this action of the body is repeated. *Q.e.d.*

Note.—We thus see that it can come to pass that we regard those things which are not existing as present, and this often happens. And it can happen that this comes to pass through other causes. But it will suffice me just as much to show one here by means of which I can so explain what I want, as if I were to show it by means of the true cause. Nor do I think that I have wandered far from the truth, since all the postulates I have assumed scarcely contain anything that is not borne out by experience, which we may not doubt after having shown that the human body as we feel it exists (Coroll. after Prop. 13, Part II.). Moreover (prev. Coroll. and Coroll. 2, Prop. 16, Part II.) we clearly understand what is the difference between, *e.g.*, the idea of Peter which con-

stitutes the essence of the mind of Peter, and the idea of
Peter as it exists in the mind of another, say, Paul. The
first directly explains the essence of the body of Peter, nor
does it involve existence save as long as Peter exists; but
the second idea indicates rather the disposition of Paul than
the nature of Peter, and so as long as this disposition of
Paul lasts his mind will regard Peter though he no longer
exists as if he were nevertheless present to him. Again, to
retain the usual phraseology, the modifications of the human
body, the ideas of which represent to us external bodies as
if they were present, we shall call the images of things,
although they do not recall the figures of things; and when
the mind regards bodies in this manner we say it imagines
them. And here, in order that I may point out where lies
error, I would have you note that the imaginations of the
mind, regarded in themselves, contain no error, or that the
mind does not err from that which it imagines, but only
in so far as it is considered as wanting the idea which cuts off
the existence of those things which it imagines as present to
itself. For if the mind while it imagined things not existing
as present to itself knew at the same time that these things
did not in truth exist, it would attribute this power of imagination to an advantage of its nature not a defect, more
especially if this faculty of imagining depends on its own
nature alone, that is (Def. 7, Part I.), if the mind's faculty of
imagining be free.

PROP. XVIII. If the human body has once been affected
at the same time by two or more bodies, when the mind
afterwards remembers any one of them it will straightway
remember the others.

Proof.—The mind (prev. Coroll.) imagines any body for
this reason, that the human body is affected and disposed
by impressions of an external body in the same way as it is
affected when certain parts of it are affected by the same
external body. But (by the hypothesis) the body was then
so disposed that the mind imagined two bodies at once.
Therefore it will imagine two bodies at the same time, and
the mind when it imagines one of them will also straightway
recall the other. *Q.e.d.*

Note.—Hence we clearly understand what is memory
(*memoria*). For it is nothing else than a certain concatena-

tion of ideas involving the nature of things which are outside the human body, and this takes place in the mind according to the order and concatenation of the modifications of the human body. I say then in the first place that it is a concatenation of those ideas only which involve the nature of things which are outside the human body, and not of those ideas which explain the nature of the same things. For those are in truth (Prop. 16, Part II.) ideas of the modifications of the human body which involve the nature both of the human body and of external bodies. I say in the second place that this concatenation takes place according to the order and concatenation of the modifications of the human body in order to distinguish it from that concatenation of ideas which takes place according to the order of the intellect through which the mind perceives things through their first causes and which is the same in all men. And hence we can clearly understand why the mind from the thought of one thing should immediately fall upon the thought of another which has no likeness to the first, *e.g.*, from the thought of the word *pomum* a Roman immediately began to think about fruit, which has no likeness to that articulate sound nor anything in common, save that the body of that man was often affected by these two, that is, the man frequently heard the word *pomum* while looking at the fruit: and thus one passes from the thought of one thing to the thought of another according as his habit arranged the images of things in his body. For a soldier, *e.g.*, when he sees the footmarks of a horse in the sand passes from the thought of the horse to the thought of the horseman, and thence to the thought of war, etc. But a countryman from the thought of a horse would pass to the thought of a plough, field, etc., and thus each one according to whether he is accustomed to unite the images of things in this or that way passes from the thought of one thing to the thought of another.

PROP. XIX. The human mind has no knowledge of the human body, nor does it know it to exist, save through ideas of modifications by which the body is affected.

Proof.—The human mind is the very idea or knowledge of the human body (Prop. 13, Part II.), which (Prop. 9, Part II.) is in God in so far as he is considered as affected by another idea of an individual thing: or because (Post. 4) the human body needs many bodies from which it is continuously regenerated, so to speak, and the order and connection of ideas is (Prop. 7, Part II.) the same as the order and connection of causes this idea will be in God in so far as he is considered as affected by the ideas of several individual things. God, therefore, has the idea of the human body, or has a knowledge of the human body, in so far as he is considered as affected by many other ideas and not in so far as he constitutes the nature of the human mind, that is (Coroll., Prop. 11, Part II.), the human mind has no knowledge of the human body. But the ideas of the modifications of the human body are in God, in so far as he constitutes the nature of the human mind, or the human mind perceives those modifications (Prop. 12, Part II.), and consequently (Prop. 16, Part II.) the human body itself, and that (Prop. 17, Part II.) as actually existing. The human mind, therefore, perceives only thus far the human body. *Q.e.d.*

Prop. XX. The idea or knowledge of the human mind is granted in God and follows in God, and is referred to him in the same manner as the idea or knowledge of the human body.

Proof.—Thought is an attribute of God (Prop. 1, Part II.), and therefore (Prop. 3, Part II.) the idea of this and of all its modifications, and consequently of the human mind (Prop. 11, Part II.), must necessarily be granted in God. Now this idea or knowledge of the human mind is not granted in God in so far as he is infinite, but in so far as he is affected by another idea of an individual thing (Prop. 9, Part II.). But the order and connection of ideas is the same as the order and connection of causes (Prop. 7, Part II.). It follows, therefore, that this idea or knowledge of the human mind is in God and is referred to God in the same manner as the knowledge or idea of the human body. *Q.e.d.*

Prop. XXI. This idea of the mind is united to the mind in the same manner as the mind is united to the body.

Proof.—That the mind is united to the body we have shown from the fact that the body is the object of the mind (Prop. 12 and 13, Part II.); and therefore by that same reason the idea of the mind is united to its object, that is the mind itself, in the same manner as the mind is united to the body. *Q.e.d.*

Note.—This proposition can be understood far more easily from what has been said in the note on Prop. 7, Part II. For there we showed that the idea of the body and the body itself, that is (Prop. 13, Part II.) the mind and body, are one and the same individual, which is conceived now under the attribute of thought, and now under the attribute of extension. Wherefore the idea of the mind and the mind itself are one and the same thing and are conceived under one and the same attribute, namely, thought. The idea of the mind, I repeat, and the mind itself follow from the same necessity in God and from the same power of thinking. For in truth the idea of the mind, that is the idea of an idea, is nothing else than the form (*forma*) of an idea in so far as it is considered as a mode of thinking without relation to its object: for if a man knows anything, by that very fact he knows he knows it, and at the same time knows that he knows that he knows it, and so on to infinity. But of this more again.

Prop. XXII. The human mind perceives not only the modifications of the body, but also the ideas of these modifications.

Proof.—The ideas of the ideas of modifications follow in God in the same way and are referred to him in the same way as the ideas of modification, which is proved in the same manner as Prop. 20, Part II. But the ideas of modifications of the body are in the human mind (Prop. 12, Part II.), that is (Coroll., Prop. 11, Part II.), in God in so far as he constitutes the essence of the human mind. Therefore, the ideas of these ideas are in God, in so far as he has the knowledge or idea of the human mind, that is (Prop. 21, Part II.) in the human mind itself, which therefore perceives not only the modifications of the human body but also the ideas of them. *Q.e.d.*

Prop. XXIII. The mind has no knowledge of itself save in so far as it perceives the ideas of the modifications of the body.

Proof.—The idea or knowledge of the mind (Prop. 20, Part II.) follows in God, and is referred to him in the same manner as the idea or knowledge of the body. But since (Prop. 19, Part II.) the human mind does not know the human body, that is (Coroll., Prop. 11, Part II.), since the knowledge of the human body is not referred to God in so far as he constitutes the nature of the human mind, therefore neither is the knowledge of the mind referred to God in so far as he constitutes the essence of the human mind, and therefore (same Coroll., Prop. 11, Part II.) the human mind thus far has no knowledge of itself. Then again the ideas of modifications by which the body is affected involve the nature of the human body itself (Prop. 16, Part II.), that is (Prop. 13, Part II.), they agree with the nature of the mind. Wherefore the knowledge of these ideas necessarily involves the knowledge of the mind. But (prev. Prop.) the knowledge of these ideas is in the human mind itself. Therefore the human mind has only thus far a knowledge of itself. *Q.e.d.*

PROP. XXIV. The human mind does not involve an adequate knowledge of the component parts of the human body.

Proof.—The parts composing the human body do not appertain to the essence of that body save in so far as they reciprocally communicate their motions in a certain ratio (*vide* Def. after Coroll., Lemma 3), and not in so far as they may be considered as individuals without relation to the human body. For the parts of the human body (Post. 1) are individuals very complex, the parts of which (Lemma 4) can be taken away from the human body without harm to the nature or form of it, and can communicate their motions (Ax. 1 after Lemma 3) to other bodies in another ratio. And therefore (Prop. 3, Part II.) the idea or knowledge of each part will be in God in so far as (Prop. 9, Part II.) he is considered as affected by another idea of an individual thing which is prior in the order of nature to that part (Prop. 7, Part II.). This also can be said of any part of the individual component of the human body, and therefore the knowledge of each component part of the human body is in God in so far as he is affected by many ideas of things, and not in so far as he has only the idea of the human body, that is (Prop. 13, Part II.) the idea which constitutes the nature of the human mind. And therefore (Coroll, Prop, 11, Part II.) the human mind does not involve an adequate knowledge of the component parts of the human body. *Q.e.d.*

PROP. XXV. The idea of each modification of the human body does not involve an adequate knowledge of the external body.

Proof.—We have shown (Prop. 16, Part II.) that the idea of the modification of the human body involves the nature of the external body in so far as the external body determines the human body in a certain way. But in so far as the external body is an individual which has no reference to the human body, its idea or knowledge is in God (Prop. 9, Part II.) in so far as God is considered as affected by the idea of the other thing which (Prop. 7, Part II.) is by nature prior to the external body. Therefore adequate knowledge of the external body is not in God in so far as he has the idea of the modification of the human body, or the idea of the modification of the human body does not involve adequate knowledge of the external body. *Q.e.d.*

PROP. XXVI. The human mind perceives no external body as actually existing save through ideas of modifications of its body.

Proof.—If the human body is affected in no way by any external body, then (Prop. 7, Part II.) neither is the idea of the human body, that is (Prop. 13, Part II.), the human mind, affected in any wise by the idea of the existence of the external body, or, in other words, it does not perceive in any way the existence of that external body. But in so far as the human body is affected in any way by any external body, thus far (Prop. 16, Part II., and its Coroll.) it perceives the external body. *Q.e.d.*

Corollary.—In so far as the human mind imagines an external body, thus far it has no adequate knowledge of it.

Proof.—When the human mind regards external bodies through the ideas of the modifications of its own body, we say it imagines (Note on Prop. 17, Part II.): nor can the human mind in any other way imagine (prev. Prop.) external bodies as actually existing. And therefore (Prop. 25, Part II.) in so far as the mind imagines external bodies, it has no adequate knowledge of them. *Q.e.d.*

PROP. XXVII. The idea of each modification of the human body does not involve adequate knowledge of the human body itself.

Proof.—Any idea of each modification of the human body involves the nature of the human body in so far as the human body itself is considered to be affected in a certain manner (Prop. 16, Part II.). But in so far as the human body is an individual which can be affected in many other ways, the idea of the modification, etc. (*vide* Proof of Prop. 25, Part II.).

PROP. XXVIII. The ideas of the modifications of the human body, in so far as they are referred to the human mind alone, are not clear and distinct but confused.

Proof.—The ideas of the modifications of the human body involve both the nature of the external bodies and that of the human body itself (Prop. 16, Part II.): and not only must they involve the nature of the human body, but also that of its parts. For modifications are modes (Post. 3) in which parts of the human body, and consequently the whole body, is affected. But (Prop. 24 and 25, Part II.) adequate knowledge of external bodies, as also of the parts composing the human body, is not in God in so far as he is considered as affected by the human mind, but in so far as he is considered as affected by other ideas. These ideas of modifications, in so far as they have reference to the human mind alone, are like consequences without premisses, that is (as is self-evident), confused ideas. *Q.e.d.*

Note.—The idea which constitutes the nature of the human mind is shown in the same manner when considered in itself not to be clear and distinct: also the idea of the human mind, and the ideas of the ideas of modifications of the human body, in so far as they have reference to the mind alone, which every one can easily see.

PROP. XXIX. The idea of the idea of each modification of the human body does not involve adequate knowledge of the human mind.

Proof.—The idea of a modification of the human body (Prop. 27, Part II.) does not involve adequate knowledge of the body itself, or, in other words, does not express its nature adequately, that is (Prop. 13, Part II.), it does not agree adequately with the nature of the mind. And therefore (Ax. 6, Part I.) the idea of this idea does not adequately express the nature of the human mind, or does not involve adequate knowledge of it. *Q.e.d.*

Corollary.—Hence it follows that the human mind, when-ever it perceives a thing in the common order of nature, has no adequate knowledge of itself, nor of its body, nor of ex-ternal bodies, but only a confused and mutilated knowledge thereof. For the mind knows not itself save in so far as it perceives ideas of modifications of the body (Prop. 23, Part II.). But it does not perceive its body save through the ideas of modifications, through which also it only perceives external bodies. And therefore in so far as it has these ideas it has no adequate knowledge of itself (Prop. 29, Part II.), nor of its body (Prop. 27, Part II.), nor of external bodies (Prop. 25, Part II.), but only (Prop. 28 and Note, Part II.) a confused and mutilated one. *Q.e.d.*

Note.—I say expressly that the mind has no adequate but only confused knowledge of itself, of its body, and of external bodies, when it perceives a thing in the common order of nature, that is, whenever it is determined externally, that is, by fortuitous circumstances, to contemplate this or that, and not when it is determined internally, that is, by the fact that it regards many things at once, to understand their agreements, differences, and oppositions one to another. For whenever it is disposed in this or any other way from within, then it regards things clearly and distinctly, as I shall show further on.

PROP. XXX. We can have only a very inadequate know-ledge of the duration of our body.

Proof.—The duration of our body does not depend on its essence (Ax. 1, Part II.), nor even on the absolute nature of God (Prop. 21, Part I.); but (Prop. 28, Part I.) it is determined for existence and action by certain causes, which are in their turn determined for existing and acting in a certain deter-mined ratio by other causes, and these by others, and so on to infinity. Therefore the duration of our body depends on the common order of nature and the disposition of things. But there is in God an adequate knowledge of the reason why things are disposed in any particular way, in so far as he has ideas of all things, and not in so far as he has only a know-ledge of the human body (Coroll., Prop. 9, Part II.). Where-fore the knowledge of the duration of our body is very inadequate in God in so far as he is considered as constituting only the nature of the human mind, that is (Coroll., Prop. 11,

Part II.), this knowledge is very inadequate in our mind. *Q.e.d.*

PROP. XXXI. We can only have a very inadequate knowledge of individual things which are outside us.

Proof.—Each individual thing, such as the human body, must be determined for existence or action in a certain manner by another individual thing: and this again by another, and so on to infinity (Prop. 28, Part I.). But as we have shown in the previous proposition that we can only have a very inadequate knowledge of the duration of our body, owing to this common property of individual things, so this must also be concluded concerning the duration of individual things, *i.e.*, that we can only have a very inadequate knowledge thereof. *Q.e.d.*

Corollary.—Hence it follows that all individual things are contingent and corruptible. For we can have no adequate knowledge concerning their duration (prev. Prop.), and this is what must be understood by the contingency of things and their liability to corruption (*vide* Note 1, Prop. 33, Part I.). For (Prop. 29, Part I.), save this, nothing is granted to be contingent.

PROP. XXXII. All ideas, in so far as they have reference to God, are true.

Proof.—Now all ideas which are in God must entirely agree with their ideals (Coroll., Prop. 7, Part II.): and therefore (Ax. 6, Part I.) they are true. *Q.e.d.*

PROP. XXXIII. There is nothing positive in ideas, wherefore they could be called false.

Proof.—If you deny this, conceive, if possible, a positive mode of thinking which would constitute the form of error or falsity. This mode of thinking cannot be in God (prev. Prop.), and outside God it cannot exist or be conceived (Prop. 15, Part I.). Therefore there is nothing positive in ideas, wherefore they could be called false. *Q.e.d.*

PROP. XXXIV. Every idea in us which is absolute, or adequate and perfect, is true.

Proof.—When we say that an adequate and perfect idea is granted in us, we say nothing else than that (Coroll., Prop.

11, Part II.) there is granted in God an adequate and perfect idea in so far as he constitutes the essence of our mind, and consequently (Prop. 32, Part II.) we say nothing else than that such an idea is true. *Q.e.d.*

PROP. XXXV. Falsity consists in privation of knowledge which is involved by inadequate or mutilated and confused ideas.

Proof.—Nothing positive is granted in ideas which could constitute their form of falsity (Prop. 33, Part II.). But falsity cannot consist in mere privation (for minds, not bodies, are said to err and be mistaken), nor in mere ignorance: for ignorance and error are two different things. Wherefore it consists in the privation of knowledge which is involved by inadequate knowledge or inadequate or confused ideas. *Q.e.d.*

Note.—In the note on Prop. 17 of this Part I explained for what reason error consists in the privation of knowledge. For the further explanation, however, I shall give an example. For instance, men are mistaken in thinking themselves free; and this opinion consists of this alone, that they are conscious of their actions and ignorant of the causes by which they are determined. This, therefore, is their idea of liberty, that they should know no cause of their actions. For that which they say, that human actions depend on the will, are words they do not fathom. For none of them know what is will and how it moves the body; those who boast of this and feign dwellings and habitations of the soul, provoke either laughter or disgust. Thus when we look at the sun we imagine that it is only some two hundred feet distant from us: which error does not consist in that imagination alone, but in the fact that while we thus imagined it we were ignorant of the cause of this imagination and the true distance. For although we may afterwards learn that the sun is some six hundred times the earth's diameter distance from us, we imagine it nevertheless to be near to us: for we do not imagine the sun to be near because we are ignorant of the true distance, but because the modification of our body involves the essence of the sun in so far as the body is affected by it.

PROP. XXXVI. Inadequate and confused ideas follow from the same necessity as adequate or clear and distinct ideas.

Proof.—All ideas are in God (Prop. 15, Part I.), and in so far as they have reference to God, they are true (Prop. 32, Part II.) and (Coroll., Prop. 7, Part II.) adequate; and therefore none are inadequate or confused save in so far as they have reference to the individual mind of any one. On this point, *vide* Prop. 24 and 25, Part II. And therefore all ideas, both adequate and inadequate, follow together from the same necessity (Coroll., Prop. 6, Part II.). *Q.e.d.*

PROP. XXXVII. That which is common to all (see Lemma 2), and that which is equally in a part and in the whole, do not constitute the essence of an individual thing.

Proof.—If you deny this, conceive, if it can be, that it does constitute the essence of an individual thing, namely, the essence of B. Then (Def. 2, Part II.) it cannot be conceived nor exist without B. And this is contrary to the hypothesis. Therefore it does not appertain to the essence of B, nor can it constitute the essence of any other individual thing. *Q.e.d.*

PROP. XXXVIII. Those things which are common to all, and which are equally in a part and in the whole, can only be conceived adequately.

Proof.—Let A be anything that is common to all bodies, and which is equally in one part of any body and in the whole. Then I say that A can only be conceived adequately. For its idea (Coroll., Prop. 7, Part II.) will necessarily be adequate in God both in so far as he has the idea of the human body, and in so far as he has ideas of its modifications, which (Prop. 16, 25, and 27, Part II.) involve in part both the nature of the human body and that of external bodies, that is (Prop. 12 and 13, Part II.), this idea will necessarily be adequate in God in so far as he constitutes the human mind, or in so far as he has ideas which are in the human mind. Therefore the mind (Coroll., Prop. 11, Part II.) necessarily adequately perceives A, and that both in so far as it perceives itself and its own or an external body: nor can A be conceived in any other manner. *Q.e.d.*

Corollary.—Hence it follows that certain ideas or notions are granted common to all men. For (Lemma 2) all bodies agree in certain things which (prev. Prop.) must adequately or clearly and distinctly be perceived by all.

PROP. XXXIX. That which is common to and a property of the human body, and certain external bodies by which the human body is used to be affected, and which is equally in the part and whole of these, has an adequate idea in the mind.

Proof.—Let A be that which is common to and a property of the human body and certain external bodies, and which is equally in the human body and in the external bodies, and which also is equally in a part and in the whole of each external body. There will be in God an adequate idea of A (Coroll., Prop. 7, Part II.), both in so far as he has the idea of the human body, and in so far as he has ideas of the given external bodies. Then let it be granted that the human body is affected by an external one through that which it has in common with it, namely, A. The idea of this modification involves the property A (Prop. 16, Part II.): and therefore (Coroll., Prop. 7, Part II.) the idea of this modification, in so far as it involves the property A, will be adequate in God in so far as he is affected by the idea of the human body, that is (Prop. 13, Part II.), in so far as he constitutes the nature of the human mind (Prop. 13, Part II.). And therefore (Coroll., Prop. 11, Part II.) this idea is also adequate in the human mind. *Q.e.d.*

Corollary.—Hence it follows that the mind is the more apt to perceive many things adequately, the more its body has things in common with other bodies.

PROP. XL. Whatever ideas follow in the mind from ideas which are adequate in the mind, are also adequate.

Proof.—This is clear. For when we say that in the mind ideas follow from other ideas which are adequate in the mind, we say nothing else than (Coroll., Prop. 11, Part II.) that an idea is granted in the divine intellect itself whose cause is God, not in so far as he is infinite nor in so far as he is affected by the ideas of many individual things, but in so far only as he constitutes the essence of the human mind.

Note I.—In these propositions I have explained the cause of notions which are called common, and which are the fundamental principles of our ratiocination. But there are other causes of certain axioms or notions which it would be advantageous to explain by this method of ours. For from these it could be concluded which notions are more useful than others, and which are of scarcely any value; and, again, which are common to all, which are clear and distinct to those alone who do not labour under misconceptions, and, finally, which are ill-founded. Then again, it would be concluded whence those notions which are called secondary, and consequently whence the axioms which are founded on them, derive their origin, and other points over which I meditated for some time. But as I have decided to make another treatise of this, and as I am afraid of wearying the reader by too great prolixity, I have decided to pass this over here. Nevertheless, lest I should omit anything that is necessary to be known, I shall briefly add the causes from which the terms called transcendental have taken their origin, such as being, thing, something. These terms have arisen from the fact that the human body, since it is limited, is only capable of distinctly forming in itself a certain number of images (I have explained what is an image in the Note on Prop. 17, Part II.): and if more than this number are formed, the images begin to be confused; and if this number of images of which the body is capable of forming in itself be much exeeded, all will become entirely confused one with the other. Since this is so, it is clear from Coroll., Prop. 17, and Prop. 18, Part II., that the mind can imagine distinctly as many bodies as images can be formed in its body at the same time. But when the images become quite confused in the body, the mind also imagines all bodies confusedly without any distinction, and, so to speak, comprehends all under one attribute, that is, under the attribute of being, of thing, etc. This also can be deduced from the fact that images are not always equally clear, and from other causes analogous to this which it is not necessary to explain here; and for the purpose which we wish to attain it suffices to consider one only. For all may be reduced to this, that these terms signify ideas extremely confused. And from similar causes have arisen those notions which are called universal or general, such as man, dog, horse, etc. I mean so many images arise in the human body, e.g., so many images of men are formed at the same time, that they overcome the power of imagining, not altogether indeed, but to such an extent that the mind cannot imagine the small differences between individuals (e.g., colour, size, etc.) and their fixed number, and only that in which all agree in so far as the body is affected by them is distinctly imagined: for in that was the body most affected by each individual, and this the mind expresses by the name of man, and predicates concerning an infinite number of individuals. For, as we have said, it cannot imagine a fixed number of individuals. But it must be noted that these notions are not formed by all in the same manner, but vary with each individual according to the variation of the thing by which the body was most often affected, and which the mind imagines or remembers the most easily. For example, those who have most often admired men for their stature, by the name of man will understand an animal of erect stature; those who are wont to regard men in another way will form another common image of men, namely, a laughing animal, a featherless biped animal, a reasoning animal, and each one will form concerning the other things universal images of things according to the disposition of his body. Wherefore it is not surprising that so many controversies should have arisen among philosophers who wished to explain things of nature merely by images of things.

Note II.—From all that has been said above it is now clearly apparent that we perceive many things and form universal notions, first, from individual things represented to our intellect mutilated, confused, and without order (Coroll., Prop. 29, Part II.), and therefore we are wont to call such perceptions knowledge from vague or casual experience (*cognitio ab experientia vaga*); second, from signs, *e.g.*, from the fact that we remember certain things through having read or heard certain words and form certain ideas of them similar to those through which we imagine things (Note, Prop. 18, Part II.). Both of these ways of regarding things I shall call hereafter knowledge of the first kind (*cognitio primi generis*), opinion (*opinio*), or imagination (*imaginatio*). Third, from the fact that we have common notions and adequate ideas of the properties of things (Coroll., Prop. 38, Coroll. and Prop. 39, and Prop. 40, Part II.). And I shall call this reason (*ratio*) and knowledge of the second kind (*cognitio secundi generis*). Besides these two kinds of knowledge there is a third, as I shall show in what follows, which we shall call intuition (*scientia intuitiva*). Now this kind of knowing proceeds from an adequate idea of the formal essence of certain attributes of God to the adequate knowledge of the essence of things. I shall illustrate these three by one example. Let three numbers be given to find the fourth, which is in the same proportion to the third as the second is to the first. Tradesmen without hesitation multiply the second by the third and divide the product by the first: either because they have not forgotten the rule which they received from the schoolmaster without any proof, or because they have often tried it with very small numbers, or by conviction of the proof of Prop. 19, Book VII., of Euclid's elements, namely, the common property of proportionals. But in very small numbers there is no need of this, for when the numbers 1, 2, 3, are given, who is there who could not see that the fourth proportional is 6? and this is much clearer because we conclude the fourth number from the same ratio which intuitively we see the first bears to the second.

PROP. XLI. Knowledge of the first kind is the only cause of falsity; knowledge of the second and third kinds is necessarily true.

Proof.—We said in the preceding note that all those ideas which are inadequate and confused appertain to knowledge of the first kind: and therefore (Prop. 35, Part II.) this knowledge is the only cause of falsity. Then as for knowledge of the second and third kinds, we said that those ideas which are adequate appertained to it; therefore (Prop. 34, Part II.) it is necessarily true. *Q.e.d.*

PROP. XLII. Knowledge of the second and third kinds and not of the first kind teaches us to distinguish the true from the false.

Proof.—This proposition is clear of itself. For he who would distinguish the true from the false must have an adequate idea of what is true and false, that is (Note 2, Prop. 40, Part II.), must know the true and false by the second and third kinds of knowledge.

PROP. XLIII. He who has a true idea, knows at that same time that he has a true idea, nor can he doubt concerning the truth of the thing.

Proof.—A true idea in us is that which is adequate in God (Coroll., Prop. 11, Part II.) in so far as he is explained through the nature of the human mind. Let us suppose, then, that there is in God, in so far as he is explained through the nature of the human mind, an adequate idea A. The idea of this idea must necessarily be granted in God, and it refers to God in the same manner as the idea A (Prop. 20, Part II., whose proof is universal in its application). But the idea A is supposed to refer to God in so far as he is explained through the nature of the human mind: therefore also the idea of the idea A must refer to God in the same manner, that is (Coroll., Prop. 11, Part II.), the adequate idea of the idea A will be in the same mind as has the adequate idea A: and therefore he who has an adequate idea or (Prop. 34, Part II.) who knows a thing truly must at the same time have an adequate idea of his knowledge or a true knowledge, that is (as is self-evident), he must at the same time be certain. *Q.e.d.*

Note.—In the note of Prop. 21 of this part I explained what was the idea of an idea, but it must be noted that the foregoing proposition is sufficiently manifest of itself. For no one who has a true idea can be ignorant of the fact that a true idea involves the greatest certainty. For to have a true idea means nothing else than to know something perfectly or best; nor can any one doubt of this unless he thinks that an idea is something mute like a picture on a painting canvas and not a mode of thinking, namely, understanding itself. And who, I ask, can know that he understands anything unless he first understands that thing itself? I mean, who can know that he is certain of anything unless he first be certain of that thing? What then can be more clear or more certain than a true idea to be a standard of truth? Clearly, just as light shows itself and darkness also, so truth is a standard of itself and falsity. And thus I think I have sufficiently answered these questions: namely, that if a true idea, in so far as it is said only to agree with its ideal, be distinguished from a false idea, then it will have no more reality or perfection than a false one (since they are distinguished merely by their extrinsic names), and consequently not even a man who has true ideas has any advantage over one who has only false ones. Then how does it come to pass that men have false ideas? And again how can any one be certain that he has ideas which agree with their ideals? Thus I think I have answered these questions. For as to the difference between a true and a false idea, it can be

seen in Prop. 35 of this part, that one bears the same relation
to the other as being bears to not-being: the causes or sources
of falsity I have most clearly shown in Prop. 19 to 35, with
the note on that proposition. And from these it is also
apparent what is the distinction between a man who has
true and one who has false ideas. As for what refers to the
last question, namely, in what way can a man know that he
has an idea which agrees with its ideal, I have shown more
than sufficiently well that it arises from this alone, that he
has an idea which agrees with its ideal, or that truth is its
own standard. Add to these that the mind, in so far as it
truly perceives a thing, is a part of the infinite intellect of
God (Coroll., Prop. 11, Part II.): and therefore it is as necessary that the clear and distinct ideas of the mind are true as
it is that those of God are true.

PROP. XLIV. It is not the nature of reason to regard things
as contingent but necessary.

Proof.—It is the nature of reason to perceive things truly
(Prop. 41, Part II.), namely (Ax. 6, Part I.), as they are in
themselves, that is (Prop. 29, Part I.), not as contingent but
necessary. *Q.e.d.*

Corollary I.—Hence it follows that it depends solely on
the imagination that we consider things whether in respect
to the past or future as contingent.

Note.—In what manner this comes about I shall explain
in a few words. We have shown above (Prop. 17, Part II.,
and its Coroll.) that the mind imagines things as present
always to itself, although they may not exist, unless causes
arise which cut off their present existence. Then (Prop.
18, Part II) we showed that if the human body has once
been affected at the same time by two external bodies,
whenever the mind subsequently recalled one of them it
would immediately recall the other, that is, it would regard
both as present to itself unless causes arose which cut off
their present existence. Moreover, no one doubts but
that we imagine time from the very fact that we imagine
some bodies to be moved slower or faster than others, or
equally fast. Let us then suppose a boy who yesterday
first of all saw Peter in the morning, at mid-day Paul,
and in the evening Simon, and to-day again saw Peter
in the morning. From Prop. 18 of this part it is clear

that as soon as he sees the morning light he will imagine the
sun to run the same course as it did the day before, and will
imagine a whole day: with the morning he will imagine
Peter, with the noon Paul, and with the evening Simon; that
is, he will imagine the existence of Paul and Simon with
relation to future time: and, on the other hand, if in the
evening hour he sees Simon, he will refer Peter and Paul to
past time by imagining them at the same time as he does
past time, and the more often he sees them in this order the
more certain will his imaginings be. But if at any time it
come to pass that one evening instead of Simon he sees James,
then the next morning he will imagine with the evening
time now Simon and now James, but not both at once, for he
is not supposed to have seen the two at the same time in
the evening, but one of them. And so his imagination will
waver, and with the future evening time he will imagine now
this one and now that one, that is, he will regard them in the
future neither as certain, but both as contingent. And this
wavering of the imagination will be the same if the imagination be of things which we regard in the same manner with
reference to past or present time, and consequently we
imagine things as contingent whether they relate to present,
past, or future time.

Corollary II.—It is the nature of reason to perceive things
under a certain species of eternity (*sub quadam æternitatis
specie*).

Proof.—It is the nature of reason to regard things not as
contingent, but as necessary (prev. Prop.). It perceives this
necessity of things (Prop. 41, Part II.) truly, that is (Ax. 6,
Part I.), as it is in itself. But (Prop. 16, Part I.) this necessity of things is the necessity itself of the eternal nature of
God. Therefore it is the nature of reason to regard things
under this species of eternity. Add to this that the bases
of reason are the notions (Prop. 38, Part II.) which explain
these things which are common to all, and which (Prop. 37,
Part II.) explain the essence of no individual thing: and
which therefore must be conceived without any relation of
time, but under a certain species of eternity. *Q.e.d.*

PROP. XLV. Every idea of every body or individual thing
actually existing necessarily involves the eternal and infinite
essence of God.

Proof.—The idea of an individual thing actually existing necessarily involves both the essence of that thing and its existence (Coroll., Prop. 8, Part II.). But individual things (Prop. 15, Part I.) cannot be conceived without God: and forasmuch as (Prop. 6, Part II.) they have God for a cause in so far as he is considered under the attribute, of which these things are modes, their ideas must necessarily (Ax. 4, Part I.) involve the conception of their attribute, that is (Def. 6, Part I.), they must involve the eternal and infinite essence of God. *Q.e.d.*

Note.—By existence I do not mean here duration, that is, existence in so far as it is conceived abstractedly and as a certain form of quantity. I speak of the very nature of existence, which is assigned to individual things by reason of the fact that they follow from the eternal necessity of the nature of God, infinite in number and in infinite ways (*vide* Prop. 16, Part I.). I speak, I say, of the very existence of individual things in so far as they are in God. For although each one is determined by another individual thing for existing in a certain manner, yet the force wherewith each of them persists in existing follows from the eternal necessity of the nature of God. Concerning which see Coroll., Prop. 24, Part I.

PROP. XLVI. The knowledge of the eternal and infinite essence of God which each idea involves is adequate and perfect.

Proof.—The proof of the previous proposition is of universal application, and whether the thing be considered as a part or a whole, its idea, whether it be of the part or whole (prev. Prop.), involves the eternal and infinite essence of God. Wherefore that which gives knowledge of the eternal and infinite essence of God is common to all, and equally in part as in whole, and therefore (Prop. 38, Part II.) this knowledge will be adequate. *Q.e.d.*

PROP. XLVII. The human mind has an adequate knowledge of the eternal and infinite essence of God.

Proof.—The human mind has ideas (Prop. 22, Part II.) from which (Prop. 23, Part II.) it perceives itself and its body (Prop. 19, Part II.) and (Coroll., Prop. 16 and 17, Part II.) external bodies as actually existing; and therefore (Prop.

45 and 46, Part II.) it has an adequate knowledge of the eternal and infinite essence of God. *Q.e.d.*

Note.—Hence we see that the infinite essence of God and his eternity are known to all.   But as all things are in God, and through him are conceived, it follows that we can deduce from this knowledge many things which we may adequately know and therefore form that third kind of knowledge of which we spoke in Note 2, Prop. 40, Part II., and of the excellence and use of which we shall have occasion to speak in the fifth part.   But that men have knowledge not so clear of God as they have of common notions arises from the fact that they cannot imagine God as they do bodies, and that they affix the name God to images of things which they are accustomed to see, and this men can scarcely avoid, for they are continually affected by external bodies.   Now many errors consist of this alone, that we do not apply names rightly to things. .For when any one says that lines which are drawn from the centre of a circle to the circumference are unequal, he means, at least at the time, something different by circle than mathematicians.   Thus when men make mistakes in calculation they have different numbers in their heads than those on the paper.   Wherefore if you could see their minds they do not err; they seem to err, however, because we think they have the same numbers in their minds as on the paper. If this were not so we should not believe that they made mistakes any more than I thought a man in error whom I heard the other day shouting that his hall had flown into his neighbour's chicken, for his mind seemed sufficiently clear to me on the subject.   And hence have arisen very many controversies, for men either do not explain their own minds, or do not rightly interpret the minds of others.   For, in truth, while they flatly contradict themselves, they think now one thing, now another, so that there may not be found in them the errors and absurdities which they find in others.

PROP. XLVIII. There is in no mind absolute or free will, but the mind is determined for willing this or that by a cause which is determined in its turn by another cause, and this one again by another, and so on to infinity.

Proof.—The mind is a fixed and determined mode of thinking (Prop. 11, Part II.), and therefore (Coroll. 2, Prop. 17, Part I.) cannot be the free cause of its actions, or it cannot have the absolute faculty of willing and unwilling: but for willing this or that it must be determined (Prop. 28, Part I.) by a cause which is determined by another, and this again by another, etc. *Q.e.d.*

Note.—In the same manner it may be shown that there cannot be found in the mind an absolute faculty of understanding, desiring, loving, etc. Whence it follows that these and such like faculties are either entirely fictitious, or nothing else than metaphysical or general entities, which we are wont to form from individual things: therefore intellect or will have reference in the same manner to this or that idea, or to this or that volition, as " stoneness " to this or that stone, or man to Peter or Paul. But the reason why men think themselves free I have explained in the appendix of Part I. But before I go any further, let this be noted, that I understand by will the faculty, not the desire, of affirming and denying: I understand, I repeat, the faculty by which the mind affirms or denies what is true or false, and not the desire by which the mind takes a liking or an aversion to anything. Now after we have shown that these faculties are general notions, which cannot be distinguished from the individual things from which we formed them, we must then inquire whether these volitions are anything else than the ideas of things. We must inquire, I say, whether there can be found in the mind any affirmation or negation save that which the idea, in so far as it is an idea, involves, on which subject see the following proposition and Def. 3, Part II., lest the thought of pictures should occur. For I do not understand by ideas, images which are formed at the back of the eye and, if you will, in the centre of the brain, but conceptions of thought.

PROP. XLIX. There is in the mind no volition or affirmation and negation save that which the idea, in so far as it is an idea, involves.

Proof.—There is not in the mind (prev. Prop.) an absolute faculty of willing and unwilling, but only individual volitions such as this or that affirmation and this or that negation. Let us conceive then any individual volition, namely, the mode of thinking, whereby the mind affirms that the three angles of a triangle are equal to two right angles. This affirmation involves the conception or idea of the triangle, that is, without the idea of the triangle it cannot be conceived. It is the same when I say that A involves the conception of B, as when I say that A cannot be conceived without B. Then this affirmation (Ax. 3, Part II.) cannot be without the idea of the triangle. Therefore this affirmation cannot exist or be conceived without the idea of the triangle. Moreover, this idea of the triangle must involve the same affirmation, namely, that its three angles are equal to two right angles. Wherefore, *vice versâ* also, this idea of the triangle cannot exist or be conceived without this affirmation: and therefore (Def. 2, Part II.) this affirmation appertains to the essence of the idea of a triangle, nor is anything else than that. And what we have said of this volition (for it was selected at random) can be said of any other volition, namely, that it is nothing but an idea. *Q.e.d.*

Corollary.—Will and intellect are one and the same thing.

Proof.—Will and intellect are nothing but individual volitions and ideas (Prop. 48, Part II., and the Note thereon). But an individual volition and idea (prev. Prop.) are one and the same thing. Therefore will and intellect are one and the same thing. *Q.e.d.*

Note.—We have thus removed the cause to which error is commonly attributed. For we have shown above that falsity consists solely in the privation of knowledge involved by mutilated and confused ideas. Wherefore a false idea, in so far as it is false, does not involve certainty. Thus when we say that a man acquiesces in what is false, and that he has no doubts concerning it, we do not say that he is certain but merely that he does not doubt, or that he acquiesces in what is false because there are no reasons which might cause his imagination to waver. On this subject, see the note on Prop. 44, Part II. Thus although a man is supposed to adhere to what is false, yet we never say that he is certain. For by certainty we understand something positive (Prop. 43, Part II., and its Note), not a privation of doubt. By the privation of certainty we understand falsity, but for the further explanation of the preceding proposition there are several warnings yet to be made. First, it is yet left for me to answer any objections which may be raised to this our doctrine. And moreover to remove any scruples I have thought it worth while to point out some of the advantages of this doctrine: I say some, for they will be better understood from what we shall say in our fifth part.

I begin then with the first point, and warn the readers to make an accurate distinction between idea, or a conception of the mind, and the images of things which we imagine. Then it is necessary to distinguish between ideas and words by which we point out things. For these three, namely, images, words, and ideas, are by most people either entirely confused or not distinguished with sufficient accuracy or care, and hence they are entirely ignorant of the fact that to know this doctrine of the will is highly necessary both for philosophic speculation and for the wise ordering of life. Those who think that ideas consist of images which are formed in us by the concourse of bodies, persuade themselves that those ideas of things like which we can form no image in the mind are not ideas, but fabrications which we invent by our own free will; they therefore regard ideas as lifeless pictures on a board, and preoccupied thus with this misconception they do not see that an idea, in so far as it is an idea, involves affirmation or negation. Then those who confuse words with the ideas, or with the affirmation which the idea involves, think that they can wish something contrary to what they feel, when they affirm or deny anything by mere words against what they feel. Any one can easily rid himself of these misconceptions if he pays attention to the nature of thought which least involves the conception of extension; and therefore he will clearly understand that an idea (since it is a mode of thinking) does not consist in the image of anything nor in words. For the essence of words and images is constituted solely by bodily motions which least involve the conception of thought.

These few warnings I think will suffice. I shall now pass on to the objections I mentioned. The first of these is that they take it for an axiom that the will can be further extended than the intellect, and is therefore different from it. But the reason why they think that the will can be further extended than the intellect is, they say, that they find we do not need a greater faculty of assenting or of affirming and denying than we have now in order to assent to infinite other things which we do not perceive, but that we do need a greater faculty of understanding. The will is then thus distinguished from the intellect, that the latter is finite and the former infinite. The second objection to us is that experience seems to teach us nothing more clearly than that we can suspend our judgment in order not to assent to things which we perceive: that this is confirmed by the fact that no one is said to be deceived in so far as he perceives anything, but in so far as he assents or dissents to it. For example, he who feigns a winged horse does not thereby grant that there is such a thing as a winged horse, that is, he is not therefore deceived unless he admits at the same time that there is such a thing as a winged horse. Therefore experience seems to teach nothing more clearly than that will, or the faculty of assenting, is free, and different from the faculty of understanding. The third objection is that one affirmation does not seem to contain more reality than another, that is, we do not seem to need more power to affirm what is true to be true than to affirm what is false to be true. But we have seen that one idea contains more reality or perfection than another; for as some objects are more excellent than others, so are some ideas more perfect than others: from this also may be inferred the difference between will and intellect. The fourth objection is: if man does not act from free will, what will happen if he remains in equilibrium between incentives to action, like Buridan's ass? Will he perish of hunger or thirst? If I admit that he will, I shall seem to have in my mind an ass or the statue of a man rather than an actual man; but if I deny it, he would then determine himself, and consequently would have the faculty of going and doing whatever he wished. Besides these, other objections may be raised; but as I am not obliged to make a demonstration of whatever any one can dream, I shall take the trouble of answering these objections only, and with the greatest possible brevity. As for the first point, I concede that the will can be further extended than the intellect, if by intellect they only understand clear and distinct ideas; but I deny that the will can be further extended than the perceptions or the faculty of conceiving. Nor do I see how the faculty of willing should be called infinite before the faculty of feeling, for just as we can by that faculty of willing affirm an infinite number of things (one after the other, for we cannot affirm an infinite number simultaneously), so also can we by the faculty of feeling, feel or perceive an infinite number of bodies (one after the

other). Then if they say that there are an infinite number
of bodies which we cannot perceive, I retort that we cannot
attain to that number by any manner of thought, and consequently by any faculty of willing; but they say that if
God wished to bring it to pass that we should perceive these
things, he would have to give us a greater faculty of perceiving
but not a greater faculty of willing than he gave us. This
is the same as if they said that if God wished to bring it to
pass that we should understand an infinite number of other
entities, that it would be necessary that he should give us a
greater intellect but not a more general idea of entity than
he gave us before, in order to grasp such infinite entities.
For we have shown that will is a general being or idea whereby
we explain all individual volitions, or that will is common
to all volitions. Since then they believe this common or
general idea of all volitions is a faculty, it is not to be wondered
at if they say that this faculty is extended beyond the
limits of the intellect to infinity; for what is universal or
general can be said alike of one, of many, and of infinite
individuals. I answer the second objection by denying
that we have free power to suspend the judgment. For
when we say that any one suspends his judgment, we say
nothing else than that he sees that he does not perceive the
thing adequately. Therefore a suspension of the judgment
is in truth a perception and not free will. To make this more
clear, conceive a boy imagining a winged horse and perceiving
nothing else. Inasmuch as this imagination involves the
existence of the horse (Coroll., Prop. 17, Part II.), and the
boy does not perceive anything that could take away from
the horse its existence, he will necessarily regard the horse
as present, nor will he have any doubts of its existence,
although he may not be certain of it. We have daily
experience of this in dreams, and I do not think there is
any one who thinks that while he sleeps he has the free power
of suspending his judgment concerning what he dreams, and
of bringing it to pass that he should not dream what he
dreams he sees; and yet it happens in dreams also that we
can suspend our judgments, namely, when we dream that
we dream. Further, I grant that no one is deceived in so far
as he perceives, that is, I grant that the imaginations of the
mind considered in themselves involve no error (Note, Prop.
17, Part II.); but I deny that a man affirms nothing in so far

as he perceives. For what else is it to perceive a winged horse than to affirm wings on a horse? For if the mind perceives nothing else save a winged horse, it will regard it as present to itself; nor will it have any reason for doubting its existence, nor any faculty of dissenting, unless the imagination of a winged horse be joined to an idea which removes existence from the horse, or unless he perceives that the idea of a winged horse that he has is inadequate, and then he will either necessarily deny the existence of the said horse or necessarily doubt it. And thus I think I have also answered the third objection, namely, that the will is something general, which is predicated of all ideas, and which only signifies that which is common to all ideas, namely, an affirmation whose adequate essence therefore, in so far as it is conceived abstractly, must be in each idea, and the same in all in this respect only; but not in so far as it is considered to constitute the idea's essence: thus far individual affirmations differ one from the other equally as much as ideas. *E.g.*, the affirmation which is involved by the idea of a circle differs from that involved by the idea of a triangle just as the idea of a circle differs from the idea of a triangle. Then again, I absolutely deny that we need equal power of thought for affirming that what is true is true, than for affirming what is false is true. For these two affirmations, if we look to the mind, have the same reciprocal relation as a being to a non-being; for there is nothing positive in ideas which can constitute the form of falsity (*vide* Prop. 35, Part II., with its Note, and the Note on Prop. 47, Part II.). It therefore must be noted how easily we are deceived when we confuse general entities with individual ones, and abstract entities and those of reason with realities. As for the fourth objection, I confess that I am prepared to admit that a man placed in such a position of equilibrium (namely, that he perceives nothing save hunger and thirst, a certain food and a certain drink which are equally distant from him), will perish of hunger and thirst. If they ask whether I do not consider that such a man should rather be regarded as an ass than a man, I answer that I do not know, as also I do not how a man should be regarded who hangs himself, or how children, fools, or madmen are to be considered.

It remains that I should point out how much this doctrine confers advantage on us for the regulating of life, which we shall easily perceive from the following points: I. Inasmuch as it teaches us to act solely according to the decree of God and to be partakers of the divine nature, the more according as our actions are more perfect and more and more understand God. This doctrine, therefore, besides bringing complete peace to the mind, has this advantage also, that it teaches us in what consists our greatest happiness or blessedness, namely, in the knowledge of God, by which we are induced to do those things which love and piety persuade us. Whence we clearly understand how far those are astray from a true estimation of virtue who expect for their virtue and best actions, as if it were the greatest slavery, that God will adorn them with the greatest rewards: as if virtue and the serving of God were not the happiness itself and the greatest liberty. II. In so far as it teaches us in what manner we should act with regard to the affairs of fortune or those which are not in our own power, that is, with regard to those things which do not follow from our nature: namely, that we should expect and bear both faces of fortune with an equal mind; for all things follow by the eternal decree of God in the same necessity as it follows from the essence of a triangle that its three angles are equal to two right angles. III. This doctrine confers advantages on social life, inasmuch as it teaches us not to despise, hate, or ridicule any one: to be angry with or envy no one. Further, it teaches us that each one should be satisfied with what he has and ready to help his neighbour, not from effeminate pity or partiality or superstition, but by the mere guidance of reason, according as the time or thing demands, as I shall show in the third part. IV. Then this doctrine confers advantages on the state in common, inasmuch as it teaches in what manner citizens should be governed, namely, that they should not be as slaves, but should do of their own free will what is best. Thus I have fulfilled what I promised at the beginning of this note, and now come to the end of the second part, in which I think I have explained the nature of the human mind and its properties at sufficient length, having regard to the difficulty of the subject, and that I have brought with me many things from which excellent conclusions of great use and most necessary to be known may be drawn, as will be seen in part from what follows.

THIRD PART

CONCERNING THE ORIGIN AND NATURE OF
THE EMOTIONS

MOST who have written on the emotions, the manner of
human life, seem to have dealt not with natural things which
follow the general laws of nature, but with things which are
outside the sphere of nature: they seem to have conceived
man in nature as a kingdom within a kingdom. For they
believe that man disturbs rather than follows the course of
nature, and that he has absolute power in his actions, and
is not determined in them by anything else than himself.
They attribute the cause of human weakness and inconstancy not to the ordinary power of nature, but to some
defect or other in human nature, wherefore they deplore,
ridicule, despise, or, what is most common of all, abuse it:
and he that can carp in the most eloquent or acute manner
at the weakness of the human mind is held by his fellows as
almost divine. Yet excellent men have not been wanting
(to whose labour and industry I feel myself much indebted)
who have written excellently in great quantity on the right
manner of life, and left to men counsels full of wisdom: yet
no one has yet determined, as far as I know, the nature and
force of the emotions and what the mind can do in opposition
to them for their constraint. I know that the most illustrious Descartes, although he also believed that the human
mind had absolute power in its actions, endeavoured to
explain the human emotions through their first causes, and
to show at the same time the way in which the mind could
have complete control over the emotions: but, in my opinion,
he showed nothing but the greatness and ingenuity of his
intellect, as I shall show in its proper place. For I wish to
revert to those who prefer rather to abuse and ridicule the
emotions and actions of men than to understand them. It
will doubtless seem most strange to these that I should
attempt to treat on the vices and failings of men in a geo-

metrical manner, and should wish to demonstrate with accurate reasoning those things which they cry out against as opposed to reason, as vain, absurd, and disgusting. This, however, is my plan. Nothing happens in nature which can be attributed to a defect of it: for nature is always the same and one everywhere, and its ability and power of acting, that is, the laws and rules of nature according to which all things are made and changed from one form into another, are everywhere and always the same, and therefore one and the same manner must there be of understanding the nature of all things, that is, by means of the universal laws and rules of nature. For such emotions as hate, wrath, envy, etc., considered in themselves, follow from the same necessity and ability of nature as other individual things: and therefore they acknowledge certain causes through which they are understood, and have certain properties equally worthy of our knowledge as the properties of any other thing, the contemplation alone of which delights us. And so I shall treat of the nature and force of the emotions, and the power of the mind over them, in the same manner as I treated of God and the mind in the previous parts, and I shall regard human actions and desires exactly as if I were dealing with lines, planes, and bodies.

DEFINITIONS

I. I call that an ADEQUATE CAUSE (*adæquata causa*) whose effect can clearly and distinctly be perceived through it. I call that one INADEQUATE or PARTIAL (*inadæquata seu partialis*) whose effect cannot be perceived through itself.

II. I say that we act or are active when something takes place within us or outside of us whose adequate cause we are, that is (prev. Def.), when from our nature anything follows in us or outside us which can be clearly and distinctly understood through that alone. On the other hand, I say we suffer or are passive when something takes place in us or follows from our nature of which we are only the partial cause.

III. By EMOTION (*affectus*) I understand the modifications of the body by which the power of action in the body is

increased or diminished, aided or restrained, and at the same
time the ideas of these modifications.

Explanation.—Thus if we can be the adequate cause of
these modifications, then by the emotion I understand an
ACTION (*actio*), if otherwise a PASSION (*passio*).

POSTULATES

I. The human body can be affected in many ways whereby
its power of acting is increased or diminished, and again in
others which neither increase nor diminish its power of action.

This postulate or axiom is dependent on Post. 1 and
Lemmas 5 and 7, which see, *post* Prop. 13, Part II.

II. The human body can suffer many changes and yet
retain the impressions or traces of objects (Post. 5, Part II.),
and consequently the same images of things (Note, Prop. 17,
Part II.).

PROPOSITIONS

PROP. I. Our mind acts certain things and suffers others:
namely, in so far as it has adequate ideas, thus far it necessarily acts certain things, and in so far as it has inadequate
ideas, thus far it necessarily suffers certain things.

Proof.—The ideas of every human mind are some adequate
and some mutilated and confused (Note, Prop. 40, Part II.).
But the ideas which are adequate in the mind of any one are
adequate in God in so far as he constitutes the essence of that
mind (Coroll., Prop. 11, Part II.), and those again which
are inadequate in the mind of any one are also in God, but
adequate (same Coroll.), not in so far as he contains in himself the essence of the given mind, but in so far as he contains
the minds of other things at the same time.   Again, from any
given idea some effect must necessarily follow (Prop. 36, Part
I.), and of this effect God is the adequate cause (Def. 1,
Part III.), not in so far as he is infinite, but in so far as he is
considered as affected by that given idea (Prop. 9, Part II.).
But of that effect of which God is the cause, in so far as he is
affected by an idea which is adequate in the mind of some
one, that same mind is the adequate cause (Coroll., Prop. 11,
Part II.).   Therefore our mind (Def. 2, Part III.), in so far
as it has adequate ideas, necessarily acts certain things: which

was the first point. Then whatever follows from an idea which is adequate in God, not in so far as he has in himself the mind of one man only, but in so far as he has in himself the minds of other things at the same time with the mind of this man, of that effect (Coroll., Prop. 11, Part II.) the mind of that man is not the adequate but merely the partial cause. And so (Def. 2, Part III.) the mind, in so far as it has inadequate ideas, necessarily suffers certain things: which was the second point. Therefore our mind, etc. *Q.e.d.*

Corollary.—Hence it follows that the mind is more or less subject to passions according as it has more or less inadequate ideas, and, on the other hand, to more action the more adequate ideas it has.

PROP. II. The body cannot determine the mind to think, nor the mind the body to remain in motion, or at rest, or in any other state (if there be any other).

Proof.—All modes of thinking have God for their cause, in so far as he is a thinking thing and not in so far as he is explained through another attribute (Prop. 6, Part II.). Therefore that which determines the mind to think is a mode of thinking and not of extension, that is (Def. 1, Part II.), it is not a body: which was the first point. Again, the motion and rest of a body must arise from another body, which also was determined for motion or rest by another body, and absolutely everything which arises in a body must have arisen from God in so far as he is considered as affected by some mode of extension and not some mode of thinking (Prop. 6, Part II.), that is, it cannot arise from the mind which (Prop. 11, Part II.) is a mode of thinking: which is the second point. Therefore the body cannot, etc. *Q.e.d.*

Note.—These points might be more clearly understood from what was said in the Note on Prop. 7, Part II., namely, that the mind and body are one and the same thing, which, now under the attribute of thought, now under the attribute of extension, is conceived. Whence it comes about that the order or concatenation of things is one, or nature is conceived now under this, now under that attribute, and consequently that the order of the actions and passions of our body are simultaneous in nature with the order of actions and passions of our mind. This also is clear from the manner in which we proved Prop. 12, Part II. And although these things are so determined that no reason of doubt can remain, yet I scarcely believe, unless I prove the matter by experience, that men can be induced to consider this with a well-balanced mind: so firmly are they persuaded that the body is moved by the mere will of the mind, or is kept at rest, and that it performs many things which merely depend on the will or ingenuity of the mind. No one has thus far determined what the body can do, or no one has yet been taught by experience what the body can do merely by the laws of nature, in so far as nature is considered merely as corporeal or extended, and what it cannot do, save when determined by the mind. For no one has yet had a sufficiently accurate knowledge of the construction of the human body as to be able to explain all its functions: in addition to which there are many things which are observed in brutes which far surpass human sagacity, and many things which sleep-walkers do which they would not dare, were they awake: all of which sufficiently shows that the body can do many things by the laws of its nature alone at which the mind is amazed. Again, no one knows in what manner, or by what means, the mind moves the body, nor how many degrees of motion it can give to the body, nor with what speed it can move it. Whence it follows when men say that this or that action arises from the mind which has power over the body, they know not what they say, or confess with specious words that they are ignorant of the cause of the said action, and have no wonderment at it. But they will say whether they know or not by what means the mind moves the body, that they have discovered by experience that, unless the mind is apt for thinking, the body remains inert: again, that it is in the power of the mind alone to speak or be silent, and that many other things are dependent solely on the will of the mind. But as for the first point, I ask them whether experience has not also taught them that when the body is inert the mind likewise is inept for thinking? For when the body is asleep, the mind, at the same time, remains unconscious, and has not the power of thinking that it has when awake. Again, I think all have found by experience that the mind is not always equally apt for thinking out its subject: but according as the body is more apt, so that the image of this or that object may cause more excitement in it, so the mind is more apt for regarding the object. But they will say that it cannot come to pass that from the laws of nature alone, in so far as nature is regarded as extended, that the causes of buildings, pictures, and things of this kind, which are made by human skill alone, can be deduced, nor can the human body, save if it be determined and led thereto by the mind, build a temple, for example. But I have already shown that they know not what a body can do, or what can be deduced from mere contemplation of its nature, and that they have known of many things which happen merely by reason of the laws of nature, which they would never have believed to happen save by the direction of the mind, as those things which sleep-walkers do at which they would be surprised were they awake; and I may here draw attention to the fabric of the human body, which far surpasses any piece of work made by human art, to say nothing of what I have already shown, namely, that from nature, considered under whatsoever attribute, infinite things follow. As for their second point, surely human affairs would be far happier if the power in men to be silent were the same as that to speak. But experience more than sufficiently teaches that men govern nothing with more difficulty than their tongues, and can moderate their desires more easily than their words. Whence it comes about that many believe that we are free in respect only to those things which we desire only moderately, for then we can restrain our desire for those things by the recol-lection of something else which we frequently recollect: and with respect to those things which we desire with such affec-tion that nothing can obliterate them from the mind we are by no means free. But in truth, if they did not experience that we do many things for which we are sorry afterwards, and that very often when we strive with adverse emotions we "see the better, yet follow the worse," there would be nothing to prevent them from believing that we do all things freely. Thus an infant thinks that it freely desires milk, an angry child thinks that it freely desires vengeance, or a timid child thinks it freely chooses flight. Again, a drunken man thinks that he speaks from the free will of the mind those things which, were he sober, he would keep to himself. Thus a madman, a talkative woman, a child, and people of such kind, think they speak by the free decision of the mind, when, in truth, they cannot put a stop to the desire to talk, just as experience teaches as clearly as reason that men think them-

selves free on account of this alone, that they are conscious
of their actions and ignorant of the causes of them; and moreover that the decisions of the mind are nothing save their
desires, which are accordingly various according to various
dispositions.   For each one moderates all his actions according to his emotion, and thus those who are assailed by conflicting emotions know not what they want: those who are
assailed by none are easily driven to one or the other.   Now
all these things clearly show that the decision of the mind
and the desire and determination of the body are simultaneous
in nature, or rather one and the same thing, which when
considered under the attribute of thought and explained
through the same we call decision (*decretum*), and when considered under the attribute of extension and deduced from
the laws of motion and rest we call determination (*deter-
minatio*), which will appear more clearly from what will be
said on the subject.   For there is another point which I wish
to be noted specially here, namely, that we can do nothing
by a decision of the mind unless we recollect having done
so before, *e.g.*, we cannot speak a word unless we recollect
having done so.   Again, it is not within the free power of the
mind to remember or forget anything.   Wherefore it must
only be thought within the free power of the mind in so far
as we can keep to ourselves or speak according to the decision
of the mind the thing we recollect.   But when we dream
that we speak, we think that we speak from the free decision
of the mind, yet we do not speak, or if we do, it is due to a
spontaneous motion of the body.   We dream again that we
conceal something from men, and think that we do so by the
same decision of the mind as that by which, when we are
awake, we are silent concerning what we know.   In the
third place, we dream that we do certain things by a decision
of the mind which were we awake we would dare not: and
therefore I should like to know whether there are in the mind
two sorts of decisions, fantastic and free?   But if our folly
is not so great as that, we must necessarily admit that this
decision of the mind, which is thought to be free, cannot be
distinguished from imagination or memory, nor is it anything
else than the affirmation which an idea, in so far as it is an
idea, necessarily involves (Prop. 49, Part II.).   And therefore these decrees of the mind arise in the mind from the same
necessity as the ideas of things actually existing.   Those

therefore, who believe that they speak, are silent, or do any-thing from the free decision of the mind, dream with their eyes open.

PROP. III. The actions of the mind arise from adequate ideas alone, but passions depend on inadequate ideas alone.

Proof.—The first thing which constitutes the essence of the mind is nothing else than the idea of the body actually existing (Prop. 11 and 13, Part II.), which (Prop. 15, Part II.) is composed of many other ideas of which (Coroll., Prop. 38, Part II.) certain are adequate and certain (Coroll., Prop. 29, Part II.) inadequate. Therefore whatever follows from the nature of the mind, and of which the mind is the proximate cause through which it must be understood, must necessarily follow from an idea adequate or inadequate. But in so far as the mind (Prop. 1, Part III.) has inadequate ideas, thus far it is necessarily passive. Therefore the actions of the mind follow from adequate ideas alone, and the mind is passive therefore merely because it has inadequate ideas. *Q.e.d.*

Note.—We see thus that passions have no reference to the mind save in so far as it has something which involves a negation, or in so far as it is regarded as a part of nature which through itself and without others cannot be clearly and distinctly perceived; and by this system of argument I could show that the passions are referred to individual things in the same manner as they are referred to the mind, nor can they be perceived in any other manner. But it is my purpose to treat of the human mind alone.

PROP. IV. Nothing can be destroyed save by an external cause.

Proof.—This proposition is self-evident. For the definition of anything affirms its essence and does not deny it: or it imposes the essence of the thing and does not take it away. And so while we regard the thing alone, and not the external cause, we can find nothing in it which can destroy it. *Q.e.d.*

PROP. V. Things are contrary by nature, that is, they cannot exist in the same subject in so far as one can destroy the other.

Proof.—If they could agree one with the other, or exist at the same time in the same subject, then something could be found in the subject which could destroy it, which (prev. Prop.) is absurd. Therefore a thing, etc. *Q.e.d.*

PROP. VI. Everything in so far as it is in itself endeavours to persist in its own being.

Proof.—Individual things are modes in which the attributes of God are expressed in a certain determined manner (Coroll., Prop. 25, Part I.), that is (Prop. 34, Part I.), they are things which express in a certain determined manner the power of God whereby he is and acts. Nor can a thing have anything within itself whereby it can be destroyed, or which takes its existence from it (Prop. 4, Part III.); but on the other hand, it is opposed to everything that could take its existence away (prev. Prop.). Therefore as much as it can, and is within itself, it endeavours to persist in its being. *Q.e.d.*

PROP. VII. The endeavour wherewith a thing endeavours to persist in its being is nothing else than the actual essence of that thing.

Proof.—From the given essence of a thing certain things necessarily follow (Prop. 36, Part I.), nor can things do anything else than that which follows necessarily from their determined nature (Prop. 29, Part I.). Wherefore the power or endeavour of anything by which it does, or endeavours to do, anything, either alone or with others, that is, the power or endeavour by which it endeavours to persist in its own being, is nothing else than the given or actual essence of that given thing. *Q.e.d.*

PROP. VIII. The endeavour wherewith a thing endeavours to persist in its own being involves no finite time but an indefinite time.

Proof.—If it involves a limited time which must determine the duration of the thing, then it would follow from the power alone by which the thing exists, that the thing after that limited time could exist no longer, but must be destroyed. But this (Prop. 4, Part III.) is absurd. Therefore the endeavour wherewith a thing endeavours to exist involves no definite time; but on the other hand, if (Prop. 4, Part III.) it is destroyed by no external cause, by the same power by which it now exists it will continue to exist for ever: therefore this endeavour involves no definite time. *Q.e.d.*

PROP. IX. The mind, in so far as it has both clear and distinct and confused ideas, endeavours to persist in its being for an indefinite period, and is conscious of this its endeavour.

Proof.—The essence of the mind is constituted of adequate and inadequate ideas (as we showed in Prop. 3, Part III.), and therefore (Prop. 7, Part III.), inasmuch as it has the first and the second, it endeavours to persist in its being, and that for an indefinite period (Prop. 8, Part III.). But since the mind (Prop. 23, Part II.) is necessarily conscious of itself through ideas of the modification of the body, so the mind (Prop. 7, Part III.) is conscious of its endeavour. *Q.e.d.*

Note.—This endeavour, when it has reference to the mind alone, is called will (*voluntas*); but when it refers simultaneously to the mind and body it is called appetite (*appetitus*), which therefore is nothing else than the essence of man, from the nature of which all things which help in its preservation necessarily follow; and therefore man is determined for acting these things. Now between appetite and desire (*cupiditas*) there is no difference but this, that desire usually has reference to men in so far as they are conscious of their appetite; and therefore it may be defined as appetite with consciousness thereof. It may be gathered from this, then, that we endeavour, wish, desire, or long for nothing because we deem it good; but on the other hand, we deem a thing good because we endeavour, wish for, desire, or long for it.

PROP. X. The idea which cuts off the existence of our body cannot be given in our mind, but is contrary thereto.

Proof.—Whatever can destroy our body cannot be granted in the same (Prop. 5, Part III.). Therefore the idea of this thing cannot be granted in God in so far as he has the idea of our body (Coroll., Prop. 9, Part II.), that is (Prop. 11 and 13, Part II.), the idea of this thing cannot be given in our mind; but on the other hand, since (Prop. 11 and 13, Part II.) the first thing which forms the essence of the mind is the idea of the body actually existing, the first and principal endeavour of our mind is to affirm (Prop. 7, Part III.) the existence of our body. And therefore the idea which denies the existence of our body is opposed to the mind, etc. *Q.e.d.*

PROP. XI. Whatever increases or diminishes, helps or

hinders the power of action of our body, the idea thereof increases or diminishes, helps or hinders the power of thinking of our mind.

Proof.—This proposition is clear from Prop. 7, Part II. or even from Prop. 14, Part II.

Note.—We see then that the mind can suffer great changes, and can pass now to a state of greater or lesser perfection; these passions explain to us the emotions of pleasure (*lætitia*) and pain (*tristitia*). In the following propositions I shall understand by pleasure the passion by which the mind passes to a higher state of perfection, and by pain the passion by which it passes to a lower state of perfection. Again, the emotion of pleasure relating simultaneously to the mind and body I call titillation or excitement (*titillatio*) or merriment (*hilaritas*); the emotions of pain, however, grief (*dolor*) or melancholy (*melancholia*). But it must be noted that titillation and grief have reference to man when one part above the rest is affected; but merriment or melancholy when all parts are equally affected. Now what was desire I have explained in the Note of Prop. 9, Part III., and besides these three I do not acknowledge any other primary emotion, for I shall show that all others follow from these in the following propositions. But before proceeding any further I must more concisely explain Prop. 10 of this part, so that it may be more clearly understood in what manner one idea can be contrary to another.

In the Note on Prop. 17, Part II., we showed that the idea which constitutes the essence of the mind involves the existence of the body as long as the body exists. Again, it follows from what we showed in Coroll., Prop. 8, Part II., and its Note, that the present existence of our mind depends on this alone, that the mind involves the actual existence of the body. Then we showed that the power of the mind by which it imagines and remembers things depends (Prop. 17 and 18, Part II., and its Note) on this, that the mind involves the actual existence of the body. Whence it follows that the present existence of the mind and its power of imagining is taken away as soon as the mind ceases to affirm the present existence of the body. But the cause on account of which the mind ceases to affirm the existence of the body, cannot be the mind itself (Prop. 4, Part III.), nor the fact that the body ceases to exist. For (Prop. 6,

Part II.) the cause on account of which the mind affirms the existence of the body is not that the body begins to exist, wherefore by the same argument it cannot cease to affirm the existence of the body, because the body ceases to exist; but (Prop. 8, Part II.) this arises from another idea which cuts off the existence of our body, and consequently of our mind, and which, therefore, is contrary to the idea which constitutes the essence of our mind.

PROP. XII. The mind, as much as it can, endeavours to imagine those things which increase or help its power of acting.

Proof.—As long as the human body is affected in a mode which involves the nature of any external body, so long the human mind regards the same body as present (Prop. 17, Part II.); and consequently (Prop. 7, Part II.), as long as the human mind regards any external body as present, that is (Note on that Prop.), as long as it imagines, so long the human mind is affected in a mode which involves the nature of the external body. And therefore as long as the mind imagines those things which increase or help the power of acting of our body, so long the body is affected in modes which increase or help its power of acting (Post. 1, Part III.), and consequently (Prop. 11, Part III.) so long the power of thinking in the mind is increased or helped. And therefore (Prop. 6 or 9, Part III.) the mind as much as it can endeavours to imagine those things. *Q.e.d.*

PROP. XIII. When the mind imagines things which diminish or hinder the power of acting of the body, it endeavours as much as it can to remember things which will cut off their existence.

Proof.—As long as the mind imagines any such thing, so long the power of the mind and body is diminished or hindered (as we have shown in the prev. Prop.), and, nevertheless, it will imagine it until the mind recalls some other thing which cuts off its present existence (Prop. 17, Part II.), that is (as we have just shown), the power of the mind and body is decreased or diminished until the mind imagines some other thing which cuts off its existence, which, therefore, the mind (Prop. 9, Part III.) as much as possible endeavours to imagine or recall. *Q.e.d.*

Corollary.—Hence it follows that the mind is averse to imagining those things which diminish or hinder its power and that of the body.

Note.—From this we clearly understand what is love (*amor*) and what hatred (*odium*), namely, that love is nothing else than pleasure accompanied by the idea of an external cause; and hate pain accompanied by the idea of an external cause. We see again that he who loves necessarily endeavours to keep present and preserve that which he loves; and, on the other hand, he who hates endeavours to remove and destroy the thing he hates. But concerning these there will be more to say later on.

PROP. XIV. If the mind were once affected at the same time by two emotions, when afterwards it is affected by one of them it will be also affected by the other.

Proof.—If the human body was affected once by two bodies at the same time, when the mind afterwards imagines one of them it will immediately recall the other (Prop. 18, Part II.). But the imaginations of our mind indicate rather the modifications of our body than the nature of external bodies (Coroll. 2, Prop. 16, Part II.). Therefore if the body, and consequently the mind (Def. 3, Part III.), was once affected by two emotions, when afterwards it may be affected by one it will also be affected by the other. *Q.e.d.*

PROP. XV. Anything can accidentally be the cause of pleasure, pain, or desire.

Proof.—Let us suppose the mind simultaneously affected by two emotions, by one which neither increases nor diminishes its power of acting, and the other which increases or diminishes it (Post. 1, Part III.). It is clear from the previous proposition that when the mind is afterwards affected by that one through its true cause which neither increases (by hypothesis) nor diminishes through itself the power of thinking, it will be affected at the same time by the other which increases or diminishes its power of thought, that is (Note, Prop. 11, Part III.), it will be affected by pleasure or pain; and therefore the former, not through itself, but accidentally, will be the cause of pleasure or pain. And in this way it may easily be shown that that thing could accidentally be the cause of desire. *Q.e.d.*

Corollary.—From the fact alone that we have regarded something with the emotion of pleasure or pain, though it were not the effecting cause, we can love or hate that thing.

Proof.—From this alone it comes to pass (Prop. 14, Part III.), that the mind, after imagining the said thing, is affected by the emotion of pleasure or pain, that is (Note, Prop. 11, Part III.), that the power of the mind or body is increased or diminished: and consequently (Prop. 12, Part III.) that the mind is desirous of, or averse to, imagining it (Coroll., Prop. 13, Part III.), that is (Note, Prop. 13, Part III.), that it loves or hates it. *Q.e.d.*

Note.—Hence we understand how it comes to pass that we love or hate certain things without having any known cause for it, but only what they call sympathy (*sympathia*), and antipathy (*antipathia*). To this also we should refer those objects which affect us with pleasure or pain merely owing to the fact that they have something in common with something that is wont to affect us with pleasure or pain, as I shall show in the following proposition. I know that certain writers who first introduced these terms, sympathy and antipathy, wished to signify thereby certain occult qualities; but nevertheless I think we may by the same terms understand known or manifest qualities.

PROP. XVI. From the fact alone that we imagine anything which has something similar to an object which is wont to affect the mind with pleasure or pain, although that in which the thing is similar to the object be not the effecting cause of those emotions, nevertheless we shall hate or love it accordingly.

Proof.—We have regarded that which is similar to the object in the object itself (by hypothesis) with the emotion of pleasure or pain; and therefore (Prop. 14, Part III.) when the mind is affected with its image, at the same time it is also affected with this or that emotion, and consequently a thing which we see to have this will be (Prop. 15, Part III.) accidentally the cause of pleasure or pain. And therefore (prev. Coroll.), although that in which it is similar to the object is not the affecting cause of these emotions, we nevertheless will love or hate it. *Q.e.d.*

PROP. XVII. If we imagine a thing which is wont to affect us with the emotion of sadness to have something similar to another thing which equally affects us with the emotion of pleasure, we will hate and love that thing at the same time.

Proof.—This thing (by hypothesis) is through itself a cause of pain, and (Note, Prop. 13, Part III.) in so far as we imagine with that emotion we hate it; and in so far as we imagine it to have something similar to another thing which is wont to affect equally with an emotion of pleasure, we love it equally with an impulse of love (prev. Prop.). And therefore we hate and love it at the same time. *Q.e.d.*

Note.—This disposition of the mind, which arises from two contrary emotions, is called a wavering of the mind (*animi fluctuatio*), and it has the same relation to the emotions as doubt has to imagination (Note, Prop. 44, Part II.); nor is there any difference between wavering of the mind and doubt save that of magnitude. But it must be noticed that I have deduced in the previous proposition these waverings of the mind from causes which cause one emotion through itself and of the other accidentally. I did that in order that they might the more easily be deduced from those which went before; and not because I deny that the waverings of the mind generally arise from an object which is the effecting cause of either emotion. For the human body (Post. 1, Part II.) is composed of many individuals of different nature, and therefore (Ax. 1, after Lemma 3, which see after Prop. 13, Part II.) it may be affected by one and the same body in many different modes; and, on the other hand, because one and the same thing can be affected in many modes, therefore it can affect one and the same part of the body in different ways. From which we can easily conceive that one and the same object can be the cause of many contrary emotions.

PROP. XVIII. A man is affected with the same emotion of pleasure or pain from the image of a thing past or future as from the image of a thing present.

Proof.—As often as a man is affected by the image of anything, he regards the thing as present, although it may not exist (Prop. 17, Part II., with its Coroll.), nor will he regard it as past or future save in so far as its image is connected with the image of time past or future (Note, Prop. 44, Part II.). Wherefore the image of the thing considered in itself is the same whether it refers to time present, past, or future, that is (Coroll. 2, Prop. 16, Part II.), the disposition of the body or emotion is the same whether the image of the thing be present, past, or future. And so the emotion of pleasure or pain is the same whether the image of the thing be present, past, or future. *Q.e.d.*

Note I.—I call a thing past or future in so far as we were or shall be affected by it. *E.g.*, in so far as we saw it or shall see it, it refreshed us or shall refresh us, it hurt us or shall hurt us, etc. For in so far as we imagine it in this manner, thus far we affirm its existence, that is, a body is affected by no emotion which excludes the existence of the thing; and therefore (Prop. 17, Part II.) the body is affected by the image of the thing in the same manner as if the thing were present. But in truth as it often happens that those who have great experience waver when they regard a thing as future or past, and are usually in doubt as to the event of it (see Note, Prop. 44, Part II.), hence it comes about that emotions which arise from similar images of things are not constant, but are usually disturbed by the images of other things, until men become assured of the issue of the thing.

Note II.—Now from what has been said we understand what is hope (*spes*), fear (*metus*), confidence (*securitas*), despair (*desperatio*), joy (*gaudium*), and disappointment (*conscientiæ morsus*). For hope is nothing else than an inconstant pleasure arisen from the image of a thing future or past, of whose event we are in doubt; fear, on the other hand, is an inconstant sadness arisen from the image of a doubtful thing. Again, if doubt be removed from these emotions, hope becomes confidence, and fear despair, that is, pleasure or pain arisen from the image of a thing which we fear or hope. Joy, again, is pleasure arisen from the image of a thing past, of whose event we were in doubt. Disappointment is this with pain substituted for pleasure.

PROP. XIX. He will be saddened who imagines that which he loves to be destroyed: if he imagines it to be preserved he is rejoiced.

Proof.—The mind, in so far as it can, tries to imagine those things which increase or help the power of acting of the body (Prop. 12, Part III.), that is (Note, Prop. 13), those things which it loves. But the imagination is aided by those things which impose existence on a thing, and, on the other hand, hindered by those things which cut off existence from a thing (Prop. 17, Part II.). Therefore the images of things which impose the existence of a thing that is loved, help the endeavour of the mind wherewith it endeavours to imagine the thing that is loved, that is (Note, Prop. 11, Part III.), they affect the mind with pleasure; and, on the other hand, those things which cut off the existence of a thing that is loved, hinder that endeavour of the mind, that is (same Note), they affect the mind with pain. And so he will be saddened who imagines that which he loves to be destroyed, etc. *Q.e.d.*

PROP. XX. He will be rejoiced who imagines what he hates to be destroyed.

Proof.—The mind (Prop. 13, Part III.) endeavours to imagine those things which cut off the existence of other things by which the body's power of acting is diminished or hindered, that is (Note on same Prop.), it endeavours to imagine those things which cut off the existence of such things as it hates. And therefore the image of a thing which cuts off the existence of that which the mind hates, helps that endeavour of the mind, that is (Note, Prop. 11, Part III.), affects the mind with joy. And so he will be rejoiced who imagines the destruction of that which he hates. *Q.e.d.*

PROP. XXI. He who imagines that which he loves to be affected by pleasure or pain, will also be affected by pleasure or pain: and these will be greater or less in the lover according as they are greater or less in the thing loved.

Proof.—The images of things (as we showed in Prop. 19, Part III.) which impose existence on the thing loved, help the mental endeavour by which it tries to imagine the thing loved. But pleasure imposes existence on the thing feeling pleasure, and the more so according as the emotion of pleasure is greater, for it is a transition to a greater state of perfection (Note, Prop. 11, Part III.). Therefore the image of pleasure in the thing loved helps the mental effort of the lover, that is (Note, Prop. 11, Part III.), it affects the lover with pleasure, and the more so according as this emotion was greater in the thing loved: which was the first point. Then in so far as a thing is affected with pain, thus far it is destroyed, the more so according to the greatness of the affecting pain (same Note, Prop. 11, Part III.): and therefore (Prop. 19,

Part III.) he that imagines what he loves to be affected with pain will also be affected with pain, and the more so according as the emotion was great in the object loved. *Q.e.d.*

PROP. XXII. If we imagine anything to affect with pleasure what we love, we are affected with love towards it: and, on the other hand, if we imagine anything to affect it with pain, we are affected with hatred towards it.

Proof.—He who affects a thing we love with pleasure or pain, likewise affects us with pleasure or pain, that is, if we imagine that the object loved is affected with pleasure or pain (prev. Prop.). But this pleasure or pain is supposed to be given in us accompanied by the idea of an external cause. Therefore (Note, Prop. 13, Part III.), if we imagine anything to affect what we love with pleasure or pain, we are affected with love or hatred towards it. *Q.e.d.*

Note.—Prop. 21 explains to us what is pity (*commiseratio*), which we may define as pain arisen from the hurt of another. But by what name to call pleasure arisen from another's good I know not. Then again, we call the love we bear towards him who benefits another, favour (*favor*), and, on the other hand, the hatred to him that misuses another, indignation (*indignatio*). It must also be noted that we pity not only a thing we have loved (as we showed in Prop. 21), but also one which we have regarded hitherto without emotion, merely because we judge it similar to ourselves (as I shall show later on): and so we favour him who benefits something similar to ourselves, and, on the other hand, are angry with him who works it evil.

PROP. XXIII. He will be rejoiced who imagines that which he hates to be affected with pain; if, on the other hand, he imagines it to be affected with pleasure, he will be saddened: and these emotions will be greater or less according as the contrary emotions were greater or less in the things hated.

Proof.—In so far as a hateful thing is affected with pain, thus far it is destroyed, and the more so according as it is affected with more pain (Note, Prop. 11, Part III.). Who, therefore (Prop. 20, Part III.), imagines a thing that he hates to be affected with pain, is inversely affected with pleasure, and the more so according as he imagines the thing hated to be affected with greater pain: which was the first point.

Again, pleasure imposes existence of the thing affected with pleasure (same Note, Prop. 11, Part III.), and the more so according as more pleasure is conceived. If any one then imagines that which he hates to be affected with pleasure, this imagination (Prop. 13, Part III.) will hinder his endeavour, that is (Note, Prop. 11, Part III.), he who hates will be affected with pain, etc. *Q.e.d.*

Note.—This pleasure can scarcely be found complete, and without any conflict of the mind. For (as I shall soon show in Prop. 27, Part III.) a man is saddened in so far as he imagines a thing similar to himself to be affected with pain: and, on the other hand, he is rejoiced if he imagines it to be affected with pleasure. But here we are regarding only hatred.

PROP. XXIV. If we imagine any one to affect a thing we hate with pleasure, we are affected with hatred towards that person. If, on the other hand, we imagine him to affect it with pain, we are affected with love towards him.

Proof.—This proposition is proved in the same manner as Prop. 22, Part III., which see.

Note.—These and such-like emotions of hatred have reference to envy (*invidia*), which is therefore nothing else than hatred itself, in so far as it is regarded as so disposing man that he rejoices at the pain of another, and is saddened at the pleasure of another.

PROP. XXV. We endeavour to affirm, concerning ourselves or what we love, everything that we imagine to affect what we love or ourselves with pleasure; and, on the other hand, we endeavour to deny, concerning ourselves and the object loved, everything that we imagine to affect us or the object loved with pain.

Proof.—What we imagine to affect a loved thing with pleasure or pain affects us also with pleasure or pain (Prop. 21, Part III.). But the mind (Prop. 12, Part III.) endeavours to imagine as much as it can those things that affect us with pleasure, that is (Prop. 17, Part II., and its Coroll.), to regard it as present; and, on the other hand (Prop. 13, Part III.), to cut off the existence of those things which affect us with pain. Therefore we endeavour to affirm, concerning ourselves or the thing loved, what we imagine will affect us or the thing loved with pleasure, and contrariwise. *Q.e.d.*

PROP. XXVI. We endeavour to affirm, concerning a thing that we hate, that which we imagine will affect it with pain, and, on the contrary, to deny all that which we imagine will affect it with pleasure.

Proof.—This proposition follows from Prop. 23, as the last one follows Prop. 21.

Note.—From this we see that it may easily come to pass that a man may think too highly of himself or an object of his love, and contrariwise concerning a thing hated. This imagination, when it refers to a man's thinking too highly of himself, is called pride (*superbia*), and is a kind of madness wherein a man dreams with his eyes open, thinking that he can do all things which he achieves only in imagination, and which therefore he regards as real, and exults in them as long as he cannot imagine those things which cut off their existence and determines his own power of action. Pride is therefore pleasure arising from a man's thinking too highly of himself. Pleasure which arises from a man's thinking too highly of another is called over-esteem or partiality (*existimatio*): and that is called disdain (*despectus*) which arises from the fact that he thinks too lowly of another.

PROP. XXVII. By the fact that we imagine a thing which is like ourselves, and which we have not regarded with any emotion to be affected with any emotion, we also are affected with a like emotion.

Proof.—The images of things are modifications of the human body the ideas of which represent to us external bodies as present (Note, Prop. 17, Part II.), that is (Prop. 16, Part II.), the ideas of which involve the nature of our body and at the same time the nature of the external body as present. If, therefore, the nature of an external body is similar to that of our own, then the idea of the external body which we imagine will involve a modification of our body similar to the modification of an external body: and consequently if we imagine any one similar to ourselves to be affected with any emotion, this imagination will express a modification of our body similar to that emotion. And therefore from the fact that we imagine a thing similar to ourselves to be affected with any emotion, we are affected in company with it by that emotion. And if we hate a thing similar to ourselves, we shall to that extent (Prop. 23, Part III.) be affected with it by a contrary emotion not a similar one. *Q.e.d.*

Note I.—This imitation of emotions, when it refers to pain, is called compassion (*commiseratio*) (see Note, Prop. 22, Part III.); when it has reference to desire it is called emulation (*œmulatio*), which then is nothing else than the desire of anything engendered in us by the fact that we imagine others similar to us to have that desire.

Corollary I.—If we imagine any one, whom we have regarded hitherto with no emotion whatever, to affect a thing similar to ourselves with pleasure, we are affected with pleasure towards that person. If, on the other hand, we imagine him to affect it with pain, we are affected with hatred towards him.

Proof.—This is shown from the prev. Prop. in the same manner as Prop. 22 from Prop. 21.

Corollary II.—We cannot hate a thing which we pity because its misery affects us with pain.

Proof.—For if we could hate it, then (Prop. 23, Part III.) we should be rejoiced at its pain, which is contrary to the hypothesis.

Corollary III.—We endeavour as much as we are able to liberate a thing we pity from its misery.

Proof.—That which affects a thing we pity with pain, affects us also with a similar pain (prev. Prop.); and therefore we endeavour to recollect everything that can take away its existence or which would destroy it (Prop. 13, Part III.), that is (Note, Prop. 9, Part III.), we desire to destroy it or we are determined for its destruction; and therefore we endeavour to liberate it from its misery. *Q.e.d.*

Note II.—This will or appetite of working good which arises from the fact that we pity the thing to which we wish to do good, is called benevolence (*benevolentia*), which is therefore nothing else than desire arisen from pity. Concerning love and hatred towards him who worked good or evil to what we imagined similar to ourselves, see Note, Prop. 22, Part III.

Prop. XXVIII. We endeavour to promote the being of everything that we imagine conducive to pleasure; but what we find repugnant or conducive to pain we endeavour to remove or destroy.

Proof.—We endeavour to imagine as much as possible what we imagine to be conducive to pleasure (Prop. 12, Part III.), that is (Prop. 17, Part II.), we endeavour as much as possible to regard it as present or actually existing. But the mind's endeavour or its power of thinking is equal and simultaneous in nature with the body's endeavour or power in acting (as clearly follows from Coroll., Prop. 7, and Coroll., Prop. 11, Part II.); therefore we endeavour absolutely to bring about its existence, or (what is the same, by Note, Prop. 9, Part III.) we desire and strive for it: which was the first point. Again, if that which we think to be the cause of pain, that is (Note, Prop. 13, Part III.), that which we hate, we imagine to be destroyed, we are rejoiced (Prop. 20, Part III.); and therefore (first part of this Prop.) we endeavour to destroy or (Prop. 11, Part III.) remove it from us, lest we should regard it as present: which was the second point. Therefore everything that is conducive to pleasure, etc. *Q.e.d.*

PROP. XXIX. We also shall endeavour to do everything which we imagine men (let it be understood in this and the following propositions that we mean men for whom we have no particular emotion) to regard with pleasure, and, on the other hand, we shall be averse to doing what we imagine men to turn away from.

Proof.—From the fact that we shall love and hate the same thing as we imagine men to love or hate (Prop. 27, Part III.), we are rejoiced or saddened at the presence of that thing (Note, Prop. 13, Part III.); and therefore (prev. Prop.) we endeavour to do everything which we imagine men to love or to regard with pleasure. *Q.e.d.*

Note.—This endeavour of doing or leaving out something, merely because we may thus please men, is called ambition (*ambitio*), especially when we thoughtlessly endeavour to please the mob and thus omit or do something to the hurt of ourselves or some one else, otherwise it is called philanthropy (*humanitas*). Again, the pleasure wherewith we imagine the action of another by which he endeavoured to please us I call praise (*laus*); but the pain wherewith we turn away from his action I call blame (*vituperium*).

PROP. XXX. If any one has done anything which he imagines to affect others with pleasure, he will be affected with pleasure accompanied by the idea of himself as the cause, or he will regard himself with pleasure. On the other hand, if he has done anything which he imagines to affect the others with pain, he regards himself then with pain.

Proof.—He who imagines that he has affected others with pleasure or pain is himself affected with pleasure or pain (Prop. 27, Part III.). But as a man (Prop. 19 and 22, Part II.) is conscious of himself through modifications by which he is determined for action, whoever has done anything which he imagines to affect others with pleasure, will be affected with pleasure accompanied by the idea of himself as the cause, or he will regard himself with pleasure, and, on the other hand, the contrary follows. *Q.e.d.*

Note.—As love (Note, Prop. 13, Part III.) is pleasure accompanied by the idea of an external cause, and hatred pain accompanied by the idea of an external cause, therefore this pleasure or pain will be a species of love and hatred. But as love and hatred have reference to external objects, we shall signify these emotions by other names. We shall call the pleasure accompanied by the idea of an external (internal?) cause honour (*gloria*), and the contrary emotion of pain shame (*pudor*)—be it understood when this pleasure or pain arises from the fact that man thinks himself praised or blamed; otherwise I shall call the pleasure accompanied by the idea of an external (internal?) cause self-complacency (*acquiescentia in seipso*), but the contrary emotion of pain I shall call repentance (*pœnitentia*). Again, as it may happen that (Coroll., Prop. 17, Part II.) the pleasure with which any one imagines that he affects others is only imaginary, and (Prop. 25, Part III.) as every one endeavours to imagine concerning himself that which he imagines to affect him with pleasure, it may easily come to pass that a vain man may become proud and imagine himself pleasing to all when he is in reality a universal nuisance.

PROP. XXXI. If we imagine any one to love, desire, or hate anything which we ourselves love, hate, or desire, by that very fact we shall love, hate, or desire it the more. But, on the other hand, if we imagine that what we love is avoided by some one, then we undergo a wavering of the mind.

Proof.—From the very fact that we imagine any one to love anything, we shall also love it ourselves (Prop. 27, Part III.). But we suppose ourselves to love it without this; there is then brought to play a new cause of love whereby our emotion is fostered: and therefore that which we love we shall love with more emotion. Again, from the fact that we imagine any one to turn away from anything, we also shall turn away from it (Prop. 27, Part III.). But if we suppose that we love it at the same time, then at the same time we shall love and turn away from a thing, or (see Note, Prop. 17, Part III.) we shall undergo a wavering of the mind. *Q.e.d.*

Corollary.—Hence, and from Prop. 28, Part III., it follows that every one endeavours as much as he can to cause every one to love what he himself loves, and to hate what he himself hates: as in the words of the poet, " As lovers let us hope and fear alike: of iron is he who loves what the other leaves." (*Ovidii Amores*, lib. 2, eleg. 19, vv. 4 and 5).

Note.—This endeavour of bringing it to pass that every one should approve of what any one loves and hates is in truth ambition (Note, Prop. 29, Part III.); and therefore we see that each one desires that all should live according to his disposition. When this is equally desired by all, they all oppose each other, and while all wish to be praised or loved, they hate each other.

Prop. XXXII. If we imagine any one to enjoy anything which only one can possess, we shall endeavour to bring it to pass that he does not possess it.

Proof.—From the fact alone that we imagine any one to enjoy anything (Prop. 27, Part III., and its Coroll. 1), we shall love that thing and desire to enjoy it. But (by the hypothesis) we imagine there to be an obstacle to this pleasure inasmuch as another may possess it: we shall therefore endeavour to bring it to pass that another should not possess it. *Q.e.d.*

Note.—We thus see that it is usually the case with most men that their nature is so constituted that they pity those who fare badly and envy those who fare well, and (prev. Prop.) with a hatred proportionate to the love we bear to the thing which we imagine some one else to possess. We see, again, that from the same property of human nature from which it follows that men are pitiful they are also envious and ambitious. Now if we would wish to consult experience, we find that she teaches us all this, more especially if we pay attention to the early years of our life. For we find that children, inasmu h as their bodies are, so to speak, in equilibrium, will laugh and cry merely because they see others laugh or cry; and whatever they see any one do they immediately desire to imitate, and they desire all things for themselves which they see give pleasure to others: clearly because the images of things, as we said, are the very modifications of the human body or modes in which the human body is affected by external causes and disposed for doing this or that.

PROP. XXXIII. When we love a thing similar to ourselves, we endeavour as much as possible to bring it about that it also should love us.

Proof.—We endeavour to imagine a thing that we love as much as we can above all others (Prop. 12, Part III.). If, therefore, the thing is similar to us, we shall endeavour to affect it with joy above the rest (Prop. 29, Part III.), or we shall endeavour as much as possible to bring it about that the thing loved should be affected with pleasure accompanied by the idea of ourselves, that is (Note, Prop. 13, Part III.), that it should love us. *Q.e.d.*

PROP. XXXIV. The greater the emotion with which we imagine a thing loved to be affected towards us, the greater will be our vain-glory.

Proof.—We endeavour (prev. Prop.) as much as we can to make the thing loved love us in return, that is (Note, Prop. 13, Part III.), to bring it about that the thing loved should be affected with pleasure accompanied with the idea of ourselves. And so the more pleasure with which we imagine the thing loved to be affected on our account, the more this endeavour is assisted, that is (Prop. 11, Part III., and its Note), the more we are affected with pleasure. But when we are pleased with the fact that we affect another thing similar to ourselves with pleasure, then we regard ourselves with pleasure (Prop. 30, Part III.). Therefore the greater the pleasure with which we imagine the thing loved to be affected on our account, the greater the pleasure with which we regard ourselves, or (Note, Prop. 30, Part III.) the more self-complacent or vain we become.   *Q.e.d.*

PROP. XXXV. If any one imagines that the thing loved is joined to another than himself with the same or a faster bond of love than that which binds it to him, he will be affected with hatred towards the object loved, and envy towards the other.

Proof.—The greater the love towards himself with which the thing loved is affected, the greater his self-complacency (prev. Prop.), that is, the greater his pleasure (Note, Prop. 30, Part III.); and therefore (Prop. 28, Part III.) he will endeavour to imagine as much as possible the thing loved to be bound to him in the tightest bond of love, and this endeavour or appetite will increase if he imagines any one else to desire the same thing for himself (Prop. 31, Part III.). But this endeavour or appetite is supposed to be hindered by the image of the thing loved, accompanied by the image of him whom the thing loved has joined to itself. Therefore (Note, Prop. 11, Part III.) he will be affected with pain accompanied by the idea of the thing loved as the cause, and at the same time the image of the other, that is (Note, Prop. 13, Part III.), he will be affected with hatred towards the object loved, and at the same time towards the other (Note, Prop. 15, Part III.), which by reason (Prop. 23, Part III.) that he enjoys the object loved, he will envy.   *Q.e.d.*

Note.—This hatred towards an object loved together with the envy of another is called jealousy (*zelotypia*), which therefore is nothing else than a wavering of the soul caused by love and hate, at the same time accompanied with the idea of a rival who is envied. Further, this hate towards the object loved will be greater according to the joy with which the jealous man was wont to be affected from the reciprocated love of the thing loved, and also according to the emotion with which he was affected towards him who now, he imagines, joins the thing loved to himself. For if he hated this person, by that very fact he will hate the object loved (Prop. 24, Part III.), for that he imagines it to affect with pleasure what he himself hates, and also (Coroll., Prop. 15, Part III.) from the fact that he is forced to join the image of the thing loved to that of him whom he hates: this state of affairs generally comes about when a man loves a woman. For he who imagines that a woman he loves prostitutes herself to another, is not only saddened by the fact that his own desire is hindered, but also, as he is forced to unite the image of the thing loved with the parts of shame and excreta of his rival, he is turned from her. To this also must be added that the jealous man is not received with the same countenance with which the thing loved was wont to greet him, on which account as a lover he will be saddened, as I shall soon show.

PROP. XXXVI. He who recollects a thing which he once enjoyed, desires to possess it under the same circumstances as those with which he first enjoyed it.

Proof.—Whatever a man sees in conjunction with a thing which has delighted him will be accidentally to him a cause of pleasure (Prop. 15, Part III.), and therefore (Prop. 28, Part III.) he will desire to possess it at the same time as the thing which delights him, or he will desire to possess the thing under the same circumstances as when he first enjoyed it. *Q.e.d.*

Corollary.—A lover will accordingly be saddened if he finds one of those attendant circumstances to be wanting.

Proof.—Now in so far as he finds one circumstance wanting, thus far he imagines something which cuts off its existence. But as he is assumed as a lover to be desirous of that one thing or circumstance (prev. Prop.), therefore (Prop. 19, Part III.) in so far as he imagines it to be wanting he is saddened. *Q.e.d.*

Note.—This sadness, in so far as it refers to the absence of that which we love, is called regret (*desiderium*).

PROP. XXXVII. The desire which arises by reason of sadness, joy, hatred, or love, is greater according as the emotion is greater.

Proof.—Sadness diminishes or hinders a man's power of action, that is (Prop. 7, Part III.), it diminishes or hinders the endeavour with which a man endeavours to persist in his being, and therefore (Prop. 5, Part III.) it is contrary to this endeavour, and whatever the power of a man affected by pain is, is directed to remove that pain. But (def. pain) the greater the pain the greater it must be opposed to the man's power of acting. Therefore the greater the pain the more will the man endeavour by his power of acting to remove it, that is (Note, Prop. 9, Part III.), the more desire or appetite with which he will endeavour to remove it. Again, since pleasure (Note, Prop. 11, Part III.) increases or helps a man's power of acting, it can easily be shown in that way that a man affected with pleasure desires nothing else than to preserve that pleasure, and that with the greater desire according as the pleasure is greater. Then since love and hatred are the emotions of pleasure and pain, it follows in the same manner that the endeavour, appetite, or desire which arises by reason of love or hatred will be greater according to the love or hatred. *Q.e.d.*

PROP. XXXVIII. If any one begins to hate a thing loved so that his love for it is clearly laid aside, he will bear greater hatred towards it on that very account than if he had never loved it, and the more so according as his former love was greater.

Proof.—Now if any one begins to hate a thing, more of his appetites are hindered than if he had not loved it. For love is a pleasure (Note, Prop. 13, Part III.) which man, as much as he can (Prop. 28, Part III.), endeavours to preserve by regarding the thing loved as present (same Note), and affecting it with pleasure as much as he can (Prop. 21, Part III.); his endeavour is greater according as (prev. Prop.) his love is greater, and so is his endeavour to bring it to pass that the thing loved should love him in return (Prop. 33, Part III.). But these endeavours are hindered by hatred towards the thing loved (Coroll., Prop. 13, and Prop. 23, Part III.). Therefore the lover (Note, Prop. 11, Part III.) will be affected with sadness on this account, and the more so according as his love was greater, that is, besides the pain whose cause is hatred there is also another cause, namely, that he loved the thing; and consequently he will regard the thing loved with a greater emotion of pain, that is (Note, Prop. 13, Part III.), he will regard it with more hatred than if he had never loved it, and the more so according as his former love was greater. *Q.e.d.*

PROP. XXXIX. He who hates any one will endeavour to do him harm unless he fears to receive a greater harm from him; and, on the other hand, he who loves some one will by the same law endeavour to do him good.

Proof.—To hate any one is the same (Note, Prop. 13, Part III.) as to imagine him the cause of pain, and therefore (Prop. 28, Part III.) he who hates anything will endeavour to remove or destroy it. But if thence he fears something more painful, or, what is the same thing, something worse, and thinks that he can avoid it by not inflicting that evil which he intended on the person he hates, he will desire to abstain from inflicting that evil (Prop. 28, Part III.), and that (Prop. 37, Part III.) with a greater endeavour than that with which he intended to inflict the evil which hitherto prevailed. The second part of the proof proceeds in the same manner as this. Therefore he who hates, etc. *Q.e.d.*

Note.—By good (*bonum*) I understand here all kind of pleasure and whatever may conduce to it, and more especially that which satisfies our fervent desires, whatever they may be; by bad (*malum*) all kinds of pain, and especially that which frustrates our desires. We have shown above (Note, Prop. 9, Part III.) that we do not desire anything because we think it good, but that we think it good because we desire it: and consequently that from which we turn we call evil or bad. Wherefore each one judges or estimates according to his own emotion what is good or bad, better or worse, best or worst. Thus a miser considers an abundance of money the best, and penury the worst. An ambitious man, on the other hand, holds nothing before honour, and turns away from nothing like shame. To an envious man nothing is more pleasing than another's misfortune, and nothing more displeasing than his good fortune: and thus each one judges according to his emotion whether a thing is good or bad, useful or hurtful. As for that emotion through which a man is so disposed that he does not want what he wants, or wants what he does not want, it is called fearfulness (*timor*), which therefore is nothing else than fear whereby a man is disposed to encounter a lesser evil in order to avoid a greater one which threatens him in the future (see Prop. 28, Part III.). But if the evil which he fears be shame, then the fearfulness is called bashfulness (*verecundia*). Finally, if the desire to avoid a future evil be hindered by the fear of another, so that the person knows not what to do, then the fear is called consternation (*consternatio*), especially if both evils feared are very great.

PROP. XL.—He who imagines himself to be hated by

another, and believes that he has given the other no cause
for hatred, will hate that person in return.

Proof.—He who imagines any one to be affected with
hatred will also be affected with hatred (Prop. 27, Part III.),
that is (Note, Prop. 13, Part III.), with sadness accompanied
with the idea of an external cause. But he (according to
the hypothesis) imagines no cause of this pain save the
person who hates him. Therefore from the fact that he
imagines himself to be hated by any one, he will be affected
with pain accompanied with the idea of the person who
hates him, or (by the same Note) he will hate that person.
Q.e.d.

Note I.—He who thinks that he has given some just cause
for hatred will (Prop. 30, Part III., and its Note) be affected
with shame. But this (Prop. 25, Part III.) rarely happens.
Moreover, this reciprocation of hatred can also arise from the
fact that hatred follows the endeavour to inflict evil on him
whom we hate (Prop. 39, Part III.). He, therefore, who
imagines that he is hated by any one, will imagine the other
as a cause of some evil or pain, and therefore will be affected
with sadness or fear accompanied by the idea of him who
hates him as the cause, that is, he will be affected with hatred
against him.

Corollary I.—He that imagines that one whom he loves
hates him, is a prey to the conflicting passions of love and
hatred; for in so far as he imagines himself to be hated by
any one, he is determined also to hate him (prev. Prop.).
But (by the hypothesis) he loves him nevertheless. Therefore
he is a prey to the conflicting passions of love and hatred.

Corollary II.—If any one imagines that an ill has been
inflicted on him by a person to whom he bore no good or
evil before, he immediately will endeavour to repay that evil
to the person in question.

Proof.—He who imagines any one to be affected with hatred
towards himself will hate that person in turn (prev. Prop.),
and (Prop. 26, Part III.) he will endeavour to remember
everything that can affect him with pain, and will endeavour,
moreover, to inflict this injury on the person (Prop. 39,
Part III.). But (by the hypothesis) the first evil he recalls
is that one done to himself. Therefore he immediately
endeavours to inflict that one in return. *Q.e.d.*

Note II.—The endeavour to inflict evil on him whom we

hate is called anger (*ira*) ; but the endeavour to inflict in
return the evil done to us is called revenge (*vindicta*).

PROP. XLI. If any one imagines himself to be loved by
some one else, and does not believe that he has given any cause
for this love (which in view of Coroll., Prop. 15, and Prop. 16,
Part III., can come to pass), he shall love that person in return.

Proof.—The proof of this proposition proceeds in the same
manner as that of the previous one: see also its note.

Note I.—If he believes that he has given just cause for
love, he will exult in it (Prop. 30, Part III., and its Note):
this is what most frequently happens (Prop. 2, Part III.); and
the contrary of this we said happens when any one imagines
that some one hates him (see Note, prev. Prop.). This reciprocal love, and consequently (Prop. 30, Part III.) the endeavour of working good to him who loves us, and who
(Prop. 39, Part III.) endeavours to do us good, is called
gratitude (*gratia seu gratitudo*). It is thus apparent that men
are far more ready to take revenge than to repay a benefit.

Corollary.—He who imagines he is loved by one whom he
hates is a prey to the conflicting emotions of hatred and love.
This is shown in the same way as was the corollary of the
previous proposition.

Note II.—If hatred prevails over love, he will endeavour
to inflict evil on the person who loves, and this is called cruelty
(*crudelitas*), more especially if he who loves is thought to
have given no special cause for hatred.

PROP. XLII. He who confers a benefit on any one, if moved
by love, or by the hope of honour, will be saddened if he
sees that the benefit is received with ingratitude.

Proof.—He who loves something similar to himself endeavours as much as possible to bring it about that he is
loved in turn by that thing (Prop. 33, Part III.). Therefore
he who confers a benefit on any one through love, does so
with the desire which holds him to be loved in return, that is
(Prop. 34, Part III.), by the hope of honour or (Note, Prop. 30,
Part III.) of pleasure: and therefore (Prop. 12, Part III.) he
will endeavour as much as possible to imagine this cause of
honour, or regard it as actually existing. But (by the hypothesis) he imagines something else that cuts off the cause of
its existence. Therefore (Prop. 19, Part III.) by that very
fact he will be saddened. *Q.e.d.*

PROP. XLIII. Hatred is increased by reciprocal hatred, and, on the other hand, can be destroyed by love.

Proof.—He who imagines that one whom he hates is affected with hatred towards him will feel to arise in himself a new hatred (Prop. 41, Part III.), while the first hatred still remains. But if, on the contrary, he imagines that one whom he hates is affected with love towards him, in so far as he imagines this he will regard himself with pleasure (Prop. 30, Part III.), and (Prop. 29, Part III.) will endeavour to please the object of his hatred, that is (Prop. 40, Part III.) he will endeavour not to hate him and not to affect him with pain: and this endeavour will be greater or less according to the emotion from which it arises (Prop. 37, Part III.). And so if it be greater than that one which arose from hatred, and through which he endeavoured to affect the thing which he hated with pain (Prop. 26, Part III.), it will prevail and will remove hatred from the mind. *Q.e.d.*

PROP. XLIV. Hatred which is entirely conquered by love passes into love, and love on that account is greater than if it had not been preceded by hatred.

Proof.—The proof proceeds in the same manner as that of Prop. 38, Part III. For he who begins to love a thing which he hated, or which he was wont to regard with pain, by the very fact that he loves will rejoice; and to this pleasure which love involves (def., Note, Prop. 13, Part III.) is added that which arises from the fact that the endeavour to remove pain which hatred involves (as we showed in Prop. 37, Part III.) is aided, accompanied by the idea of him whom he hated as cause.

Note.—Though this is so, no one will endeavour to hate anything or to be affected with pain in order to enjoy this increased pleasure, that is, no one desires to work evil to himself with the hope of recovering from this evil, nor desires to be ill for the sake of recovering. For each one will endeavour to preserve his being and remove as much as possible all pain. But if the contrary is conceived, that a man can desire to hate some one in order to love him subsequently with a greater love, he will always desire to hate him. For the greater the hatred may be, the greater will be the subsequent love, and therefore he will always desire that his hatred for him should become more and more; and by the same system of reasoning, a man would wish to become more and more ill in order to enjoy more pleasure from the subsequent convalescence, and therefore he would always desire to be ill, which is absurd (Prop. 6, Part III.).

PROP. XLV. If one imagines that any one similar to himself is affected with hatred towards another thing similar to himself whom he himself loves, then he will hate the first of these two.

Proof.—The thing loved has reciprocal hatred towards him who hates it (Prop. 40, Part III.). And therefore the lover who imagines that any one hates the thing he loves, by that very fact imagines the thing beloved to be affected by hatred, that is (Note, Prop. 13, Part III.), by pain: and consequently (Prop. 21, Part III.) he will be saddened, and that accompanied by the idea of him who hates the thing beloved as a cause, that is (Note, Prop. 13, Part III.), he will hate that person. *Q.e.d.*

PROP. XLVI. If any one has been affected with pleasure or pain by another person of a class or nation different to his own, and that accompanied by the idea of that person under the general name of that class or nation as the cause of the pleasure or pain, he will love or hate not only that person, but all of that class or nation.

Proof.—The proof of this is clear from Prop. 16, Part III.

PROP. XLVII. Joy which arises from the fact that we imagine a thing which we hate to be destroyed or affected by some evil never arises without some pain in us.

Proof.—This is clear from Prop. 27, Part III. For in so far as we imagine a thing similar to ourselves to be affected with pain we are saddened.

Note.—This proposition can also be shown from the Coroll., Prop. 17, Part II. For as often as we recall a thing, although it may not actually exist, we still regard it as present, and the body is affected in the same manner. Wherefore in so far as the memory of that thing is strong, man is determined to regard it with pain, which determination, while the image of this thing lasts, is hindered by the recollection of those things which cut off its existence, but it is not removed. And therefore the man is only rejoiced in so far as this determination is hindered; and hence it comes about that this pleasure which arises from the evil suffered by the thing which we hate is repeated as often as we recall the thing. For as we have said, when the image of that thing is aroused, inasmuch as it involves the existence of that thing, it determines the man to regard it with the same pain with which he was wont to regard it when it existed. But inasmuch as he joins the images of other things to the image of this thing, and these things cut off its existence, so this determination to be affected with pain is hindered at once, and the man rejoices again, and this as often as the repetition takes place. And this is the very reason why men rejoice as often as they recall past evils suffered by any one, and why they delight to relate perils from which they have escaped. For when they imagine any peril, they regard the same as future and are determined to fear it; but this determination is coerced by the idea of freedom, which they annexed to the idea of this peril when they were delivered from it, and which renders them secure again: and so once more they are rejoiced.

PROP. XLVIII. Love and hatred, for example, towards Peter, are destroyed, if the pain which the latter involves, and the pleasure which the former involves, are connected to the idea of another thing as a cause; and each of them will be diminished in so far as we imagine Peter not to be the only cause of either.

Proof.—This is obvious from the mere definition of love and hatred, which see in the Note on Prop. 13, Part III. For pleasure is called love towards Peter, and pain hatred towards him merely on this account, that he is regarded as the cause of this or that effect. When this then is either wholly or partly removed, the emotion towards Peter is either wholly or partly removed. *Q.e.d.*

PROP. XLIX. Love or hatred towards a thing which we imagine to be free must be greater than the love or hatred towards a necessary thing, provided both are subject to the same cause.

Proof.—A thing which we imagine to be free must (Def. 7, Part I.) be perceived through itself without any others. If, therefore, we imagine it to be the cause of the aforesaid pleasure or pain, by that very fact (Note, Prop. 13, Part III.)

we shall love or hate it, and that (prev. Prop.) with the greatest love or hatred that can arise from the given emotion. But if we imagine the thing which is the cause of the given effect to be necessary, then (Def. 7, Part I.) we shall imagine it not alone, but together with other things, to be the cause of the given effect and therefore (prev. Prop.) our love or hatred towards it will be less. *Q.e.d.*

Note.—Hence it follows that men, inasmuch as they consider themselves free, prosecute each with greater reciprocal love or hatred than other things: to this is added the imitation of emotions, of which see Prop. 27, 34, 40, and 43, Part III.

PROP. L. Anything can be accidentally the cause of hope or fear.

Proof.—This proposition is shown in the same way as Prop. 15, Part III., which see, together with the note on Prop. 18, Part III.

Note.—Things which are accidentally the cause of hope or fear are called good or bad omens (*bona aut mala omina*). Now in so far as these omens are the cause of hope or fear they are (see def. hope and fear, Note 2, Prop. 18, Part III.) the cause of pleasure or pain, and consequently (Coroll., Prop. 15, Part III.) thus far we love or hate them, and (Prop. 28, Part III.) we endeavour to attract them as means to obtain that which we hope for, or to remove them as obstacles or causes of fear. Moreover, it follows from Prop. 25, Part III., that we are so constituted by nature that we easily believe what we hope, but with difficulty what we fear, and that we form too high or too low estimates of these things. From this has arisen superstition, by which men are assailed on all sides. However, I do not think it worth while to point out here the waverings of the mind which arise from hope or fear, since it follows merely from the definition of these emotions that fear cannot be granted without hope nor hope without fear (as I shall explain more in detail in its proper place), and since in so far as we hope or fear anything we love or hate it. And therefore whatever we have said concerning love and hatred any one can apply to hope or fear.

PROP. LI. Different men can be affected by one and the same object in different manners, and one and the same man can be affected by one and the same object in different ways at different times.

Proof.—The human body (Post. 3, Part II.) is affected by external bodies in many ways. Therefore two men can be affected in different ways at the same time, and therefore (Ax. 1, after Lemma 3, after Prop. 13, Part II.) they can be affected in various ways by one and the same object. Again (Post. 3, Part II.), the human body can be affected now in this mode and now in that, and consequently (same Axiom) it can be affected by one and the same object at different times in different ways. *Q.e.d.*

Note.—We thus see that it can come to pass that what one loves another hates; and what one fears another fears not; and that one and the same man may now love what before he hated, and now dares what he feared before, etc. Again, inasmuch as each forms an opinion according to his emotion as to what is good or bad, or what is better or worse (see Note, Prop. 39, Part III.), it follows that men can vary both in opinion and in emotion (this can be although the human mind is a part of the divine intellect, as we have shown in the Note on Prop. 13, Part II.); and hence it comes about that when we compare some people with others, we distinguish them merely by the difference of their emotions, and that we call some intrepid, some timid, and some by some other name. *E.g.*, I call that man intrepid (*intrepidus*) who despises danger which I am wont to fear; and moreover, if I pay attention to the fact that his desire to work evil to him whom he hates, and good to him whom he loves, is not hindered by fear of the danger which is great enough to restrain me, I call him daring (*audax*). Then, again, he appears to me timid (*timidus*) who fears some danger which I am wont to despise; and if I pay more attention to this, that his desire is hindered by the fear which cannot restrain me, I call him pusillanimous (*pusillanimis*), and thus all will pass judgment. Again, from this nature of men and instability of judgment, namely, that man often forms opinion of things merely from his emotion, and that the things which he thinks make for pleasure or pain, and which therefore (Prop. 28, Part III.) he endeavours to promote into happening or remove, are often only imaginary, to say nothing of the other points I showed in Part II., on the uncertainty of things, we can easily conceive that man can easily be the cause both that he is rejoiced or saddened, or, in other words, he can be affected with pleasure or pain accompanied by the idea of himself as the cause. And therefore we can easily understand what repentance and self-complacency are, namely, that repentance is pain accompanied by the idea of oneself as cause, and self-complacency is pleasure accompanied by the idea of oneself as cause; and these emotions are most strong because men think themselves free (*vide* Prop. 49, Part III.).

PROP. LII. We cannot regard an object which we have seen before together with some others, or which we imagine to have nothing that is not common to many, as long as one which we imagine to have something singular about it.

Proof.—As soon as we imagine the object which we have seen with others, we immediately recall the others (Prop. 18, Part II., with its Note), and thus from regarding one we immediately pass to the regarding of another. And this is the case with an object which we imagine to have nothing that is not common to many. For we suppose by that very fact that we are regarding in it nothing that we have not seen with the others. But when we suppose that we imagine something singular in any object, something that we have never seen before, we say nothing else than that the mind, while it regards that object, has nothing else in itself to the regarding of which it may pass from the regarding of this object. And therefore it is determined for the regarding of that alone. Therefore we cannot regard, etc. *Q.e.d.*

Note.—This modification of the mind or admiration of an individual thing is called, in so far as it happens in the mind alone, wonder (*admiratio*); but if called up by an object which we fear it is said to be consternation (*consternatio*), for wonderment at something evil holds man suspended in regarding it, that he cannot think of the other things by means of which he may liberate himself from it. But if that at which we wonder be the prudence, industry, or anything of this kind of any man, inasmuch as we regard that man as excelling us by far in this, then the wonder is called veneration (*veneratio*), otherwise horror (*horror*), if we wonder at a man's rage, envy, etc. Again, if we admire the prudence, etc., of a man whom we love, our love by that very fact will become greater (Prop. 12, Part III.), and this love joined to wonder or veneration we call devotion (*devotio*). And in a like manner we may conceive hatred, hope, confidence, and other emotions joined to wonder; and thus we could deduce more emotions than could be expressed in our ordinary vocabulary. Hence it is apparent that the names of the emotions are taken rather from vulgar use than from an accurate knowledge of them.

To wonder is opposed contempt (*contemtus*), of which this for the most part is the cause, namely, that inasmuch as we see some one wonder at, love, or fear something, or something seems at the first sight similar to things which we wonder at, love, or fear (Prop. 15, with its Note, and Prop. 27, Part III.), we are determined to wonder at, to love, or fear that thing, etc. But if from the presence or accurate scrutiny of that thing we are forced to deny all that concerning that same thing which could be the cause of wonder, fear, or love, etc., then the mind remains determined to think rather of those things which are not in the thing than of those which are in it: while, on the other hand, by reason of the presence of the object, it is more wont to consider those things which are in it. Now as devotion arises from the wonder at a thing which we love, so derision (*irrisio*) arises from the contempt of a thing which we hate or fear, and disdain (*dedignatio*) arises from the contempt of foolishness, just as veneration arises from the wonder at prudence. We can, moreover, conceive love, hope, honour, and other emotions joined to contempt, and thence deduce other emotions which we are not wont to know by particular names.

PROP. LIII. When the mind regards itself and its power of acting it is rejoiced, and the more so, the more distinctly it imagines itself and its power of acting.

Proof.—Man does not know himself save through the modifications of his body, and the ideas of these modifications (Props. 19 and 23, Part II.). Therefore when it happens that the mind can regard itself, it is assumed by that very fact to pass to a greater state of perfection, that is (Note, Prop. 11, Part III.), to be affected with pleasure, and the more so according as it can imagine itself and its power of acting more distinctly. *Q.e.d.*

Corollary.—This pleasure is more and more fostered the more a man imagines himself to be praised by others. For the more he imagines himself to be praised by others, the greater, by that very fact, the pleasure with which he magines others to be affected, and that accompanied by the idea of himself as cause (Note, Prop. 29, Part III.). And therefore (Prop. 27, Part III.) the greater will be the joy accompanied by an idea of himself with which he is affected. *Q.e.d.*

Prop. LIV. The mind endeavours to imagine those things only which impose its power of action on it.

Proof.—The endeavour or power of the mind is the same as the essence of the mind (Prop. 7, Part III.). But the essence of the mind (as is self-manifest) only affirms that which the mind is and can do; and not that which it is not and cannot do. And therefore it endeavours to imagine only that which affirms or imposes its power of acting. *Q.e.d.*

Prop. LV. When the mind imagines its want of power it is saddened by that fact.

Proof.—The essence of the mind affirms only that which the mind is and can do, or it is the nature of the mind only to imagine those things which impose its power of acting (prev. Prop.). When therefore we say that the mind, while regarding itself, imagines its weakness, we say nothing else than that, while the mind endeavours to imagine something which imposes its power of acting, that endeavour is hindered or (Note, Prop. 11, Part III.) that it is saddened. *Q.e.d.*

Corollary.—This pain or sadness is fostered more and more if one imagines himself to be reviled by others, which can be proved in the same manner as the Coroll., Prop. 53, Part III.

Note.—This pain, accompanied by the idea of our weakness, is called humility (*humilitas*); the pleasure, on the other hand, which arises from the contemplation of oneself is called self-love (*philautia*) or self-complacency. And as this is repeated as often as a man regards his virtues or his power of acting, it therefore comes to pass that every one is fond of relating his own exploits and displaying the strength both of his body and his mind, and that men are on this account a nuisance one to the other. From which it likewise follows that men are naturally envious (see Note, Prop. 24, and Note, Prop. 32, Part III.), or, in other words, prone to rejoice at the weakness of their equals and to be saddened at their strength. For as often as one imagines his actions he is affected with pleasure (Prop. 53, Part III.), and the more so according as he imagines them more distinctly or to express more perfection, that is (by what was said in Note 1, Prop. 40, Part II.), according as he can the better distinguish them from others and regard them as singular. Wherefore each person will derive the greatest pleasure from the contemplation of himself when he regards something in himself which he denies in others. But if that which he affirms of himself has reference to the general idea of man and beast, he will not be so greatly pleased; and on the other hand, he will be saddened if he imagines his actions, when compared to those of others, to be weaker, which sadness (Prop. 28, Part III.) he will endeavour to remove by wrongly interpreting the actions of others, or by adorning his own as much as possible. It is therefore apparent that men have a natural proclivity to hatred and envy, which, moreover, is aided by their education. For parents are wont to encourage their children to virtue solely by the promise of honour or the fostering of envy. Yet perhaps some one will hesitate at this point, saying that very often we wonder at the virtues of men and venerate them. In order to remove this scruple, I shall add this corollary.

Corollary II.—No one envies the virtue of any one save his equal.

Proof.—Envy is hatred itself (see Note, Prop. 24, Part III.) or (Note, Prop. 13, Part III.) sadness, that is (Note, Prop. 11, Part III.), a modification by which a man's power of acting or endeavour is hindered. But man (Note, Prop. 9, Part III.) endeavours or desires to do nothing save what can follow from his given nature. Therefore man desires to attribute to himself no power of acting or (what is the same thing) no virtue which is proper to another nature and alien to his own. And therefore his desire cannot be hindered nor he himself saddened by the fact that he regards some virtue in some one dissimilar to himself, and consequently he cannot envy him; but he can envy his equal, who is supposed to be of the same nature as himself. *Q.e.d.*

Note.—When we said in the Note on Prop. 52, Part III., that we venerate a man by reason of the fact that we wonder at his prudence, courage, etc., we meant that that comes about (as can be seen of the Prop. itself) because we imagine those virtues to be possessed by that person alone and not common to our nature: and therefore we do not envy them any more than we envy height in a tree or courage in a lion, etc.

PROP. LVI. There are as many species of pleasure, pain, desire, and consequently any emotion which is composed of these, such as wavering of the mind, or which is derived from these, such as love, fear, hope, hate, etc., as there are species of objects by which we are affected.

Proof.—Pleasure and pain, and consequently the emotions which are composed of or derived from these, are passions (Note, Prop. 11, Part III.); we also are passive in so far as we have inadequate ideas (Prop. 1, Part III.), and in so far as we have them alone are we passive (Prop. 3, Part III.), that is (see Note 1, Prop. 40, Part II.), we are only necessarily passive in so far as we imagine, or (see Prop. 17, Part II., with its Note) in so far as we are affected by an emotion which involves the nature of our body and the nature of an external body. The nature, therefore, of each passion must so be explained necessarily that the nature of the object by which we are affected may be expressed. The pleasure which arises from the object, *e.g.* A, involves the nature of the object A, and the pleasure which arises from the object B involves the nature of that object B: and therefore these two pleasures are of different nature because they arise from causes of different nature. Thus also the emotion of sadness which arises from one object is different in nature from the sadness which arises from another cause, which also must be understood of love, hate, hope, fear, wavering of the mind, etc.: and therefore there are as many species of pleasure, pain, love, etc., as there are species of objects by which we are affected. But desire is the essence or nature of every one in so far as it is conceived as determined from any given disposition of the person to do anything (see Note, Prop. 9, Part III.). Therefore, according as each one is affected by external causes with this or that kind of pleasure, pain, love, hatred, that is, according as his nature is constituted in this or that manner, so will his desire be this or that, and the nature of one desire necessarily different to the nature of another as much as the emotions from which each one has arisen differ one from the other. Therefore there are as many species of desires as there are species of pleasure, pain, love, etc., and consequently (from what has already been shown) as there are species of objects by which we are affected. *Q.e.d.*

Note.—Among the species of emotions, which (prev. Prop.) are of great number, the best known are luxury (*luxuria*), drunkenness (*ebrietas*), lust (*libido*), avarice (*avaritia*), and ambition (*ambitio*), which are only varieties of love or desire: which explain the nature of this or that emotion according to the objects to which they refer. For by luxury, drunkenness, lust, avarice, and ambition we understand nothing else than an immoderate love or desire for feasting, drinking, lechery, riches, and honour. Moreover, these emotions, in so far as we distinguish them from others merely by the object to which they refer, have no opposites. For temperance, sobriety, chastity, which we are wont to contrast with luxury, drunkenness, lust, etc., are not emotions or passions, but indicate strength of mind which moderates these emotions. The remaining species of emotions I cannot explain here (for they are as many as there are objects), nor, if I could, would it be necessary. For it suffices for what we have in view, namely, to determine the strength of the emotions and the power of the mind in moderating them, to have a definition of each emotion of universal application. It suffices, I say, for us to understand the common properties of the emotions and mind, so that we may be able to determine of what kind and quantity is the power of the mind in moderating and checking the emotions. And so, although there is a great difference between this and that emotion of love, hate, or desire, *e.g.*, as the love for children and the love for a wife, it is not our place to take note of these differences or inquire any further into the origin and nature of the emotions.

PROP. LVII. Any emotion of every individual differs from the emotion of another only in so far as the essence of one differs from the essence of another.

Proof.—This Prop. is clear from Ax. 1, which see after Lemma 1, Note, Prop. 13, Part II. But nevertheless we shall prove it from the definitions of the three primary emotions.

All emotions have reference to desire, pleasure, or pain, as the definitions which we gave of them show. But desire is the nature and essence of everything (see its def. in Note,

Prop. 9, Part III.): therefore the desire of one individual differs from the desire of another only inasmuch as the essence of one differs from the essence or nature of the other. Pleasure and pain are passions by which the power or endeavour of every person to persist in his own being is increased or diminished, aided or hindered (Prop. 11, Part III., and its Note). But by endeavour to persist in its being, in so far as it refers to the mind and body at the same time, we understand appetite and desire (Note, Prop. 9, Part III.); therefore pleasure and pain are desire itself, or appetite, in so far as it is increased or diminished by external causes, helped or hindered, that is (same Note), they are the nature of every one. And therefore the pleasure or pain of one person differs only from the pleasure or pain of another in so far as the nature or essence of one differs from the nature or essence of another: and consequently any emotion of an individual, etc. *Q.e.d.*

Note.—Hence it follows that the emotions of animals, which are called irrational (for we can in no wise doubt that brutes feel now we know the origin of the mind), differ only from the emotions of man inasmuch as their nature differs from the nature of man. Horse and man are filled with the desire of procreation: the desire of the former is equine, while that of the latter is human. So also the lusts and appetites of insects, fish, and birds must vary. Thus although each individual lives content and rejoices in the nature he has, yet the life in which each is content and rejoices is nothing else than the idea or soul of that individual: and therefore the joy of one only differs in nature from the joy of another in so far as the essence of one differs from the essence of another. Again, it follows from the previous proposition that there is a considerable difference between the joy of, *e.g.*, a drunkard and that which possesses a philosopher: which I wished to mention here by the way. This is what I have to say of the emotions which refer to man in so far as he is passive. It remains that I should add a few points which refer to him in so far as he is active.

PROP. LVIII. Besides pleasure and desire, which are passions, there are other emotions of pleasure and desire which refer to us in so far as we are active.

Proof.—When the mind conceives itself and its power of

acting, it rejoices (Prop. 53, Part III.). But the mind necessarily regards itself when it conceives a true or adequate idea (Prop. 43, Part II.). But the mind conceives certain adequate ideas (Note 2, Prop. 40, Part II.). Therefore it will also rejoice in so far as it conceives adequate ideas, that is (Prop. 1, Part III.), in so far as it is active. Again, the mind endeavours to persist in its being (Prop. 9, Part III.) in so far as it has both clear and distinct ideas and confused ones. But by endeavour we understand desire (Note, Prop. 9, Part III.). Therefore desire also has reference to us in so far as we understand, or (Prop. 1, Part III.) in so far as we are active. *Q.e.d.*

PROP. LIX. Among all the emotions which have reference to the mind, in so far as it is active, there are none which have not reference to pleasure or desire.

Proof.—All emotions have reference to pleasure, pain, or desire, as the definitions which we gave of them show. But we understand by pain that the mind's power of thinking is diminished or hindered (Prop. 11, Part III., and its Note), and therefore the mind in so far as it is saddened has its power of understanding, that is, its power of acting (Prop. 1, Part III.), diminished or hindered. And therefore no emotions of pain can be referred to the mind in so far as it is active, but only emotions of pleasure or desire which (prev. Prop.) thus far have reference to the mind. *Q.e.d.*

Note.—All actions which follow from the emotions which have reference to the mind, in so far as it is active or understands, I refer to fortitude (*fortitudo*), which I distinguish into two parts, courage or magnanimity (*animositas*) and nobility (*generositas*). For I understand by courage the desire by which each endeavours to preserve what is his own according to the dictate of reason alone. But by nobility I understand the desire by which each endeavours according to the dictate of reason alone to help and join to himself in friendship all other men. And so I refer those actions which work out the good of the agent to courage, and those which work out the good of others to nobility. Therefore temperance, sobriety, and presence of mind in danger, etc., are species of courage; but modesty, clemency, etc., are species of nobility. And thus I think I have explained and shown through their primary causes the principal emotions and waverings of the mind which arise from the composition of the three primary emotions, namely, pleasure, pain, and desire. And it is apparent from these propositions that we are driven about by external causes in many manners, and that we, like waves driven about by contrary winds, waver and are unconscious of the issue and of our fate. But I said I have shown not all that can be given, but only the principal conflictions of the mind. For proceeding in the same way as above, we can easily show that love is united to repentance, disdain, and shame, etc. But I think it will be clear to all from the preceding propositions that the emotions can be compounded one with another in so many ways, and so many variations can arise from these combinations, that it were impossible to express them by any number. But for my purpose it suffices to have enumerated the principal ones; for the rest which I have omitted would be to satisfy the curious, not those who seek the profit of this. It remains, however, to be noted concerning love what very often happens while we are enjoying the thing which we desired, that the body from the enjoyment acquires a new disposition, by which it is determined in another way, and other images of things are aroused in it, and at the same time the mind begins to imagine and desire other things. *E.g.*, when we imagine something which is wont to delight us with its flavour, we desire to enjoy it, that is, to eat it. But as soon as we enjoy it the stomach is filled and the body's desire is turned in another direction. But if while the body is in this condition the image of this food, inasmuch as it is present, be stimulated, and consequently the endeavour or desire of eating it be stimulated, the new condition of the body will feel disgust at this desire or endeavour, and consequently the presence of the food which before we desired will now be odious to us, and this is what we call satiety or weariness (*fastidium aut tædium*). For the rest, I have neglected the external modifications of the body which are observable in emotions such as tremor, pallor, sobbing, and laughter, because they refer to the body without any relation to the mind. Again, as there are certain things to be noted with reference to the definitions of the emotions, I shall repeat them in this order, with such notes as I think necessary.

DEFINITIONS OF THE EMOTIONS

I. Desire (*cupiditas*) is the very essence of man in so far as it is conceived as determined to do something by some given modification of itself.

Explanation.—We said above in the Note on Prop. 9, Part III., that desire was appetite with a consciousness of itself: and that appetite was the very essence of man in so far as it is determined to do such things as will serve for its preservation. But in the same note I also gave warning that in truth I recognise no difference between human appetite and desire. For whether a man be conscious of his appetite or whether he be not, his appetite remains the same notwithstanding: and therefore, lest I seem guilty of tautology, I did not wish to explain desire by means of appetite, but I endeavoured at the same time to define it in such a way that I might comprehend in one all the endeavours of human nature which we signify by the name of appetite, will, desire, or impulse. I might indeed have said that desire was the very essence of man in so far as it is conceived as determined to do something; but from this definition (Prop. 23, Part II.) it would not follow that the mind could be conscious of its appetite or desire. Therefore, in order to involve the cause of this consciousness, it was necessary to add (same Prop.), in so far as it is conceived as determined by some modification of itself. For by modification of human nature we understand any disposition of that nature, whether it be innate, or whether it be conceived under the attribute of thought or extension alone, or whether it have reference to both at the same time. Hence by the name of desire I understand any endeavours, impulses, appetites, or volitions, which are various, according to the various dispositions of the said man, and often opposed one to the other as a man is drawn in different directions and knows not whither to turn.

II. Pleasure (*lætitia*) is man's transition from a less state of perfection to a greater.

III. Pain (*tristitia*) is man's transition from a greater state of perfection to a lesser.

Explanation.—I say transition, for pleasure is not perfection itself: for if a man were born with the perfection to which he passes, he would possess it without the emotion of pleasure; and the contrary to this makes it still more apparent. For that pain consists of a transition from a greater to a less perfection, and not of that less perfection itself, no one can deny, since man cannot thus far be saddened in so far as he participates in any perfection. Nor can we say that pain consists of the privation of a greater perfection, for privation is nothing. But the emotion of sadness or pain is an action (*actus*), which therefore cannot be anything else than the action of passing to a lesser state of perfection, that is, an action by which the power of action of a man is lessened or hindered (see Note, Prop. 11, Part III.). As for the definitions of laughter, giggling, melancholy, and grief, I omit them inasmuch as they have reference rather to the body, and are only species of pleasure or pain.

IV. Wonder (*admiratio*) is the imagination of anything, in which the mind accordingly remains without motion because the imagination of this particular thing has no connection with the rest (see Prop. 52, with its Note).

Explanation.—In the Note on Prop. 18, Part II., we showed what was the reason that the mind from the contemplation of one thing passes at once to the contemplation of another, namely, that inasmuch as the images of those things were so intertwined and so arranged that one followed another, which therefore cannot be conceived if the image be new; but the mind will remain transfixed in the contemplation of that thing until it is determined by other causes for thinking otherwise. The imagination of a new thing, therefore, considered in itself, is of the same nature as other imaginations, and on that account I do not count wonder among the emotions, nor do I see why I should do so, since this distraction of the mind arises from no positive reason which attracts the mind from other things, but only from the fact that the cause is wanting why the mind, from the regarding of one thing, should pass to the thinking of others. I recognise, therefore (as I intimated in the Note of Prop. 11, Part III.), only three primary emotions, namely, pleasure, pain, and desire; nor have I spoken of wonder for any other reason than that it is customary to speak of certain emotions which arise from the three primary ones by other names when they have reference to objects which we wonder at; and this same reason moves me to put forward also a definition of contempt (*contemtus*).

V. Contempt is the imagination of anything which touches the mind so little that the mind is moved by the presence of that thing to think rather of things which are not contained in the thing than those which are contained in it (see Note, Prop. 52, Part III.).

The definitions of veneration and scorn I pass over here, for I know not any emotions which arise therefrom.

VI. Love (*amor*) is pleasure accompanied by the idea of an external cause.

Explanation.—This definition sufficiently explains the essence of love. That one given by authors who define that love is the wish of the lover to unite himself to the object loved, does not explain the essence of love, but a property thereof: and as the essence of love has not been perceived sufficiently by the authors in question, they accordingly have neither a clear conception of its property, and accordingly their definition is considered by all to be exceedingly obscure. But let it be remarked that when I say that it is a property of the essence of love that the lover wishes to be united to the object of his love, I do not understand by will or wish, consent, deliberation, or free decision (for this we have shown to be fictitious in Prop. 48, Part II.), nor even the wish of the lover to be united with the object of his love when it is absent, nor of continuing in its presence when it is present (for love can be conceived without either of these desires); but by wish I understand the satisfaction which is in the love by reason of the presence of the object loved, by which the pleasure of the lover is maintained, or at least cherished.

VII. Hatred (*odium*) is pain accompanied by the idea of an external cause.

Explanation.—What must be noted here can easily be perceived from what was said in the explanation of the previous definition (see, moreover, Note, Prop. 13, Part III.).

VIII. Inclination (*propensio*) is pleasure accompanied by the idea of anything which by accident is the cause of pleasure.

IX. Aversion (*aversio*) is pain accompanied by the idea

of anything which is accidentally the cause of that pain (see Note, Prop. 15, Part III.).

X. Devotion (*devotio*) is love towards him whom we admire or wonder at.

Explanation.—That wonder arises from the novelty of a thing we showed in Prop. 52, Part III. If, therefore, it comes to pass that we often imagine that which we wonder at, then we shall cease to wonder: and thus we see that devotion can easily degenerate into simple love.

XI. Derision (*irrisio*) is pleasure arisen from the fact that we imagine what we despise to be present in what we hate.

Explanation.—In so far as we despise a thing which we hate, thus far we deny its existence (Note, Prop. 52, Part III.), and thus far we rejoice (Prop. 20, Part III.). But as we suppose that man hates what he derides, it follows that this joy is not very staple (see Note, Prop. 47, Part III.).

XII. Hope (*spes*) is an uncertain pleasure arisen from the idea of a thing past or future, the event of which we still doubt to some extent.

XIII. Fear (*metus*) is an uncertain pain arisen from the idea of something past or future of whose event we doubt somewhat (see Note 2, Prop 18, Part III.).

Explanation.—It follows from these definitions that fear cannot be without hope nor hope without fear. For he that depends on hope and doubts the event of a thing, is supposed to imagine something which cuts off the existence of that thing in the future: and therefore thus far he is pained (Prop. 19, Part III.), and consequently, while he depends on hope he has fears as to the event of the thing. He, on the other hand, that is in fear, that is, who doubts concerning the event of a thing which he hates, imagines also something which cuts off the existence of that thing: and therefore (Prop. 20, Part III.) he rejoices, and consequently thus far has hope that it will not come to pass.

XIV. Confidence (*securitas*) is pleasure arisen from the idea of a past or future thing of which the cause of doubt is overborne.

XV. Despair (*desperatio*) is pain arisen from the idea of a thing past or future of which all cause of doubt is removed.

Explanation.—Confidence therefore arises from hope, and

despair from fear, when all cause of doubt as to the event of a thing is removed, which takes place because a man imagines a thing past or future to be present, or because he imagines other things which cut off the existence of those things which brought doubt to him. For although we may never be certain as to the event of individual things (Note, Prop. 31, Part II.), it can nevertheless come to pass that we have no doubt concerning their event. For we have shown that it is a different thing not to doubt concerning a thing (see Note, Prop. 49, Part II.) and to be certain about it: and therefore it may come to pass that we are affected with the same emotion of pleasure or pain from the image of a thing past or future as from the image of a thing present, as we showed in Prop. 18, Part III., which see, together with its second note.

XVI. Joy (*gaudium*) is pleasure accompanied by the idea of a past thing which surpassed our hope in its event.

XVII. Disappointment (*conscientiæ morsus*) is pain accompanied by the idea of a past thing which surpassed our hope in its event.

XVIII. Pity (*commiseratio*) is pain accompanied by the idea of an ill which happened to another whom we imagine similar to ourselves (see Note, Prop. 22, and Note, Prop. 27, Part III.).

Explanation.—Between pity and compassion (*misericordia*) there seems to be no difference save perhaps this, that pity has reference to a particular emotion, while compassion to a habit.

XIX. Favour (*favor*) is love towards some one who has benefited another.

XX. Indignation (*indignatio*) is hatred towards some one who has maltreated another.

Explanation.—I know that these names, according to common usage, have other meanings, but it is my purpose not to explain the meanings of words, but the nature of things, and to explain them in such words whose meanings, according to current use, are not entirely different from the meaning which I wish to attach to them: this warning should suffice once for all. As for the cause of these emotions, see Coroll. 1, Prop. 27, and Coroll., Prop. 22, Part III.

XXI. Partiality (*existimatio*) is estimating something too highly by reason of love.

XXII. Disparagement (*despectus*) is estimating something too lowly by reason of hatred.

Explanation.—Partiality is therefore an effect or property of love, while disparagement is an effect or property of hate: and therefore partiality may also be defined as love in so far as it thus affects man so that he estimates a thing too highly, and on the other hand, disparagement as hatred in so far as it thus affects man that he underestimates him whom he hates (see on this point Note, Prop. 26, Part III.).

XXIII. Envy (*invidia*) is hatred in so far as it so affects man that he is pained at the good fortune and rejoiced at the evil fortune of another.

Explanation.—Envy is commonly opposed or contrasted with compassion (*misericordia*), which therefore may be thus defined despite the usual meaning of the word.

XXIV. Compassion (*misericordia*) is love in so far as it so affects man that he rejoices at the good fortune of another and is saddened at his evil fortune.

Explanation.—For the rest concerning envy, see Note, Prop. 24, and Note, Prop. 32, Part III. These are emotions of pleasure and pain which are accompanied by the idea of an external thing as cause, either through itself or by accident. I now pass on to those emotions which the idea of a thing internal accompany as cause.

XXV. Self-complacency (*acquiescentia in seipso*) is pleasure arising from the fact that man regards himself and his power of acting.

XXVI. Humility (*humilitas*) is pain arising from the fact that man regards his want of power or weakness.

Explanation.—Self-complacency is opposed to humility in so far as by it we understand pleasure which arises from the fact that we regard our power of acting; but in so far as we understand by it pleasure accompanied by the idea of some deed which we think we have done by the free decision of the mind, it is opposed to repentance, which can thus be defined by us:

XXVII. Repentance (*pœnitentia*) is pain accompanied by

the idea of some deed which we think we have done by the free decision of the mind.

Explanation.—We have shown the causes of these emotions in Note, Prop. 51, 53, 54, 55, and its Note, Part III. Concerning the free decision of the mind, however, see Note, Prop. 35, Part II. But here, moreover, this notable point arises, that it is not wonderful that pain should follow all those actions which according to custom are called wicked (*pravus*), and those which are called right (*rectus*) should be followed by pleasure. For we can understand from what has been said above that this most certainly depends upon education. Parents, by reprobating wicked actions and reproving their children on the committal of them, and on the other hand, by persuading to and praising good or right actions, have brought it about that the former should be associated with pain and the latter with pleasure. This also is proved by experience. For custom and religion are not the same to all: but on the contrary, what is sacred to some is profane to others, and what is honourable to some is disgraceful to others. Therefore, according as each has been educated, so he repents of or glories in his actions.

XXVIII. Pride (*superbia*) is over-estimation of oneself by reason of self-love.

Explanation.—Pride is different from partiality, for the latter has reference to the over-estimation of an external object, while the former has reference to self-over-estimation. However, as partiality is the effect or property of love, so pride is that of self-love (*philautia*), which therefore may be defined as love of self, or self-complacency, in so far as it thus affects man so as to over-estimate himself (see Note, Prop. 26, Part III.). There is no contrary to this emotion. For no one under-estimates oneself by reason of self-hate, that is, no one under-estimates himself in so far as he imagines that he cannot do this or that. For whatever a man imagines that he cannot do, he imagines it necessarily, and by that very imagination he is so disposed that in truth he cannot do what he imagines he cannot do. For so long as he imagines that he cannot do this or that, so long is he determined not to do it: and consequently, so long it is impossible to him that he should do it. However, if we pay attention to these things, which depend solely on opinion, we shall be able to conceive that it is possible that a man should under-estimate himself. For it can well come to pass that any one, while sadly regarding his weakness, should imagine that he is despised by all, and that while all other men are thinking of nothing less than of despising him. A man, moreover, may under-estimate himself if he deny himself something in the present with relation to future time of which he is uncertain: as, for example, if he should deny that he can conceive anything certain, or desire or do anything save what is wicked and disgraceful, etc. We could, moreover, say that any one under-estimates himself when we see that he dares not do certain things from too great a fear of shame which others who are his equals do without any fear. We can therefore oppose this emotion to pride; I shall call it self-despising or dejection (*abjectio*). For as self-complacency arises from pride, so self-despising arises from humility: and this therefore may thus be defined:

XXIX. Self-despising or dejection (*abjectio*) is under-estimating oneself by reason of pain.

Explanation.—We are wont, nevertheless, to contrast pride with humility, but then more when we regard their effects than their nature. For we are wont to call him proud who praises himself too much (see Note, Prop. 30, Part III.), who relates only his own great deeds and only the evil ones of others, who wishes to be before others, and who lives with that gravity and adornment which is natural to those who are far above him in rank. On the other hand, we call him humble who often blushes, who confesses his faults, and relates the virtues and great deeds of others, who yields to all, who walks with a bowed head, and neglects to take upon himself any ornament of dress. But these emotions of humility and self-despising are very rare, for human nature considered in itself strives as much as possible against them (see Prop. 15 and 54, Part III.); and therefore those who are believed to be most abject and humble are usually most ambitious and envious.

XXX. Honour or glory (*gloria*) is pleasure accompanied by the idea of some action of ours which we imagine others to praise.

XXXI. Shame (*pudor*) is pain accompanied by the idea of some action of our own which we imagine others to blame.

Explanation.—Concerning these see Note, Prop. 30, Part III. But this difference must be noted, namely, the difference between shame and bashfulness (*verecundia*). For shame is pain which follows the deed of which we are ashamed; but bashfulness is the fear or dread of shame by which a man is prevented from committing a shameful action. To bashfulness impudence is usually opposed, which in truth is not an emotion, as I shall show in its place; but the names of emotions (as I have already pointed out) have more reference to use than nature. And thus I have completed what I proposed to explain, namely, the emotions which arise from pleasure or pain. I now proceed to those which I refer to desire.

XXXII. Regret (*desiderium*) is the desire or appetite of possessing something which is fostered by the memory of that thing, and at the same time hindered by the memory of other things which cut off the existence of the thing desired.

Explanation.—When we remember anything, as I have already said often, we are so disposed by that act of remembering that we regard it with the same emotion as if it were present; but this disposition or endeavour, while we are awake, is very often hindered by the images of things which cut off the existence of that thing which we remember. When, therefore, we remember something which affects us with a kind of pleasure, by that very fact we endeavour to regard it as present with the same emotion of pleasure; but this endeavour is immediately checked by the recollection of things which cut off its existence. Wherefore regret is in truth pain which is opposed to that pleasure which arises from the absence of that thing which we hate, concerning which see Note, Prop. 47, Part III. But as the name regret seems to have reference to desire, I have therefore referred this emotion to the emotions arising from desire.

XXXIII. Emulation (*æmulatio*) is the desire of anything which is engendered in us from the fact that we imagine others to desire it also.

Explanation.—He that runs away because he sees others do so, or who is afraid because he sees that others are, or also he who, because he sees some other burning his hand, draws his hand towards him and moves his body as if his own hand were burnt, is said to imitate the emotions of any other, but not to emulate him: not because we know any difference between the cause of imitation and the cause of emulation, but because it has become customary to call him who imitates what we think to be honourable, useful, or pleasant, emulous. As for the rest concerning the cause of emulation, see Prop. 27, Part III., with its Note. The reason why envy is generally united to this emotion can be seen from Prop. 32, Part III., with its Note.

XXXIV. Gratefulness or gratitude (*gratia seu gratitudo*) is the desire or zeal for love by which we endeavour to benefit him who has benefited us from a similar emotion of love (see Prop. 39, with the Note on Prop. 41, Part III.).

XXXV. Benevolence (*benevolentia*) is the desire of benefiting those whom we pity (see Note, Prop. 27, Part III.).

XXXVI. Anger (*ira*) is the desire whereby through hatred we are incited to work evil to him whom we hate (see Prop. 39, Part III.).

XXXVII. Vengeance (*vindicta*) or revenge is the desire by which we are incited through reciprocated hatred to work evil to him who has worked evil to us from a similar emotion (see Coroll. 2, Prop. 40, Part III., with its Note).

XXXVIII. Cruelty or savageness (*crudelitas seu sævitas*) is the desire whereby any one is incited to work evil to one whom we love or whom we pity.

Explanation.—Cruelty is opposed to clemency (*clementia*), which is not a passion, but a power of the mind wherewith man moderates his desire for anger and revenge.

XXXIX. Timidity (*timor*) is the desire of avoiding a greater evil which we fear by encountering a lesser one (see Note, Prop. 39, Part III.).

XL. Daring (*audacia*) is the desire whereby any one is incited to do anything with a danger which his equals dare not encounter.

XLI. Cowardice (*pusillanimitas*) belongs to him whose desire is hindered by the fear or dread of a danger which his equals dare to undergo.

Explanation.—Cowardice therefore is nothing else than the fear of some evil which many are not wont to fear: wherefore I do not refer it to the emotions of desire. I wished, however, to explain it here, because in so far as we regard desire it is really opposed to the emotion of daring.

XLII. Consternation (*consternatio*) belongs to him whose desire of avoiding an evil is hindered by his wonderment at the evil which he fears.

Explanation.—Consternation is therefore a species of cowardice. But as consternation arises from a double fear, it can be more conveniently defined as fear which holds a man stupefied or hesitating in such a manner that he cannot remove the difficulty in his way. I say stupefied in so far as we understand his desire of removing his evil to be hindered by wonder; I say hesitating, on the other hand, in so far as we conceive that desire to be hindered by the fear of another evil which equally torments him: so that it comes about that he knows not which of the two to avoid. On this see Note, Prop. 39, and Note, Prop. 52, Part III. As for cowardice and daring, see Note, Prop. 51, Part III.

XLIII. Politeness or modesty (*humanitas seu modestia*) is the desire of doing such things as please men and omitting such as do not.

XLIV. Ambition (*ambitio*) is the immoderate desire of glory or honour.

Explanation.—Ambition is the desire by which all the emotions (Prop. 31 and 27, Part III.) are fostered and encouraged: and thus this emotion can scarcely be overcome. For as long as man is held by any desire, he is also held by this. "The very best men," says Cicero (*pro Archia*, cap. 2; cf. *Tuscul. disput.* I., cap. 15), "are especially guided by glory. Philosophers, who write on the despising of glory, affix their names to their books," etc.

XLV. Luxury (*luxuria*) is the immoderate desire or even love of feasting.

XLVI. Drunkenness (*ebrietas*) is the immoderate desire, and love, of drinking.

XLVII. Avarice (*avaritia*) is the immoderate desire or love of riches.

XLVIII. Lust (*libido*) is desire and love in sexual intercourse.

Explanation.—Whether this desire for sexual intercourse be moderate or not, it is wont to be called lust. Moreover, these last five emotions (as I gave notice of in the Note, Prop. 56, Part III.) have no contraries. For modesty is a species of ambition (see Note, Prop. 29, Part III.). I also gave warning that temperance (*temperantia*), sobriety (*sobrietas*), and chastity (*castitas*) indicate strength of mind, and are not passions. It may, however, come to pass that an avaricious man or an ambitious or timid one may refrain from over-eating, over-drinking, or sexual intercourse, yet avarice, drunkenness, and timidity are not contrary to luxury, drunkenness, and chastity. For an avaricious man would wish to gorge himself on the meat and drink of another; an ambitious man will moderate himself in nothing provided that he think his excesses secret; and if he live among people drunken and lustful, the fact that he is ambitious will make him more prone to those vices. Lastly, a timid man does what he does not wish to do. For although an avaricious man will throw all his wealth into the sea for the purpose of saving his life, he remains nevertheless avaricious; and if a lustful man is pained in such a way that he cannot indulge himself as usual, he does not thereby cease to be lustful. So that, to put it absolutely, these emotions have not so great regard for the acts themselves of feasting, drinking, etc., as for the desire or love for them. Nothing, therefore, can be opposed to these emotions save nobility and magnanimity (*generositas et animositas*), of which I shall speak presently.

The definitions of jealousy (*zelotypia*) and the other waverings of the mind I pass over in silence, for they arise from emotions which we have already described, and many of them have no names, which shows that for ordinary use it suffices to know them in general. It follows, however, from the definitions of the emotions which I have explained, that they all have arisen from desire, pleasure, or pain, or rather only these three exist, each of which is wont to be called by various names, by reason of its various relations and extrinsic marks. If, therefore, we regard these three primary emotions and what we said above concerning the nature of the mind, we can thus define the emotions in so far as they have reference to the mind itself.

GENERAL DEFINITION OF THE EMOTIONS

Emotion, which is called passiveness of the soul (*pathema animi*), is a confused idea wherewith the mind affirms a greater or less power of existing (*vis existendi*) of its body or of any part of it than before, and which being granted, the mind is thereby determined to think of one thing rather than of another.

Explanation.—I say, in the first place, that emotion, or passion of the soul, is a "confused idea." For we have shown that the mind only thus far suffers or is passive (see Prop. 3, Part III.) in so far as it has inadequate or confused ideas. I say again, wherewith the mind affirms a greater or less power of existing of its body or any part of it than before. For all the ideas of bodies which we have, indicate rather the actual disposition of our own body (Coroll. 2, Prop. 16, Part III.) than the nature of the external body; but this idea, which constitutes the form (*forma*) of the emotion, must indicate or express the disposition of the body, or of some part of it which the body or that part possesses by reason of the fact that its power of acting or existing is increased or diminished, aided or hindered. But it must be noted when I say "a greater or less power of existing than before," that I do not understand that the mind compares the present condition of the body with the past, but that the idea which constitutes the form of the emotion affirms something concerning the body whereby more or less reality is really involved than before. And inasmuch as the essence of the mind consists of this (Prop. 11 and 13, Part II.), that it affirms the actual existence of its body, and as we understand by perfection the very essence of the thing, it follows, therefore, that the mind passes to a greater or less perfection when it happens to affirm something concerning its body, or some part of it, which involves more or less reality than before. When, therefore, I said above that the mind's power of thinking was increased or diminished, I wished nothing else to be understood than that the mind had formed an idea of its body, or some part of it, which expressed more or less reality than it had affirmed concerning its body. For the excellence of ideas and the actual power of thinking is estimated from the excellence of the object. I added, moreover, "and which being granted, the mind is thereby determined to think of this rather than of that," in order that, besides the nature of pleasure and pain which the first part of the definition explains, I might also express the nature of desire.

FOURTH PART

ON HUMAN SERVITUDE, OR THE STRENGTH
OF THE EMOTIONS

PREFACE

HUMAN lack of power in moderating and checking the emotions I call servitude. For a man who is submissive to his emotions is not in power over himself, but in the hands of fortune to such an extent that he is often constrained, although he may see what is better for him, to follow what is worse (see Ovid, *Metam.*, VII. 20). I purpose accordingly in this part to show the reason for this, and what there is good and bad in the emotions. But before I begin I must preface something concerning perfection and imperfection, and then good and bad.

He that determines to do anything, and finishes it, calls it perfect, and that not only himself, but any one else who rightly knows, or thinks he knows, the mind of the author of that work or his design. For example, if any one sees some work (which I suppose not yet finished), and knows that the design of the author of that work is to build a house, he will call that house imperfect, and on the contrary, perfect as soon as he sees it brought to the finish which its author determined to give to it. But if any one sees some piece of work the like of which he had never seen, and does not know the mind of the artificer, he clearly will not know whether the work be perfect or not. This seems to have been the first meaning of these words. But afterwards, when men began to form general ideas and to think out general notions for houses, buildings, towers, etc., and to prefer certain notions to others, it came to pass that every one called that perfect which he saw to agree with the general notion which he had formed of that sort of thing, and on the contrary, imperfect what he saw less agree with his general notion, although in the opinion of the artificer it might be correct.

There seems to be no other reason that men should call natural things which are not made with human hands perfect or imperfect: for men are wont to form general notions of natural as well as artificial things, which they regard as models to which nature looks for guidance (for they think she does nothing without some end in view). When, therefore, they see something to take place in nature which less agrees with the exemplary notion which they have of that kind of thing, they think that nature has been guilty of error and has gone astray to have left that thing imperfect. We see thus that men have been wont to call things of nature perfect or imperfect from prejudice rather than from a true knowledge, for we showed in the appendix of the first part that nature does not act with an end in view: for that eternal and infinite being we call God or nature acts by the same necessity as that by which it exists, for we showed that it acts from the same necessity of its nature as that by which it exists (see Prop. 16, Part I.). Therefore the reason or cause why God or nature acts, or why they exist, is one and the same; therefore, as God exists with no end in view, he cannot act with any end in view, but has no beginning or end either in existing or acting. A cause, then, that is called final is nothing save human appetite itself in so far as it is considered as the beginning or primary cause of anything. E.g., when we say that habitation is the final cause of this or that house, we understand nothing else than this, that man had a desire of building a house from his imagining the conveniences of domestic life. Wherefore habitation, in so far as it is considered as a final cause, is nothing save this individual appetite (or desire), which in truth is the effecting cause which is considered as primary because men are commonly ignorant of the causes of their appetites. For they are, as I have already said, conscious of their actions and appetites, but ignorant of the causes by which they are determined to desire anything. The common saying of the vulgar, that nature sometimes is guilty of error and goes astray and produces imperfect things, I count among the false beliefs which I dealt with in the appendix of Part I. Therefore perfection and imperfection are in truth only modes of thinking, namely notions, which we are wont to invent owing to the fact that we compare reciprocally individuals of the same species or kind. And on that account (see above, Def. 6, Part II.) I said that by reality and perfection I understood the same thing. For we are wont to refer all individuals of nature to one class which we call most general, namely, to the notion of being which appertains absolutely to all individuals of nature. In so far as we refer the individuals of nature to this one class, and compare them reciprocally, and find that some have more reality or perfection than others, thus far we call some more perfect than others; and in so far as we attribute to them something which involves negation, as term, end, weakness, etc., thus far we call them imperfect, inasmuch as they do not affect our mind as much as those which we call perfect, and not because there is something wanting in them which is part of their nature, or that nature has gone astray. For nothing belongs to the nature of anything except that which follows from the necessity of the nature of the effecting cause, and whatever follows from the necessity of the nature of the effecting cause, necessarily happens.

As for the terms good and bad, they also mean nothing positive in things considered in themselves, nor are they anything else than modes of thought, or notions, which we form from the comparison of things mutually. For one and the same thing can at the same time be good, bad, and indifferent. E.g., music is good to the melancholy, bad to those who mourn, and neither good nor bad to the deaf. Although this be so, these words must be retained by us. For inasmuch as we desire to form an idea of man as a type of human nature to which we may look, we must retain these words for our use in the sense I have spoken of. Therefore, in the following propositions I shall understand by good what we certainly know to be a means of our attaining that type of human nature which we have set before us; and by bad, that which we know certainly prevents us from attaining the said type. Again, we shall call men more perfect or imperfect in so far as they approach or are distant from this type. For most specially must it be noted that when I say a man passes from a less to a greater perfection, and the contrary, that I do not understand that he is changed from one essence or form into another, e.g., a horse would be equally destroyed if it were changed into a man as if it were changed into an insect; but that his power of acting, in so far as this is understood by his nature, we conceive to be

increased or diminished. Finally, by perfection in general I
shall understand, as I said, reality, that is, the essence of anything, in so far as it exists and operates in a certain manner,
without any consideration of time. For no individual thing
can be said to be more perfect because it has remained in
existence longer: the duration of things cannot be determined by their essence, since the essence of things does not
involve a certain and determined time of existing; but
everything, whether it be more or less perfect, shall persist
in existing with the same force with which it began to exist,
so that in this all things are equal.

DEFINITIONS

I. By GOOD (*bonum*) I understand that which we certainly
know to be useful to us.

II. But by BAD (*malum*) I understand that which we certainly know will prevent us from partaking any good.

Concerning these definitions, see the foregoing preface
towards the end.

III. I call individual things CONTINGENT (*contingentes*) in so
far as while we regard their essence alone, we find nothing
which imposes their existence necessarily, or which necessarily excludes it.

IV. I call the same individual things POSSIBLE (*possibiles*)
in so far as while we regard the causes by which they must
be produced, we know not whether they are determined to
produce them.

In the Note 1, Prop. 33, Part I., I made no distinction
between possible and contingent, because it was not necessary
to distinguish them accurately there.

V. In the following propositions I shall understand by
CONTRARY EMOTIONS (*affectus contrarii*) those which draw a
man in different directions, although they may be of the
same kind, as luxury and avarice, which are species of love,
and are contrary not by nature but by accident.

VI. What I understand by emotion towards a thing
future, present, or past, I have explained in Notes 1 and 2,
Prop. 18, Part III., which see.

But it is the place here to note that we can only distinctly imagine distance of time, like that of space, up to a certain limit, that is, just as those things which are beyond two hundred paces from us, or whose distance from the place where we are exceeds that which we can distinctly imagine, we are wont to imagine equally distant from us and as if they were in the same plane, so also those objects whose time of existing we imagine to be distant from the present by a longer interval than that which we are accustomed to imagine, we imagine all to be equally distant from the present, and refer them all to one moment of time.

VII. By END (*finis*), with which in view we do anything, I understand a desire.

VIII. By VIRTUE (*virtus*) and POWER (*potentia*) I understand the same thing, that is (Prop. 7, Part III.), virtue, in so far as it has reference to man, is his essence or nature in so far as he has the power of effecting something which can only be understood by the laws of that nature.

AXIOM. There is no individual thing in nature than which there is none more powerful or stronger; but whatever is given, there is also something stronger given by which that given thing can be destroyed.

PROPOSITIONS

PROP. I. Nothing positive, which a false idea has, is removed by the presence of what is true in so far as it is true.

Proof.—Falsity consists solely of the privation of knowledge which is involved by inadequate ideas (Prop. 35, Part II.). Nor do these have anything positive, by reason of which they are called false (Prop. 33, Part II.); but on the contrary, in so far as they have reference to God, they are true (Pop. 32, Part II.). If, therefore, that which is positive, possessed by a false idea, were removed by the presence of what is true in so far as it is true, then a true idea would be removed by itself, which (Prop. 4, Part III.) is absurd. Therefore nothing positive, etc.   *Q.e.d.*

Note.—This proposition is understood more clearly from Coroll. 2, Prop. 16, Part II. For imagination is an idea which indicates rather the present disposition of the human body than the nature of an external body, not indeed distinctly, but confusedly: whence it comes about that the mind is said to err. *E.g.*, when we look at the sun, we imagine it to be about two hundred paces distant from us, in which we are deceived as long as we are ignorant of the true distance. When the distance is known the error is removed, but not the imagination, that is, the idea of the sun which explains its nature in so far only as the body is affected by it; and therefore, although we know the real distance, nevertheless we imagine that we are close to it. For, as I said in the Note, Prop. 35, Part II., we do not think that the sun is near to us because we are ignorant of the true distance, but because the mind imagines the magnitude of the sun in so far as the body is affected by it. Thus when the rays of the sun falling on the surface of water are reflected to our eyes, then we imagine it as if it were in the water, although we know its proper place. And thus other imaginations by which the mind is deceived, whether they indicate the natural disposition of the body or whether that its power of acting is increased or diminished, are not contrary to what is true, nor do they vanish at its presence. It happens indeed that when we falsely fear some evil, that the fear vanishes when we hear a true account; but the contrary also happens when we fear an evil which is certain to come, and our fear vanishes when we hear a false account. And therefore these imaginations do not vanish at the presence of truth in so far as it is truth, but because other imaginations stronger than these arrive and cut off the present existence of the things which we imagine, as we showed in Prop. 17, Part II.

PROP. II. We are passive in so far as we are a part of nature which cannot be conceived through itself without others.

Proof.—We are said to be passive when something takes place in us of which we are only the partial cause (Def. 2, Part III.), that is (Def. 1, Part III.), something which cannot be deduced solely from the laws of our nature. We are passive, therefore, in so far as we are part of nature which cannot be conceived through itself without other parts. *Q.e.d.*

PROP. III. The force with which man persists in existing is limited, and is far surpassed by the power of external causes.

Proof.—This is clear from the axiom of this part. For with a given man there is given something, say A, stronger than he, and given A, there is given something, say B, stronger than A, and so on to infinity. And therefore the power of man is limited by the power of some other thing, and infinitely surpassed by the power of external causes. *Q.e.d.*

PROP. IV. It cannot happen that a man should not be a part of nature, and that he should be able not to suffer changes, save those which can be understood through his nature alone, and of which he is the adequate cause.

Proof.—The power with which individual things, and consequently man, preserves his being is the very power of God or nature (Coroll., Prop. 24, Part I.), not in so far as he is infinite, but in so far as he can be explained through actual human essence (Prop. 7, Part III.). Therefore the power of man, in so far as it is explained through his actual essence, is a part of the infinite power of God or nature, that is, of his essence (Prop. 34, Part I.): which was the first point. Again, if it can come to pass that a man can suffer no changes save those that can be understood through the nature alone of that man, it would follow (Prop. 4 and 6, Part III.) that he cannot perish, and that he will live of necessity for ever. But this must follow from a cause whose power is finite or infinite, namely, from the mere power of man, that he would be able to remove changes which arise from external causes from him, or from the infinite power of nature by which all individual things are so directed that man can suffer no other changes than those which serve for his preservation. But the first point (from the prev. Prop., whose application is universal) is absurd. Therefore, if it could come to pass that man should suffer no changes save those that can be understood through the mere nature of man himself, and consequently, as we have already shown, that he should exist for ever, this would have to follow from the infinite power of God. Consequently (Prop. 16, Part I.) the order of the whole of nature would have to be deduced in so far as it is considered under the attributes of thought and extension from the necessity of divine nature, in so far as it is considered as affected by the idea of some man. And therefore (Prop. 21, Part I.) it would follow that man was infinite, which (by the first part of this proof) is absurd. It cannot therefore happen that a man should suffer no changes save those of which he is the adequate cause. *Q.e.d.*

Corollary.—Hence it follows that man is always necessarily liable to passions, that he always follows the common order of nature and obeys it, and that he accommodates himself to it as much as the nature of things demands.

PROP. V. The force and increase of any passion, and its persistence in existing, are not defined by the power whereby we endeavour to persist in existing, but by the power of an external cause compared with our own.

Proof.—The essence of passion cannot be explained merely through our essence (Def. 1 and 2, Part III.), that is (Prop. 7, Part III.), the power of passion cannot be defined by the power with which we endeavour to persist in our being; but (as in Prop. 16, Part II., was shown) it must necessarily be defined by the power of some external cause compared with our own. *Q.e.d.*

PROP. VI. The force of any passion or emotion can so surpass the rest of the actions or the power of a man that the emotion adheres obstinately to him.

Proof.—The force and increase of any passion, and its persistence in existing, is defined by the power of an external cause compared with ours (prev. Prop.): and therefore (Prop. 3, Part IV.) it can surpass a man's power, etc. *Q.e.d.*

PROP. VII. An emotion can neither be hindered nor removed save by a contrary emotion and one stronger in checking emotion.

Proof.—An emotion, in so far as it has reference to the mind, is an idea wherewith the mind affirms a greater or less force of existing of its body than before (General Definition of the Emotions, which will be found towards the end of the third part). When, therefore, the mind is assailed by any emotion, the body is affected at the same time by a modification whereby its power of acting is either increased or diminished. Now this modification of the body (Prop. 5, Part IV.) receives from its cause the force for persisting in its being, which therefore can neither be restrained nor removed save by a bodily cause (Prop. 4, Part III.) which

affects the body with a modification contrary to that one
(Prop. 5, Part III.) and stronger than it (Ax., Part IV.).
And therefore (Prop. 12, Part II.) the mind is affected by
the idea of a modification stronger and contrary to the
previous one, that is (Gen. Def. Emo.), the mind will be
affected with an emotion stronger and contrary to the
former which cuts off the existence of or takes away the
former: and thus the emotion can neither be checked nor
removed save by a contrary and stronger emotion. *Q.e.d.*

Corollary.—An emotion, in so far as it has reference to the
mind, can neither be hindered nor destroyed save through
the idea of a contrary modification of the body and one
stronger than the modification which we suffer. For the
emotion which we suffer cannot be checked or removed save
by an emotion stronger than it and contrary to it (prev.
Prop.), that is (Gen. Def. Emo.), save through the idea of a
modification of the body stronger than and contrary to the
modification which we suffer.

Prop. VIII. The knowledge of good or evil is nothing
else than the emotion of pleasure or pain, in so far as we are
conscious of it.

Proof.—We call that good or evil which is useful or the
contrary for our preservation (Def. 1 and 2, Part IV.), that
is (Prop. 7, Part III.), which increases or diminishes, helps
or hinders our power of acting. And so, in so far as (see
def. pleasure and pain, Note, Prop. 11, Part III.) we perceive
anything to affect us with pleasure or pain, we call it good
or evil; and therefore the knowledge of good or evil is
nothing else than the idea of pleasure or pain which follows
necessarily from the emotion of pleasure or pain (Prop. 22,
Part II.). But this idea is united to the emotion in the
same manner as the mind is united to the body (Prop. 21,
Part II.), that is (as was shown in the Note on that Prop.),
this idea is not distinguished in truth from that emotion or
(Gen. Def. Emo.) from the idea of the modification of the body
save in conception alone. Therefore this knowledge of good
and evil is nothing else than emotion itself, in so far as we
are conscious of it. *Q.e.d.*

Prop. IX. An emotion whose cause we imagine to be with
us at the present is stronger than if we did not imagine it to
be present.

Proof.—Imagination is the idea wherewith the mind regards a thing as present (see def. in Note, Prop. 17, Part II.) which nevertheless indicates rather the disposition of the human body than the nature of the external body (Coroll. 2, Prop. 16, Part II.). Imagination is therefore an emotion (Gen. Def. Emo.) in so far as it indicates the disposition of the body. But imagination (Prop. 17, Part II.) is more intense as long as we imagine nothing which cuts off the present existence of the external object. Therefore an emotion also, whose cause we imagine to be with us in the present, is more intense or stronger than if we did not imagine it to be present with us. *Q.e.d.*

Note.—When I said above, in Prop. 18, Part III., that we are affected with the same emotion by a future or past thing as if the thing which we imagine were present, I expressly gave warning that it was true in so far as we regard the image alone of the thing (for it is of the same nature, whether we imagined it or not), but I did not deny that it becomes weaker when we regard other things as present to us which cut off the present existence of the future thing. I neglected to call attention to this then, as I had determined to treat on the force of the emotions in this part.

Corollary.—The image of a thing future or past, that is, of a thing which we regard with reference to time future or past, to the exclusion of time present, is, under similar conditions, weaker than the image of a thing present, and consequently the emotion towards a thing future or past is, *cæteris paribus*, less intense than the emotion towards a thing present.

PROP. X. Towards a future thing which we imagine to be close at hand we are more intensely affected than if we imagine the time of its existing to be further distant from the present; and by the recollection of a thing which we imagine to have passed not long ago we are more intensely affected also than if we imagine it to have passed long ago.

Proof.—For in so far as we imagine a thing to be close at hand or just to have past, we imagine that which will exclude the presence of the thing less than if we imagine its future time of existing to be further away from the present, or if it had passed away long ago (as is self-evident): therefore (prev. Prop.) we shall be affected towards it more intensely. *Q.e.d.*

Note.—From what we noted in Def. 6, Part IV., it follows that we are affected equally mildly towards objects which are distant from the present by a longer space of time than we can determine by imagining, although we know them to be also distant by a long space of time one from the other.

PROP. XI. The emotion towards a thing which we imagine to be necessary is more intense, *cæteris paribus,* than towards a thing possible, contingent, or not necessary.

Proof.—In so far as we imagine anything to be necessary we affirm its existence, and on the contrary, we deny the existence of a thing in so far as we imagine it not necessary (Note 1, Prop. 33, Part I.): and accordingly the emotion towards a thing necessary is more intense, *cæteris paribus,* than towards a thing not necessary.   *Q.e.d.*

PROP. XII. The emotion towards a thing which we know to be non-existent at the present time, and which we imagine possible, is more intense, *cæteris paribus,* than that towards a thing contingent.

Proof.—In so far as we imagine the thing as contingent, we are affected by no image of another thing which imposes its existence on it (Def. 3, Part IV.); but, on the other hand (according to the hypothesis), we imagine certain things cut off its present existence. But in so far as we imagine the thing to be possible in the future, we imagine certain things which impose existence on it (Def. 4, Part IV.), that is (Prop. 18, Part III.), which foster hope or fear: and therefore emotion towards a thing possible is more intense. *Q.e.d.*

Corollary.—Emotion towards a thing which we know to be non-existent in the present, and which we imagine as contingent, is far more mild than if we imagine the thing to be present with us.

Proof.—Emotion towards a thing which we imagine to exist in the present is more intense than if we imagined it as future (Coroll., Prop. 9, Part IV.), and it is far more intense if we imagine the future time not to be far distant from the present (Prop. 10, Part IV.). Therefore the emotion towards a thing whose time of existing we imagine to be far distant from the present is far more mild than if we imagine it as present, and nevertheless is more intense (prev. Prop.)

than if we imagined that thing as contingent. Therefore the emotion towards a thing contingent is far more mild than if we imagined the thing to be with us at the present. *Q.e.d.*

PROP. XIII. Emotion towards a thing contingent, which we know does not exist in the present, is far more mild, *cæteris paribus*, than emotion towards a thing past.

Proof.—In so far as we imagine a thing as contingent, we are affected by the image of no other thing which imposes the existence of that thing (Def. 3, Part IV.); but, on the contrary (by hypothesis), we imagine certain things which cut off its present existence. But in so far as we imagine it with reference to time past, we are supposed to imagine something which restores it to memory, or which excites the image of the thing (see Prop. 18, Part II., with its Note), and thus far accordingly it brings it to pass that we regard it as if it were present (Coroll., Prop. 17, Part II.). And therefore (Prop. 9, Part IV.) emotion towards a thing contingent, which we know does not exist in the present, is more mild, *cæteris paribus*, than emotion towards a thing past. *Q.e.d.*

PROP. XIV. A true knowledge of good and evil cannot restrain any emotion in so far as the knowledge is true, but only in so far as it is considered as an emotion.

Proof.—An emotion is an idea whereby the mind affirms a greater or less force of existing of its body (Gen. Def. Emo.), and therefore (Prop. 1, Part IV.) it has nothing positive which can be removed by the presence of what is true; and consequently a true knowledge of good and evil, in so far as it is true, cannot restrain any emotion. But in so far as it is an emotion (Prop. 8, Part IV.), if it is stronger than the emotion to be restrained, thus far only (Prop. 7, Part IV.) it can hinder or restrain an emotion. *Q.e.d.*

PROP. XV. Desire which arises from a true knowledge of good and evil can be destroyed or checked by many other desires which arise from emotions by which we are assailed.

Proof.—From a true knowledge of good and evil, in so far as this (Prop. 8, Part IV.) is an emotion, there necessarily arises desire (Def. Emo. 1), which is the greater according as the emotion from which it arises is greater (Prop. 37, Part III.). But inasmuch as this desire (by the hypothesis) arises from the fact that we truly understand something, it follows also that it is within us in so far as we are active (Prop. 3, Part III.). And therefore it must be understood through our essence alone (Def. 2, Part III.), and consequently (Prop. 7, Part III.) its force and increase must only be defined by human power. Again, the desires which arise from the emotions by which we are assailed are greater according as the emotions are the more intense; and therefore their force and increase (Prop. 5, Part IV.) must be defined by the power of the external causes, which, if compared with our own power, indefinitely surpasses our power (Prop. 3, Part IV.). And therefore the desires which arise from similar emotions can be more intense than that which arises from the knowledge of good and evil; and therefore (Prop. 7, Part IV.) they will be able to check or destroy it. *Q.e.d.*

PROP. XVI. The desire which arises from the knowledge of good and evil, in so far as this knowledge has reference to the future, can more easily be checked or destroyed than the desire of things which are pleasing in the present.

Proof.—Emotion towards a thing which we imagine to be future is less intense than towards a thing present (Coroll., Prop. 9, Part IV.). But the desire which arises from the knowledge of good and evil, although this knowledge should concern things which are good in the present, can be destroyed or checked by any haphazard desire (prev. Prop., whose proof is universal). Therefore the desire which arises from such knowledge, in so far as it has reference to the future, can be more easily destroyed or checked, etc. *Q.e.d.*

PROP. XVII. Desire which arises from true knowledge of good and evil, in so far as this concerns things contingent, can be far more easily restrained than the desire for things which are present.

Proof.—This proposition is proved in the same manner as the previous one, from Coroll., Prop. 12, Part IV.

Note.—Thus I think I have shown the reason why men are guided rather by opinion than by true reason, and why a true knowledge of good and evil often excites disturbances of the mind, and often yields to all manner of lusts.   Whence is arisen the saying of the poet: *Video meliora proboque, deteriora sequor*—" The better I see and approve, the worse I follow " (Ovid, *Metam.*, VII. 20).   This also Ecclesiastes seems to have had in mind when he said, " He who increaseth knowledge, increaseth sorrow."   I have not written this, however, with the aim of proving or concluding therefrom that it is better to be ignorant than to have knowledge, or that a wise man has no advantage over a fool in the moderating of his emotions, but because it is necessary to know both the power and want of power of our nature, so that we may determine what reason can do in the moderating of the desires and what it cannot; and in this part I have said I shall deal only with human want of power.   For I have determined to treat of the power of reason over the emotions separately.

Prop. XVIII. Desire which arises from pleasure is stronger, *cæteris paribus*, than the desire which arises from pain.

Proof.—Desire is the very essence of man (Def. Emo. 1), that is (Prop. 7, Part III.), the endeavour wherewith man endeavours to persist in his being.   Wherefore desire which arises from pleasure is helped or increased by the emotion of pleasure itself (def. pleasure in Note, Prop. 11, Part III.); but that desire which arises from sadness or pain is diminished or hindered by the emotion of pain (same Note).   And therefore the force of desire which arises from pleasure must be defined by human power, and at the same time, by the power of an external cause; but that which arises from pain must only be defined by human power: and therefore the former is stronger than the latter.   *Q.e.d.*

Note.—In these few propositions I have explained the causes of human impotence and inconstancy, and why men do not follow the precepts of reason.   It remains, however, that I should show what is that which reason prescribes for us, and which of the emotions agree with the laws of human reason, and which, on the other hand, are contrary to them. But before I begin to prove this in full in the geometrical method we follow, it would be well to show here briefly at first the dictates of reason, so that those things which I mean may be understood and perceived more easily by all. Since reason postulates nothing against nature, it postulates, therefore, that each man should love himself, and seek what is useful to him—I mean what is truly useful to him—and desire whatever leads man truly to a greater state of perfection, and finally, that each one should endeavour to preserve his being as far as it in him lies. This is as necessarily true as that the whole is greater than the part (see Prop. 4, Part III.). Again, as virtue is nothing else (Def. 8, Part IV.) than to act according to the laws of one's own nature, and no one endeavours to preserve his being (Prop. 7, Part III.) save according to the laws of his own nature, it follows hence, firstly, that the basis of virtue is the endeavour to preserve one's own being, and that happiness consists in this, that man can preserve his own being; secondly, that virtue should be desired by us on its own account, and there is nothing more excellent or useful to us on which account we should desire it; thirdly, that those who commit suicide are powerless souls, and allow themselves to be conquered by external causes repugnant to their nature. Again, it follows from Post. 4, Part II., that we can never bring it about that we need nothing outside ourselves for our preservation, and that in order to live we need have no commerce with things which are without us. If, moreover, we looked at our minds, our intellect would be more imperfect if the mind were alone and understood nothing save itself. Many things are therefore without us which are very useful to us, and therefore much to be desired. Of these, none can be considered more excellent than those which agree with our nature. For (to give an example) if two individuals of the same nature were to combine, they would form one individual twice as strong as either individual: there is therefore nothing more useful to man than man. Nothing, I say, can be desired by men more excellent for their self-preservation than that all with all should so agree that they compose the minds of all into one mind, and the bodies of all into one body, and all endeavour at the same time as much as possible to preserve their being, and all seek at the same time what is useful to them all as a body. From which it follows that men who are governed by reason, that is, men who, under the guidance of reason, seek what is useful to them, desire nothing for themselves which they do not also desire for the rest of mankind, and therefore they are just, faithful, and honourable.

*G 481

These are the dictates of reason which I purposed in these few words to point out before I proceed to prove them in greater detail, which I did for this reason, that, if it were possible, I might attract the attention of those who believe that this principle, namely, that each should seek out what is useful to himself, is the basis not of virtue and piety, but of impiety. Therefore, after I have shown briefly that the contrary is the case, I proceed to prove it in the same manner as that in which we have proceeded so far.

PROP. XIX. Each one necessarily desires or turns from, by the laws of his nature, what he thinks to be good or evil.

Proof.—The knowledge of good and evil (Prop. 8, Part IV.) is the emotion of pleasure or pain in so far as we are conscious of it: and therefore (Prop. 28, Part III.) every one necessarily desires what he thinks to be good, and turns from what he thinks to be evil. But this desire is nothing else than the very essence or nature of man (def. desire, which see in Note, Prop. 9, Part III., and Def. Emo. 1). Therefore every one, from the laws of his nature alone, necessarily desires or turns away from, etc. *Q.e.d.*

PROP. XX. The more each one seeks what is useful to him, that is, the more he endeavours and can preserve his being, the more he is endowed with virtue; and, on the contrary, the more one neglects to preserve what is useful, or his being, he is thus far impotent or powerless.

Proof.—Virtue is human power itself, which is defined by the essence of man alone (Def. 8, Part IV.), that is (Prop. 7, Part III.), which is defined by the endeavour alone wherewith he endeavours to persist in his own being. The more, therefore, he endeavours and succeeds in preserving his own essence, the more he is endowed with virtue, and consequently (Prop. 4 and 6, Part III.) in so far as he neglects to preserve his being he is thus far wanting in power. *Q.e.d.*

Note.—No one, therefore, unless he is overcome by external causes and those contrary to his nature, neglects to desire what is useful to himself and to preserve his being. No one, I say, from the necessity of his nature, but driven by external causes, turns away from taking food, or commits suicide, which can take place in many manners. Namely, any one can kill himself by compulsion of some other who twists

back his right hand, in which he holds by chance his sword,
and forces him to direct the sword against his own heart; or,
like Seneca by the command of a tyrant, he may be forced
to open his veins, that is, to avoid a greater evil by encountering a less; or again, latent external causes may so dispose
his imagination and so affect his body, that it may assume
a nature contrary to its former one, and of which an idea
cannot be given in the mind (Prop. 10, Part III.). But that
a man, from the necessity of his nature, should endeavour to
become non-existent, or change himself into another form,
is as impossible as it is for anything to be made from nothing,
as every one with a little reflection can easily see.

PROP. XXI. No one can desire to be blessed, to act well,
or live well, who at the same time does not desire to be, to
act, and to live, that is, actually to exist.

Proof.—The proof of this proposition, or rather the thing
itself, is self-evident, and appears from the definition of
desire. For the desire (Def. Emo. 1) of being blessed, of
acting well, and of living well, etc., is the very essence of
man, that is (Prop. 7, Part III.), the endeavour wherewith
each one endeavours to preserve his own being. Therefore
no one can desire, etc. *Q.e.d.*

PROP. XXII. No virtue can be conceived as prior to this
virtue of endeavouring to preserve oneself.

Proof.—The endeavour of preserving oneself is the very
essence of a thing (Prop. 7, Part III.). If, therefore, any
virtue can be conceived as prior to this one, namely, this
endeavour, the essence of the thing would therefore be conceived (Def. 8, Part IV.) prior to itself, which, as is self-
manifest, is absurd. Therefore no virtue, etc. *Q.e.d.*

Corollary.—The endeavour of preserving oneself is the
first and only basis of virtue, for prior to this principle
nothing else can be conceived (prev. Prop.), and without it
(Prop. 21, Part IV.) no virtue can be conceived.

PROP. XXIII. Man, in so far as he is determined to do
anything, by the fact that he has inadequate ideas cannot
absolutely be said to act from virtue, but only in so far as he
is determined by the fact that he understands.

Proof.—In so far as a man is determined to do something

by the fact that he has inadequate ideas, so far is he passive
(Prop. 1, Part III.), that is (Def. 1 and 2, Part III.), he does
something which cannot be perceived through its own
essence alone, that is (Def. 8, Part IV.), which does not follow
from his virtue.   But in so far as he is determined to do
something, by the fact that he understands, he is active
(Prop. 1, Part III.), that is (Def. 2, Part III.), he does something which can be perceived through his own essence alone
or (Def. 8, Part IV.) which follows adequately from his virtue.
Q.e.d.

PROP. XXIV. To act absolutely according to virtue is
nothing else in us than to act under the guidance of reason,
to live so, and to preserve one's being (these three have the
same meaning) on the basis of seeking what is useful to
oneself.

Proof.—To act absolutely from virtue is nothing else
(Def. 8, Part IV.) than to act according to the laws of one's
own nature.   But we only act so in so far as we understand
(Prop. 3, Part III.).   Therefore to act according to virtue
is nothing else in us than to act, to live, and preserve our
being according to the guidance of reason, on the basis of
seeking what is useful to oneself.   *Q.e.d.*

PROP. XXV. No one endeavours to preserve his being for
the sake of anything else.

Proof.—The endeavour wherewith each thing endeavours
to persist in its own being is defined by the essence of the
thing alone (Prop. 7, Part III.), and from this alone, and
not from the essence of any other thing, it necessarily follows
(Prop. 6, Part III.) that each one endeavours to preserve
his own essence.   The proposition is also obvious from
Coroll., Prop. 22, Part IV.   For if man were to endeavour
to preserve his being for the sake of anything else, then that
thing would be the primary basis of his virtue (as is self-
manifest), which (by that Coroll.) is absurd.   Therefore no
one endeavours, etc.   *Q.e.d.*

PROP. XXVI. Whatever we endeavour to do under the
guidance of reason is nothing else than to understand; nor
does the mind, in so far as it uses reason, judge anything
useful to itself save what is conducive to understanding.

Proof.—The endeavour to preserve oneself is nothing else than the essence of the thing (Prop. 7, Part III.) which, in so far as it exists as such, is conceived to have force for persisting in existing (Prop. 6, Part III.), and for doing those things which necessarily follow from its given nature (see the def. of desire in Note, Prop. 9, Part III.). But the essence of reason is nothing else than the mind itself in so far as it understands clearly and distinctly (see def. in Note 2, Prop. 40, Part II.). Therefore (Prop. 40, Part II.), whatever we endeavour to do under the guidance of reason is nothing else than to understand. Again, as this endeavour of the mind, whereby, in so far as it reasons, it tries to possess its own being, is nothing other than to understand (first part of this Prop.), therefore this endeavour to understand (Coroll., Prop. 22, Part IV.) is the first and only basis of virtue. Nor do we endeavour to understand for the sake of any end, but, on the contrary, the mind, in so far as it reasons, cannot conceive anything as good to itself save what is conducive to understanding (Def. 1, Part IV.).

PROP. XXVII. We know nothing to be certainly good or evil save what is truly conducive to understanding or what prevents us from understanding.

Proof.—The mind, in so far as it reasons, desires nothing else than to understand, nor does it judge anything useful to itself save what is conducive to understanding (prev. Prop.). But the mind (Prop. 41 and 43, Part II., with its Note) has no certainty in things save in so far as it has adequate ideas, or, what (Prop. 40, Note 2, Part II.) is the same thing, in so far as it reasons. Therefore we understand nothing to be certainly good save what is conducive to understanding, and, on the contrary, that to be bad which can prevent us from understanding. *Q.e.d.*

PROP. XXVIII. The greatest good of the mind is the knowledge of God, and the greatest virtue of the mind is to know God.

Proof.—The greatest thing that the mind can understand is God, that is (Def. 6, Part I.), a being absolutely infinite, and without which nothing can either be (Prop. 15, Part I.) or be conceived. Therefore (Prop. 26 and 27, Part IV.) the thing of the greatest use or good to the mind (Def. 1, Part IV.)

is the knowledge of God. Again, the mind, in so far as it understands, thus far only is active (Prop. 1 and 3, Part III.), and thus far (Prop. 23, Part IV.) can it be absolutely said that it acts according to virtue. To understand, therefore, is the absolute virtue of the mind. But the greatest thing that the mind can understand is God (as we have just proved). Therefore the greatest virtue of the mind is to understand or know God. *Q.e.d.*

PROP. XXIX. No individual thing whose nature is altogether different to ours can aid or hinder our power of doing things, and absolutely nothing can be either good or bad save if it have something in common with us.

Proof.—The power of any individual thing, and consequently (Coroll., Prop. 10, Part II.) the power of man, by which he exists and works, is only determined by another individual thing (Prop. 28, Part I.) whose nature (Prop. 6, Part II.) must be understood through the same attribute through which human nature is conceived. Therefore our power of acting, in whatever way it may be conceived, can be determined, and consequently aided or hindered, by the power of some other thing which has something in common with us, and not by the power of something whose nature is altogether different to ours; and inasmuch as we call that good or bad which is the cause of pleasure or pain (Prop. 8, Part IV.), that is (Prop. 11, Note, Part III.), which increases or diminishes, aids or hinders our power of acting, therefore the thing whose nature is entirely different to ours can be neither good nor bad to us. *Q.e.d.*

PROP. XXX. Nothing can be bad through that which it has in common with our nature; but in so far as it is bad, thus far it is contrary to us.

Proof.—We call that bad which is the cause of pain (Prop. 8, Part IV.), that is (by def., which see in Note, Prop. 11, Part III.), which decreases or diminishes our power of acting. If, therefore, anything through that which it has in common with us were bad to us, it would therefore be able to diminish or hinder what it has in common with us, which (Prop. 4, Part III.) is absurd. Therefore nothing through that which it has in common with us can be bad to us; but, on the other hand, in so far as it is bad, that is (as we have just shown), in so far as it can diminish or hinder our power of action, thus far (Prop. 5, Part III.) it is contrary to us. *Q.e.d.*

PROP. XXXI. In so far as anything agrees with our nature, thus far it is necessarily good.

Proof.—In so far as anything agrees with our nature it cannot (prev. Prop.) be bad. It will therefore be either good or indifferent. If we suppose this, that it is neither good nor bad, then nothing (Ax., Part IV.) will follow from its nature which can serve for the preservation of our nature, that is (by hypothesis), which serves for the preservation of the thing itself. But this is absurd (Prop. 6, Part III). It will therefore be, in so far as it agrees with our nature, necessarily good. *Q.e.d.*

Corollary.—Hence it follows that the more a thing agrees with our nature, the more useful or good it is to us, and, on the other hand, the more useful anything is to us, the more it agrees with our nature. For in so far as it does not agree with our nature it will necessarily be different to our nature or contrary to it. If it is different, then (Prop. 29, Part IV.) it can be neither good nor bad; if it is contrary, it will therefore be contrary to that which agrees with our nature, that is (prev. Prop.), contrary to good or bad. Nothing, therefore, save in so far as it agrees with our nature, can be good; and therefore the more it agrees with our nature, the more useful it is to us, and contrariwise. *Q.e.d.*

PROP. XXXII. In so far as men are liable to passions they cannot thus far be said to agree in nature.

Proof.—Things which are said to agree in nature are understood to agree in power (Prop. 7, Part III.), but not in want of power or negation, and consequently (see Note, Prop. 3, Part II.) in passion. Wherefore men, in so far as they are liable to passions, cannot be thus far said to agree in nature. *Q.e.d.*

Note.—This also is self-manifest. For he that says that black and white agree in this alone, that neither of them is red, absolutely affirms that black and white agree in nothing. Thus also, if any one say that man and stone agree in this alone, that they both are finite, powerless, or do not exist by the necessity of their own natures, or again, that they are indefinitely surpassed by the power of external causes, he absolutely affirms that man and stone agree in nothing. For those things which agree in negation alone, or in what they have not, in truth agree in nothing.

Prop. XXXIII. Men can differ in nature in so far as they are assailed by emotions which are passions, and thus far one and the same man is variable and inconstant.

Proof.—The nature or essence of emotion cannot be explained through our essence or nature alone (Def. 1 and 2, Part III.), but by the power, that is (Prop. 7, Part III.), by the nature of external causes compared with our own, it must be defined. Whence it comes about that there are as many species of each emotion as there are species of objects by which we are affected (Prop. 56, Part III.), and that men are affected by one and the same object in different manners (Prop. 51, Part III.), and thus far disagree in nature, and moreover, that one and the same man (Prop. 51, Part III.) is affected in different manners towards the same object, and thus far is variable, etc. *Q.e.d.*

Prop. XXXIV. Men, in so far as they are assailed by emotions which are passions, can be contrary one to the other.

Proof.—A man, *e.g.* Peter, can be the cause that Paul is saddened, inasmuch as he has something similar to a thing which Paul hates (Prop. 16, Part III.), or inasmuch as Peter possesses alone something which Paul also loves (Prop. 32, Part III., with its Note), or on other accounts (for the principal, see Note, Prop. 55, Part III.). And therefore it hence comes to pass that Paul hates Peter (Def. Emo. 7), and consequently it may easily happen (Prop. 40, Part III., with its Note) that Peter hates Paul on the other hand, and therefore (Prop. 39, Part III.) that they endeavour to work each other reciprocal harm, that is (Prop. 30, Part IV.), that they become contrary one to the other. But the emotion of pain is always a passion (Prop. 59, Part III.): therefore men, in so far as they are assailed by emotions which are passions, can be contrary one to the other. *Q.e.d.*

Note.—I said that Paul may hate Peter, inasmuch as he imagines him to possess what he himself loves. Whence at the first glance it seems that these two, from the fact that they love the same thing, and consequently agree in nature, are hateful one to the other; and therefore if this is true, Prop. 30 and 31 of this part are false. But if we are willing to examine the matter fairly, we shall see that these statements entirely agree. For these two are not hateful to each other in so far as they agree in nature, that is, in so far as they both love the same thing, but in so far as they disagree one with the other. For in so far as they both love the same thing, by that very fact the love of each of them is fostered (Prop. 31, Part III.), that is (Def. Emo. 6), by that very fact the pleasure of each is fostered. Wherefore it is far from being the case that in so far as they love the same thing and agree in nature they are hateful one to the other; but the cause of this thing is, as I said, nothing else than that they are supposed to disagree in nature. For we suppose Peter to have the idea of the thing loved possessed by him, and Paul, on the other hand, the idea of the thing loved lost to him. Whence it comes about that the first is affected with pleasure, and the second with pain: and thus far they are contrary one to the other. And in this manner we can easily show that the other causes of hatred depend on this alone, that men disagree in nature, and not on the fact that they agree.

Prop. XXXV. In so far as men live under the guidance of reason, thus far only they always necessarily agree in nature.

Proof.—In so far as men are assailed by emotions which are passions they can be different in nature (Prop. 33, Part IV.) and contrary one to the other (prev. Prop.). But men are said to be active only in so far as they live under the guidance of reason (Prop. 3, Part III.), and therefore whatever follows from human nature, in so far as it is defined by reason, must (Def. 2, Part III.) be understood through human nature alone as its proximate cause. But inasmuch as each one desires according to the laws of his own nature what is good, and endeavours to remove what he thinks to be bad (Prop. 19, Part IV.), and inasmuch as that which we judge to be good or bad, according to the dictate of reason, is necessarily good or bad (Prop. 41, Part II.), therefore men, in so far as they live according to the dictates of reason, do those things which are necessarily good to human nature, and consequently to each man, that is (Coroll., Prop. 31, Part IV.), which agree with the nature of each man. And therefore men also necessarily agree one with the other in so far as they live according to the mandate of reason. *Q.e.d.*

Corollary I.—There is no individual thing in nature more useful to man than one who lives under the guidance of reason. For that is most useful to man which mostly agrees with his nature (Coroll., Prop. 31, Part IV.), that is (as is self-evident), man. But man is absolutely active according to the laws of his nature when he lives under the guidance of reason (Def. 2, Part III.), and thus far only can he agree necessarily with the nature of another man (prev. Prop.). Therefore there is nothing more useful to man than a man, etc. *Q.e.d.*

Corollary II.—As each man seeks that most which is useful to him, so men are most useful one to the other. For the more each man seeks what is useful to him and endeavours to preserve himself, the more he is endowed with virtue (Prop. 20, Part IV.), or, what is the same thing (Def. 8, Part IV.), the more power he is endowed with to act according to the laws of his nature, that is (Prop. 3, Part III.), to live under the guidance of reason. But men agree most in nature when they live under the guidance of reason (prev. Prop.). Therefore (prev. Coroll.) men are most useful one to the other when each one most seeks out what is useful to himself. *Q.e.d.*

Note.—What we have just shown is borne witness to by experience daily with such convincing examples that it has become a proverb: Man is a God to man. Yet it rarely happens that men live according to the instructions of reason, but among them things are in such a state that they are usually envious of or a nuisance to each other. But nevertheless they are scarcely able to lead a solitary life, so that to many the definition that man is a social animal must be very apparent; and in truth things are so ordered that from the common society of men far more conveniences arise than the contrary. Let satirists therefore laugh to their hearts' content at human affairs, let theologians revile them, and let the melancholy praise as much as they can the rude and barbarous isolated life: let them despise men and admire the brutes—despite all this, men will find that they can prepare with mutual aid far more easily what they need, and avoid far more easily the perils which beset them on all sides, by united forces: to say nothing of how much better it is, and more worthy of our knowledge, to regard the deeds of men rather than those of brutes.

PROP. XXXVI. The greatest good of those who follow virtue is common to all, and all can equally enjoy it.

Proof.—To act from virtue is to act from the instruction of reason (Prop. 24, Part IV.), and whatever we endeavour to do from reason is understanding (Prop. 26, Part IV.). And therefore (Prop. 28, Part IV.) the greatest good of those who follow virtue is to know God, that is (Prop. 47, Part II., and its Note), the good which can be possessed equally by all men, in so far as they are of the same nature. *Q.e.d.*

Note.—But if any one ask, What if the greatest good of those who follow virtue were not common to all? would it not then follow as above (see Prop. 34, Part IV.), that men who live according to the mandate of reason, that is (Prop. 35, Part IV.), men, in so far as they agree in nature, would be contrary one to the other? He has this answer for himself, that it arises not accidentally but from the very nature of reason that the greatest good of man should be common to all, clearly because it is deduced from human essence itself in so far as it is defined by reason, and inasmuch as a man can neither be nor be conceived without the power of enjoying the greatest good. For it belongs (Prop. 47, Part II.) to the essence of the human mind to have an adequate knowledge of the eternal and infinite essence of God.

PROP. XXXVII. The good which each one who follows virtue desires for himself, he also desires for other men, and the more so the more knowledge he has of God.

Proof.—Men, in so far as they live under the guidance of reason, are most useful to men (Coroll. 1, Prop. 35, Part IV.); and therefore (Prop. 19, Part IV.) we endeavour, under the guidance of reason, to bring it about that men live under the guidance of reason. But the good which each person who lives according to the dictate of reason, that is (Prop. 24, Part IV.), who follows virtue, desires for himself, is to understand (Prop 26, Part IV.); therefore the good which he desires for himself, he desires

also for other men.   Again, desire, in so far as it has reference
to the mind, is the very essence of the mind (Def. Emo. 1);
but the essence of the mind consists of knowledge (Prop. 11,
Part II.) which involves knowledge of God (Prop. 47, Part
II.), and without which (Prop. 15, Part I.) it cannot exist or
be conceived.   And therefore, according as the essence of
the mind involves a greater knowledge of God, so the desire
with which he who follows virtue desires the good which he
desires for himself for others, will be greater.   *Q.e.d.*

   Another Proof.—A man will love the good which he desires
for himself and loves, with greater constancy, if he sees that
others love it also (Prop. 31, Part III.).   And therefore
(Coroll., same Prop.) he will endeavour to bring it about that
others also will like it.   And as this good (prev. Prop.) is
common to all, and all may enjoy it, he will endeavour,
therefore (by the same reason), to bring it to pass that all
enjoy it, and (Prop. 37, Part III.) the more so the more he
enjoys it.   *Q.e.d.*

   Note I.—He who endeavours from emotion alone to bring
it to pass that others love what he loves, and that others
should live according to his liking, acts from impulse, and
is hateful more especially to those whom other things please,
and who accordingly endeavour with the same impulse to
bring it about that others should live according to their idea
of life.   Again, as the greatest good which men desire from
emotion is often such that only one can possess it, it comes
about that those who love are not constant in mind, and
while they delight to praise the things they love, yet at the
same time they fear to be believed.   But he who endeavours
to lead the rest by reason, not impulse, acts humanely and
benignly, and is most constant in mind.   Again, whatever
we desire and do of which we are the cause, in so far as we
have the idea of God or in so far as we know God, I refer to
Religion (*religio*).   The desire, however, of doing good, which
is engendered in us by reason of the fact that we live according to the precepts of reason, I call Piety (*pietas*).   Again,
the desire wherewith a man who lives according to the instruction of reason is so held that he wishes to unite others to
him in friendship, I call Honesty (*honestas*), and that honest
which men who live under the guidance of reason praise;
and, on the other hand, that base (*turpe*) which is opposed to
the making of friendship.   Besides this, I have shown what

are the basements of a state. Now the difference between true virtue and weakness can easily be perceived from what has been said above, namely, that true virtue is nothing else than living according to the precepts of reason; and therefore weakness consists in this alone, that man allows himself to be led by things which are outside him, and is determined by them to do those things which the common disposition of external things postulates, and not those postulated by his own nature considered in itself. Now these are the things which I promised to prove in the Note of Prop. 18, Part IV., from which it is apparent that that law not to slaughter animals has its foundation more in vain superstition and womanish pity than true reason. The reason wherewith we seek what is useful to us teaches us the necessity of uniting ourselves with our fellow-men, but not with brutes and things which are different from the human species in nature; but we have over them the same right as they over us. Again, as every one's right is defined by his virtue or power, men have far more right over beasts than beasts over men. I do not deny that beasts feel; but I deny that on that account we should not consult our necessity and use them as much as we wish and treat them as we will, since they do not agree with us in nature, and their emotions are in nature different from human emotions (see Note, Prop. 57, Part III.). It remains that I should explain what is just and what unjust, what is sin and what merit. On these points see the following note.

Note II.—In the appendix of the first part I promised to explain what was praise and blame, merit and sin, just and unjust. As for praise and blame, I have explained them in the Note of Prop. 29, Part III. I must now say something concerning the rest; but before doing that I must say something concerning the natural and civil state of man.

Every man exists by consummate right of nature, and consequently every man does by reason of this right those things which follow from the necessity of his nature; and therefore each man judges for himself, by his consummate right of nature, what is good or bad, and consults his advantage according to his disposition (see Prop. 19 and 20, Part IV.), and revenges himself (Coroll. 2, Prop. 40, Part III.), and endeavours to preserve what he loves and to destroy what he hates (Prop. 28, Part III.). If men lived according to the dictate of reason, each one would possess (Coroll. 1, Prop. 35, Part IV.) his right without any loss to another; but because they are liable to emotions (Coroll., Prop. 4, Part IV.) which far surpass human power or virtue (Prop. 6, Part IV.), they are therefore often drawn in different directions (Prop. 33, Part IV.) and are contrary one to the other (Prop. 34, Part IV.), while they need each other's help (Note, Prop. 35, Part IV.).   It is necessary, then, in order that men may live in concord and be of help to each other, that they should give up their natural right and render themselves reciprocally secure, and determine to do nothing that will be injurious to another.   The manner in which this can come to pass, namely, that men, who are necessarily liable to emotions (Coroll., Prop. 4, Part IV.), and inconstant and variable (Prop. 33, Part IV.), can mutually render themselves secure and have trust one in the other, is clear from Prop. 7, Part IV., and Prop. 39, Part III., namely, that no emotion can be checked save by another emotion stronger than and contrary to the emotion to be checked, and that every one refrains from inflicting evil through fear of incurring a greater evil.   By this law society (*societas*) can be held together, provided it keep for itself the right every one has of vindicating wrong done to him, and judging what is good and evil, and if it have also the power of prescribing a common system of life and behaviour, and of making laws and forcing them to be respected, not by reason, which cannot check emotions (Note, Prop. 17, Part IV.), but by threats.   This society, ratified with laws and power of keeping itself together, is called state (*civitas*), and those who are protected by this right are called citizens (*cives*).   From which we can easily understand that nothing can exist in a natural state which can be called good or bad by common assent, since every man, who is in a natural state, consults only his own advantage, and determines what is good or bad according to his own fancy and in so far as he has regard for his own advantage alone and holds himself responsible to no one save himself by any law; and therefore sin cannot be conceived in a natural state, but only in a civil state, where it is decreed by common consent what is good or bad, and each one holds himself responsible to the state.   Therefore sin (*peccatum*) is nothing else than disobedience, which is thus punishable by right of the state alone; and on the other hand obedience is considered a merit in a citizen, because he who rejoices in the advantages of a state is thereby judged worthy. Again, in a natural state no one is master of anything by common consent, nor can there be anything in nature which can be said to belong to this man and not to that, but all things belong equally to all men; and accordingly in a natural state no wish of rendering to each man his own can be conceived, nor of taking away from a man what belongs to him, that is, in a state of nature nothing takes place that can be called just or unjust, but only in a civil state, where it is determined by common consent what belongs to this man or that. From this it is apparent that just and unjust, sin and merit, are merely extrinsic notions, not attributes which explain the nature of the mind. But I have said enough of this.

PROP. XXXVIII. That is useful to man which so disposes the human body that it can be affected in many modes, or which renders it capable of affecting external bodies in many modes, and the more so according as it renders the body more apt to be affected in many modes or to affect other bodies so; and, on the contrary, that is harmful (*noxius*) to man which renders the body less apt for this.

Proof.—The more the body is rendered apt for this, the more the mind is rendered apt for perceiving (Prop. 14, Part II.): and therefore that which disposes the body in that way and renders it apt for this, is necessarily good or useful (Prop. 26 and 27, Part IV.), and more useful the more apt it renders the body for this, and, on the contrary (by the same Prop. 14, Part II., inversed, and Prop. 26 and 27, Part IV.), that is harmful which renders the body less apt for this. *Q.e.d.*

PROP. XXXIX. Whatever brings it to pass that the proportion of motion and rest which the parts of the human body hold one to the other is preserved, is good; and contrariwise, that is bad which brings it about that the parts of the human body have another proportion mutually of motion and rest.

Proof.—The human body needs for its preservation many other bodies (Post. 4, Part II.); but that which constitutes the form of the human body consists of this, that its parts convey one to the other their motions mutually in a certain ratio (Def. before Lemma 4, which see after Prop. 13, Part II.). Therefore that which brings it about that the proportion of motion and rest which the parts of the body have one to the other is preserved, preserves the form of the human body, and consequently brings it to pass (Post. 3 and 6, Part II.) that the human body can be affected in many ways, and also that it can affect external bodies in many ways: and therefore (prev. Prop.) it is good. Again, that which brings it to pass that the parts of the human body assume some other proportion of motion and rest, bring it to pass (same Def., Part II.) that the human body assumes another form, that is (as is self-evident, and as we gave notice towards the end of the preface of this part), that the human body is destroyed, and consequently rendered entirely inapt for being affected in many modes: and therefore (prev. Prop.) it is bad. *Q.e.d.*

Note.—What evil or good this can do to the mind is explained in the fifth part. But it must be noted here, that I understand the body to suffer death when its parts are so disposed that they assume one with the other another proportion of motion and rest. For I do not dare to deny that the human body can be changed into another nature entirely different to its own, although the circulation of the blood and the other signs whereby a body is thought to live be preserved. For there is no reason which obliges me to state that a body does not die unless it is changed into a corpse: indeed experience seems to persuade the contrary. For it comes to pass at times that a man suffers such changes that it is difficult to say he is the same, as I have heard related of a certain Spanish poet, who had been seized with a certain sickness, and although he recovered from it, remained in such darkness as to his past life that he did not think the tales and tragedies he had written were his own, and could easily have been mistaken for a grown-up child had he forgotten how to speak. And if this seems incredible, what shall we say of children whose nature a man of advanced age deems so different from his own that he could not be persuaded that he ever was a child if he did not judge of his own from the example of others? But lest I gather material for the superstitious to raise new questions about, I had rather leave this question without further discussion.

PROP. XL. Whatever is conducive of the common society of men, or whatever brings it about that men live together in peace and agreement, is useful, and, on the contrary, that is bad which induces discord in the state.

Proof.—Whatever brings it about that men live together in agreement, brings it about at the same time that they live under the guidance of reason (Prop. 35, Part IV.), and therefore (Prop. 26 and 27, Part IV.) it is good: and (by the same argument) that, on the other hand, is bad which fosters discord. *Q.e.d.*

PROP. XLI. Pleasure clearly is not evil but good; but pain, on the contrary, is clearly evil.

Proof.—Pleasure (Prop. 11, Part III., with its Note) is an emotion by which the power of acting of the body is increased or aided; but pain contrariwise is an emotion whereby the body's power of acting is diminished or hindered; and therefore (Prop. 38, Part IV.) pleasure is certainly good, etc. *Q.e.d.*

PROP. XLII. There cannot be too much merriment, but it is always good; but, on the other hand, melancholy is always bad.

Proof.—Merriment (see its def. in Note, Prop. 11, Part III.) is pleasure which, in so far as it has reference to the body, consists of this, that all the parts of the body are equally affected, that is (Prop. 11, Part III.), that the body's power of acting is increased or aided in such a way as all the parts preserve the same proportions of motion and rest one with the other; and therefore (Prop. 39, Part IV.) merriment is always good, and can have no excess. But melancholy (whose def. see in the same Note, Prop. 11, Part III.) is pain which, in so far as it has reference to the body, consists of this, that the body's power of acting is absolutely diminished or hindered; and therefore (Prop. 38, Part IV.) it is always bad. *Q.e.d.*

PROP. XLIII. Titillation can be excessive and be bad; but grief may be good in so far as titillation or pleasure is bad.

Proof.—Titillation is pleasure which, in so far as it has reference to the body, consists of this, that one or several parts of the body are affected beyond the rest (see its def.

in Note, Prop. 11, Part III.); the power of this emotion can be so great that it surpasses the remaining actions of the body (Prop. 6, Part IV.), and it may become very fixedly adhered to this, and accordingly prevent the body from being ready to be affected by many other modes; and therefore (Prop. 38, Part IV.) it can be bad. Again, grief which, on the other hand, is pain, considered in itself cannot be good (Prop. 41, Part IV.). But inasmuch as its force and increase is defined by the power of an external cause compared with our own (Prop. 5, Part IV.), we can therefore conceive infinite degrees and modes of the forces of this emotion (Prop. 3, Part IV.); and so we can conceive such a mode or grade which can restrain titillation so that it is not excessive, and thus far (by the first part of this Prop.) bring it about that the body should not be rendered less apt; and thus far it will be good. *Q.e.d.*

PROP. XLIV. Love and desire can be excessive.

Proof.—Love is pleasure accompanied (Def. Emo. 6) by the idea of an external cause. Therefore titillation (Note, Prop. 11, Part III.) accompanied by the idea of an external cause is love; and therefore love (prev. Prop.) can be excessive. Again, desire is the greater according as the emotion from which it arose is greater (Prop. 37, Part III.). Wherefore, as an emotion can surpass all the other actions of man, so also can desire which arises from that emotion surpass other desires, and so it can have the same excess as we proved in the previous proposition titillation to have. *Q.e.d.*

Note.—Merriment, which we said to be good, can be more easily conceived than observed. For the emotions by which we are daily assailed have reference rather to some part of the body which is affected beyond the others, and so the emotions as a rule are in excess, and so detain the mind in the contemplation of one object that it cannot think of others; and although men are liable to many emotions, and therefore few are found who are always assailed by one and the same emotion, yet there are not wanting those to whom one and the same emotion adheres with great pertinacity. We see that men are sometimes so affected by one object that, although it is not present, yet they believe it to be present with them; when this happens to a man who is not asleep, we say that he is delirious or insane; nor are they

The Strength of the Emotions 173

thought less mad who are fired with love, and who spend
night and day in dreaming of their ladylove or mistress, for
they cause laughter. But when a miser thinks of nothing
save money and coins, or an ambitious man of nothing save
honour, these are not thought to be insane, for they are
harmful, and are thought worthy of hatred. But in truth,
avarice, ambition, lust, etc., are nothing but species of
madness, although they are not enumerated among diseases.

PROP. XLV. Hatred can never be good.

Proof.—We endeavour to destroy the man whom we hate
(Prop. 39, Part III.), that is (Prop. 37, Part IV.), we
endeavour to do something which is bad. Therefore, etc.
Q.e.d.

Note I.—Let it be noted that here and in the following
propositions I only understand by hatred that towards men.

Corollary I.—Envy, derision, contempt, rage, revenge,
and the other emotions which have reference to hatred or
arise from it, are bad, which is clear from Prop. 39, Part III.,
and Prop. 37, Part IV.

Corollary II.—Whatever we desire owing to the fact that
we are affected with hatred is evil and unjust in the state;
which is also obvious from Prop. 39, Part III., and from the
definition of evil or disgraceful, which see in the Note on
Prop. 3, Part IV.

Note II.—Between derision (which we said to be bad in
the first Coroll.) and laughter (*risus*) I admit there is a great
difference. For laughter and also jocularity are merely
pleasure; and therefore, provided they are not in excess,
they are good in themselves (Prop. 41, Part IV.). Nothing,
therefore, save gloomy and mirthless superstition prohibits
laughter. For why is it more becoming to satisfy hunger
and thirst than to disperse melancholy? My reason is this,
and I have convinced myself of it: No deity, nor any one
save the envious, is pleased with my want of power or my
misfortune, nor imputes to our virtue, tears, sobs, fear, and
other things of this kind which are significant of a weak
man; but, on the contrary, the more we are affected with
pleasure, thus we pass to a greater perfection, that is we
necessarily participate of the divine nature. To make use
of things and take delight in them as much as possible (not
indeed to satiety, for that is not to take delight) is the part

of a wise man. It is, I say, the part of a wise man to feed himself with moderate pleasant food and drink, and to take pleasure with perfumes, with the beauty of growing plants, dress, music, sports, and theatres, and other places of this kind which man may use without any hurt to his fellows. For the human body is composed of many parts of different nature which continuously stand in need of new and varied nourishment, so that the body as a whole may be equally apt for performing those things which can follow from its nature, and consequently so that the mind also may be equally apt for understanding many things at the same time. This manner of living agrees best with our principles and the general manner of life: from which it follows that this manner of life is the best of all, and in all ways to be commended, nor is there any need for us to be more clear or more detailed on this subject.

PROP. XLVI. He who lives under the guidance of reason endeavours as much as possible to repay his fellow's hatred, rage, contempt, etc., with love and nobleness.

Proof.—All emotions of hatred are bad (Coroll. 1, prev. Prop.): and therefore he who lives according to the precepts of reason will endeavour as much as possible to bring it to pass that he is not assailed by emotions of hatred (Prop. 19, Part IV.), and consequently (Prop. 37, Part IV.) he will endeavour to prevent any one else from suffering those emotions. But hatred is increased by reciprocated hatred, and, on the contrary, can be demolished by love (Prop. 43, Part III.) in such a way that hatred is transformed into love (Prop. 44, Part III.). Therefore he who lives under the guidance of reason will endeavour to repay another's hatred, etc., with love, that is nobleness (whose def. see in Note, Prop. 59, Part III.). *Q.e.d.*

Note.—He who wishes to revenge injuries by reciprocal hatred will live in misery. But he who endeavours to drive away hatred by means of love, fights with pleasure and confidence: he resists equally one or many men, and scarcely needs at all the help of fortune. Those whom he conquers yield joyfully, not from want of force but increase thereof. All these things follow so clearly from the definitions alone of love and intellect that there is no need for me to point them out.

Prop. XLVII. The emotions of hope and fear cannot be in themselves good.

Proof.—The emotions of hope and fear are not given without pain. For fear is (Def. Emo. 13) sadness or pain, and hope (see explanation of Def. Emo. 12, and 13) is not given without fear. And thus (Prop. 41, Part IV.) these emotions cannot be in themselves good, but only in so far as they can restrain an excess of pleasure (Prop. 43, Part IV.). *Q.e.d.*

Note.—To this must be added that these emotions indicate a want of knowledge and weakness of mind; and on this account, confidence, despair, joy, and disappointment are significant of a weak mind. For although confidence and joy are emotions of pleasure, they imply that pain has preceded them, namely, hope and fear. Therefore the more we endeavour to live under the guidance of reason, the less we endeavour to depend on hope, and the more to deliver ourselves and make ourselves free from fear and overcome fortune as much as possible, and finally to direct our actions by the certain advice of reason.

Prop. XLVIII. The emotions of partiality and disparagement are always bad.

Proof.—Now these emotions (Def. Emo. 21 and 22) are opposed to reason, and therefore (Prop. 26 and 27, Part IV.) they are bad. *Q.e.d.*

Prop. XLIX. Partiality easily renders the man who is over-estimated, proud.

Proof.—If we see any one praises more than justly what is in us through love we are easily exulted (Note, Prop. 41, Part III.), or we are affected with pleasure (Def. Emo. 30), and we easily believe whatever good we hear said about us (Prop. 25, Part III.). And therefore we esteem ourselves beyond the limits of justice through self-love, that is (Def. Emo. 28) we easily become proud. *Q.e.d.*

Prop. L. Pity in a man who lives under the guidance of reason is in itself bad and useless.

Proof.—Now pity (Def. Emo. 18) is sadness, and therefore (Prop. 41, Part IV.) is bad in itself. The good which follows from it, namely, that we endeavour to free the man whom we pity from his misery (Coroll., Prop. 27, Part III.), we desire to do from the mere command of reason (Prop. 37, Part IV.), nor can we do anything which we know to be good save under the guidance of reason (Prop. 27, Part IV.). And therefore pity in a man who lives under the guidance of reason is bad and useless in itself. *Q.e.d.*

Corollary.—Hence it follows that a man who lives according to the dictate of reason endeavours as far as possible not to be touched with pity.

Note.—He who rightly knows that all things follow from the necessity of divine nature, and come to pass according to the eternal natural and regular laws, will find nothing at all that is worthy of hatred, laughter, or contempt, nor will he feel compassion; but as far as human virtue can go, he will endeavour to act well, as people say, and to rejoice. To this must be added that he who is easily touched by the emotions of pity, and is moved to tears at the misery of another, often does something of which he afterwards repents: both inasmuch as we can do nothing according to emotion which we can certainly know to be good, and inasmuch as we are easily deceived by false tears. I am speaking here expressly of a man who lives under the guidance of reason. For he who is moved neither by reason nor pity to help others is rightly called inhuman, for (Prop. 27, Part III.) he seems to be dissimilar to man.

PROP. LI. Favour is not opposed to reason, but can agree with it and arise from it.

Proof.—Now favour is love towards him who has benefited another (Def. Emo. 19): and therefore it can have reference to the mind in so far as it is said to be active (Prop. 59, Part III.), that is (Prop. 3, Part III.), in so far as it understands; and therefore it agrees with reason, etc. *Q.e.d.*

Another Proof.—He who lives under the guidance of reason desires for others the good he desires for himself (Prop. 37, Part IV.). Wherefore, by the very fact that he sees some one benefit another, his own endeavour to benefit is aided, that is (Prop. 11, Part III.), he is rejoiced, and that (by the hypothesis) accompanied by the idea of him who wrought the other good; and therefore (Def. Emo. 19) he favours him. *Q.e.d.*

Note.—Indignation, as it is defined by us (Def. Emo. 20), is necessarily bad (Prop. 45, Part IV.). But it must be noted that when sovereign power with the desire of preserving the peace punishes a citizen who has wrought another an injury, we do not say that it is indignant with the citizen when it punishes him, inasmuch as it is not imbued with hatred to ruin the citizen, but with a sense of duty.

PROP. LII. Self-complacency can arise from reason, and that self-complacency which arises from reason alone is the greatest.

Proof.—Self-complacency is pleasure arisen from the fact that man regards himself and his power of acting (Def. Emo. 25). But the true power of acting of man or his virtue is reason itself (Prop. 3, Part III.), which man clearly and distinctly regards (Prop. 40 and 43, Part II.). Therefore self-complacency arises from reason. Again, man while he regards himself perceives nothing clearly and distinctly, save those things which follow from his power of acting (Def. 2, Part III.), that is (Prop. 3, Part III.), which follow from his power of understanding. Therefore from this self-regarding the greatest self-complacency possible arises. *Q.e.d.*

Note.—Self-complacency is the greatest good we can expect. For (as we have shown in Prop. 25, Part IV.) no one endeavours to preserve his being for the sake of some end; and inasmuch as this self-complacency is more and more cherished and encouraged by praises (Coroll., Prop. 53, Part III.), and, on the contrary (Coroll. 1, Prop. 55, Part III.), disturbed more and more by blame, we are led in life principally by the desire of honour, and under the burden of blame we can scarcely endure it.

PROP. LIII. Humility is not a virtue, or it does not arise from reason.

Proof.—Humility is pain which arises from the fact that man regards his own want of power (Def. Emo. 26). But in so far as man knows himself by true reason, thus far he is supposed to understand his essence, that is (Prop. 7, Part III.), his power. Wherefore if man, while he regards himself, perceives any weakness of his, it arises not from the fact that he understands himself, but (as we showed in Prop. 55, Part III.) from the fact that his power of acting is hindered. But if we suppose that man conceives his weakness from the fact

that he understands something more powerful than himself,
whose knowledge determines his power of acting, then we
conceive nothing else than that man distinctly understands
himself (Prop. 26, Part IV.), or that thus his power of acting
is aided. Whreefore humility or pain, which arises from the
fact that man regards his weakness, does not arise from true
contemplation or reason, and is not a virtue but a passion.
Q.e.d.

PROP. LIV. Repentance is not a virtue, or, in other words,
it does not arise from reason, but he who repents of an action
is twice as unhappy or as weak as before.

Proof.—The first part of this proposition is proved in the
same manner as the preceding proposition. The second
part is clear merely from the definition of this emotion (see
Def. Emo. 27). For the man allows himself to be overcome
first by evil desire and then by pain.

Note.—Inasmuch as men rarely live according to the
dictates of reason, these two emotions, namely, humility and
repentance, and beside these hope and fear, work more good
than evil: and so, as we must sin, it is better to sin in that.
For if men who are powerless in mind should all become
equally proud, they would be shamed with nothing, nor
would they fear anything wherewith they may be united as
with chains and held together. If the mob is not in fear, it
threatens in its turn. Wherefore it is not to be wondered at
that the prophets, who consulted the advantage not of a few,
but of the commonwealth, should have so greatly commended
humility, repentance, and reverence. And in truth those
who are liable to these emotions can be led far easier than
others to live under the guidance of reason, that is, to be free
and enjoy the life of the blessed.

PROP. LV. The greatest pride or dejection is the greatest
ignorance of self.

Proof.—This is clear from Def. Emo. 28 and 29.

PROP. LVI. The greatest pride or dejection indicates the
greatest weakness of mind.

Proof.—The primary basis of virtue is self-preservation
(Coroll., Prop. 22, Part IV.), and that under the guidance of
reason (Prop. 24, Part IV.). He, therefore, who knows not

himself, knows not the basis of all virtues, and consequently is ignorant of all virtues. Again, to act from virtue is nothing else than to act under the guidance of reason (Prop. 24, Part IV.), and he who acts under the guidance of reason must necessarily know that he acts under the guidance of reason (Prop. 43, Part II.). He, therefore, who has the greatest ignorance of himself, and consequently (as we have just shown) of all the virtues, acts the least from virtue, that is (as is clear from Def. 8), he is most weak in his mind; and therefore (prev. Prop.) the greatest pride or dejection indicates the greatest weakness of mind. *Q.e.d.*

Corollary.—Hence it follows most clearly that proud and dejected people are most liable to emotions.

Note.—However, dejection can be more easily corrected than pride, since the latter is an emotion of pleasure, while the other is an emotion of pain; and therefore (Prop. 18, Part IV.) the former is the stronger of the two.

PROP. LVII. A proud man loves the presence of parasites or flatterers, but the presence of noble people he hates.

Proof.—Pride is pleasure arisen from the fact that man over-estimates himself (Def. Emo. 28 and 6); this opinion a proud man endeavours as much as possible to foster (see Note, Prop. 13, Part III.). And therefore he will love the presence of parasites or flatterers (the definitions of these are omitted, for they are too well known), and as for the company or presence of noble men, he will hate it. *Q.e.d.*

Note.—It would be too long to enumerate here all the evils of pride, for the proud are liable to all emotions, but to none less than to the emotions of love and pity. But I must not be silent concerning the fact that a man is called proud who under-estimates his fellows; and therefore pride in this case must be defined as pleasure arisen from a false opinion whereby a man considers himself above his fellows. And dejection contrary to this pride must be defined as pain arisen from the false opinion whereby a man thinks himself below his fellows. But we can easily conceive from this position that a proud man is necessarily envious (see Note, Prop. 55, Part III.), and hates those most who are most praised by reason of virtue, nor can his hatred be easily overcome by their love or benefit (Note, Prop. 41, Part III.), and that he delights only in the presence of those who deceive his weak mind and from being merely foolish make him mad. Although dejection is contrary to pride, yet a dejected man is nearest to a proud one. For since his pain arises from the fact that he compares his weakness with the strength or virtue of others, his pain will be removed, that is, he will be rejoiced, if his imagination be occupied in the contemplation of the vices of others, whence the proverb has arisen: It is a comfort to the unhappy to have companions in misery; and on the other hand, he will be more saddened the more he thinks himself beneath them: whence it comes about that none are so prone to envy as the dejected, and that these endeavour to observe the deeds of men with the greatest care, more with the object of carping at them than of correcting them, and that they praise and glory in dejection alone, but in such a way that they still seem dejected. Now these things follow from this emotion with the same necessity as it does from the nature of a triangle that its three angles are equal to two right angles; and I have already said that I call these and like emotions bad in so far as I have regard for human advantage. But the laws of nature have respect for the general order of nature of which man is a part, which I have paused to mention in passing lest any one should think me to wish to relate the vices of men and their absurdities, and not to show the nature and properties of things. For, as I said in the preface of Part III., I regard human emotions and their properties in the same manner as the remaining things of nature. And surely human emotions indicate, if not human power and art, at least that of nature, no less than many other things which we wonder at and in whose contemplation we delight. But I pass on to note those things of the emotions which bear advantage to men or which work them evil.

PROP. LVIII. Honour is not opposed to reason, but can arise from it.

Proof.—This is clear from Def. Emo. 30, and from the definition of honourable, which see in Note 1, Prop. 37, Part IV.

Note.—What is called vainglory or empty honour is self-complacency, which is fostered only by the opinion of the mob; and when this ceases, so also does the self-complacency cease, that is (Note, Prop. 52, Part IV.), the greatest good which each person loves. Whence it comes about that he

whose honour depends on the opinion of the mob, must day
by day strive with the greatest anxiety, act and scheme in
order to retain his reputation.   For the mob is varied and
inconstant, and therefore if a reputation is not carefully
preserved it dies quickly.   Every one desires to obtain for
himself the applause of the mob, and so one easily represses
the reputation of the other, from which, since the struggle is
for what is esteemed the greatest good, an enormous burning
desire arises in one of suppressing the other in whatever
manner possible, and he that comes out victor has more
honour or glory from having done harm to others than from
having profited himself.   This honour or self-complacency
is in truth vain, for it is nothing.

What must be noted concerning shame can easily be
gathered from what we said of pity and repentance.   This
only will I add, that just as compassion so also shame,
although it is not a virtue, is nevertheless good in so far as
it indicates in the man who is overcome with shame a desire
to live honourably, just as agony is good in so far as it
shows that the injured part is not yet putrefied.   Wherefore, although a man who is ashamed of some deed is in
truth pained, he is nevertheless more perfect than a shame-
less person who has no desire of living honourably.

And these are the points which I undertook to note
concerning the emotions of pleasure and pain.   As for
desires, these are either good or bad in so far as they arise
from good or bad emotions.   But all in truth, in so far as
they are engendered in us by emotions which are passions,
are blind (as can easily be gathered from what has been said
in Note, Prop. 44, Part IV.), nor would they be of any use
at all if men could easily be led to live according to the
dictates of reason alone, as I shall now show in a few words.

Prop. LIX. For all actions for which we are determined
by an emotion which is a passion we can be determined
without that emotion by reason alone.

Proof.—To act from reason is nothing else (Prop. 3 and
Def. 2, Part III.) than to do those things which follow from
the necessity of our nature considered in itself.   But pain
is bad in so far as it diminishes or hinders this power of acting
(Prop. 41, Part IV.).   Therefore from this emotion we can
be determined for no action which we could not do if we were

led by reason. Moreover, pleasure is bad in so far as it prevents man from being ready for action (Prop. 41 and 43, Part IV.). And therefore we can be determined for no action which we could not do if we were led by reason. Again, in so far as pleasure is good it agrees with reason (for it consists of this, that man's power of acting is increased or aided), nor is it a passion save in so far as it does not increase man's power of acting to the extent that he perceives himself and his actions adequately (Prop. 3, Part III., with its Note). Wherefore if a man affected with pleasure is led to such perfection that he conceives himself and his actions adequately, he will be as apt, nay more apt, for those actions for which he was determined by emotions which are passions. But all emotions have reference either to pleasure, pain, or desire (see explan. Def. Emo. 4), and desire (Def. Emo. 1) is nothing else than the endeavour to act. Therefore for all actions for which we are determined by an emotion which is a passion we can be determined by reason alone. *Q.e.d.*

Another Proof.—Each action is said to be bad in so far as it arises from the fact that we are affected with hatred or any other evil emotion (see Coroll. 1, Prop. 45, Part IV.). But no action considered in itself is good or evil (as we showed in the preface of this part), but one and the same action is now good and now bad. Therefore to that same action which is now evil, or which arises from some evil emotion, we can be led by reason (Prop. 19, Part IV.). *Q.e.d.*

Note.—These points will be explained more clearly by an example—namely, the action of striking, in so far as it is considered physically, and in so far as we pay attention to this alone, that a man raises his arm, clenches his fist and brings it down with all the force of his arm, is a virtue which is conceived from the construction of the human body. If, therefore, a man moved by hatred or rage is determined to clench his fist and move his arm, this comes about, as we showed in the second part, because one and the same action can be united to certain images of things; and therefore both from those images of things which we conceive confusedly and from those which we conceive clearly and distinctly, we can be determined for one and the same action. It is therefore apparent that every desire which arises from an emotion which is a passion would be of no use if men were guided by reason. Let us see now why desire which arises from an emotion which is a passion is called blind by us.

PROP. LX. Desire which arises from pleasure or pain which has reference to one or certain parts of the body but not all has no advantage to man as a whole.

Proof.—Let it be supposed that a part, *e.g.* A, of a body is so aided by the force of some external cause that it overcomes the rest (Prop. 6, Part IV.). This part will not endeavour to lose its forces in order that the other parts may perform their functions, or it would then have the force or power of losing its forces, which (Prop. 6, Part III.) is absurd. That part will therefore endeavour, and consequently (Prop. 7 and 12, Part III.) the mind also will endeavour, to preserve its condition; and therefore desire which arises from such an emotion of pleasure will not bring advantage to the body as a whole. Then if, on the other hand, it is supposed that the part A is hindered in such a way that the remaining parts overcome it, it may be proved in the same manner that the desire which arises from pain will not bring advantage to the body as a whole. *Q.e.d.*

Note.—As pleasure has reference generally (Note, Prop. 44, Part IV.) to one part of the body, we therefore desire as a rule to preserve our being without having regard to our health as a whole. To which must be added that the desires by which we are usually held (Coroll., Prop. 9, Part IV.) have regard only for present not future time.

PROP. LXI. Desire which arises from reason can have no excess.

Proof.—Desire (Def. Emo. 1) absolutely considered is the very essence of man in so far as it is conceived as determined in any manner to do anything. Therefore desire which arises from reason, that is (Prop. 3, Part III.), which is engendered in us in so far as we are active, is the very essence or nature of man in so far as it is conceived as determined to do those things which are adequately conceived through the essence of man alone (Def. 2, Part III.). If, therefore, this desire can have excess, then human nature considered in itself can exceed itself, or could do more than it can do, which is a manifest contradiction. And therefore this desire cannot have excess. *Q.e.d.*

PROP. LXII. In so far as the mind conceives a thing according to the dictate of reason, it will be equally affected whether the idea be of a thing present, past, or future.

Proof.—Whatever the mind conceives under the guidance of reason, it conceives entirely under a certain species of eternity or necessity (Coroll. 2, Prop. 44, Part II.), and is affected with the same certainty (Prop. 43, Part II., and its Note). Wherefore, whether the idea be of a thing future, past, or present, the mind will conceive it by the same necessity and will be affected with the same certainty; and whether the idea be of a thing present, past, or future, it will nevertheless be equally true (Prop. 41, Part II.), that is (Def. 4, Part II.), it will have, nevertheless, the same properties of an adequate idea. And therefore in so far as the mind conceives a thing according to the dictates of reason it is affected in the same manner, whether the idea be of a thing future, past, or present. *Q.e.d.*

Note.—If we could have an adequate knowledge of the duration of things, and could determine by reason their times of existing, we should regard things future and present with the same emotion, and the mind would desire, as if it were present, the good which it conceives as future: and consequently it would neglect necessarily a lesser present good for a greater future one, and it would desire in no wise what was good in the present, but the cause of future ill, as we shall soon show. But we can only have a most inadequate idea of the duration of things (Prop. 31, Part II.), and we must determine things' time of existing by imagination alone (Note, Prop. 44, Part II.), which is not equally affected by the image of a thing present and one future. Whence it comes about that the true knowledge of good and evil which we have is only abstract or general, and the judgment which we make of the order of things and the connection of causes, so as to be able to determine what is good or bad for us in the present, is rather imaginary than real. And therefore it is not wonderful that desire which arises from the knowledge of good and evil, in so far as this has reference to the future, can be more easily restrained by the desire of things which are pleasant in the present, concerning which see Prop. 18, Part IV.

PROP. LXIII. He that is led by fear to do good in order to avoid evil is not led by reason.

The Strength of the Emotions 185

Proof.—All emotions which have reference to the mind in so far as it is active, that is (Prop. 3, Part III.), which have reference to reason, are none other than the emotions of pleasure and desire (Prop. 59, Part III.). And therefore (Def. Emo. 13) he that is led by fear to do good in order to avoid evil is not led by reason. *Q.e.d.*

Note I.—The superstitious, who know better how to reprobate vice than to teach virtue, and who do not endeavour to lead men by reason, but to so inspire them with fear that they avoid evil rather than love virtue, have no other intention than to make the rest as miserable as themselves; and therefore it is not wonderful that for the most part they are a nuisance and hateful to men.

Corollary.—By reason of the desire which arises from reason we directly follow what is good and indirectly avoid what is evil.

Proof.—The desire which arises from reason can only arise from the emotion of pleasure which is not a passion (Prop. 59, Part III.), that is, from pleasure which cannot be excessive (Prop. 61, Part IV.), and not from pain. And accordingly this desire (Prop. 8, Part IV.) arises from the knowledge of good, and not from that of evil. And therefore under the guidance of reason we directly desire what is good, and thus far only we avoid what is evil. *Q.e.d.*

Note II.—This corollary can be explained by the example of a sick and healthy man. The sick man eats what he dislikes from a fear of death; but a healthy man enjoys his food, and thus reaps more benefit from life than if he feared death and desired to avoid it directly. Thus a judge who is not imbued with hatred or rage, etc., but merely with love for public safety, and condemns the guilty to death, is led by reason alone.

PROP. LXIV. The knowledge of evil is inadequate knowledge.

Proof.—The knowledge of evil (Prop. 8, Part IV.) is pain itself in so far as we are conscious of it. But pain is a transition to a lesser state of perfection (Def. Emo. 3), which on that account cannot be understood through the essence itself of man (Prop. 6 and 7, Part III.). And accordingly (Def. 2, Part III.) it is a passion which (Prop. 3, Part III.) depends on inadequate ideas, and consequently (Prop. 29, Part II.) the knowledge of evil is inadequate. *Q.e.d.*

Corollary.—Hence it follows that if the human mind had only adequate ideas it would form no notion of evil.

PROP. LXV. Under the guidance of reason we follow the greater of two things which are good and the lesser of two things which are evil.

Proof.—A good thing which prevents us from enjoying a greater good is in truth an evil, for good and bad is said of things (as we showed in the preface of this part) in so far as we compare them one with the other, and (for the same reason) a lesser evil is in truth a good. Wherefore (Coroll., prev. Prop.) under the guidance of reason we desire or follow only the greater of two things which are good and the lesser of two which are evil. *Q.e.d.*

Corollary.—We may follow under the guidance of reason the lesser evil as if it were the greater good, and neglect the lesser good as the cause of a greater evil. For the evil which is here called lesser is in truth good, and, on the other hand, the good is evil. Wherefore (Coroll., prev. Prop.) we desire the former and avoid the latter. *Q.e.d.*

PROP. LXVI. Under the guidance of reason we desire a greater future good before a lesser present one, and a lesser evil in the present " before a greater in the future " (Van Vloten's version).

Proof.—If the mind could have adequate knowledge of a future thing, it would be affected with the same emotion towards a future thing as towards a present one (Prop. 62, Part IV.). Wherefore, in so far as we have regard to reason, as we are supposed to do in this proposition, whether the greater good or evil be supposed future or present, the thing is the same. And therefore (Prop. 65, Part IV.) we desire a greater future good before a lesser present one. *Q.e.d.*

Corollary.—We desire under the guidance of reason a lesser present evil which is the cause of a greater future good, and we avoid a lesser present good which is the cause of a greater future evil. The proof of this corollary bears the same relation to that of the previous proposition as the Coroll. of Prop. 65 bore to Prop. 65 itself.

Note.—If these statements are compared with what we showed concerning the force of the emotions in this part up to the eighteenth proposition, we shall easily see what is the difference between a man who is led by opinion or emotion and one who is led by reason. The former, whether he will or not, performs things of which he is entirely ignorant; the latter is subordinate to no one, and only does those things which he knows to be of primary importance in his life, and which on that account he desires the most; and therefore I call the former a slave, but the latter free, concerning whose habits and manner of life we may here say a few words.

PROP. LXVII. A free man thinks of nothing less than of death, and his wisdom is a meditation not of death but of life.

Proof.—A free man, that is, one who lives according to the dictate of reason alone, is not led by the fear of death (Prop. 63, Part IV.), but directly desires what is good (Coroll., same Prop.), that is (Prop. 24, Part IV.), to act, to live, and preserve his being on the basis of seeking what is useful to him. And therefore he thinks of nothing less than of death, but his wisdom is a meditation of life. *Q.e.d.*

PROP. LXVIII. If men were born free they would form no conception of good and evil as long as they were free.

Proof.—I said that he was free who is led by reason alone. He, therefore, who is born free and remains free has only adequate ideas, and accordingly has no conception of evil (Coroll., Prop. 64, Part IV.), and consequently (for good and evil are correlative) none of good. *Q.e.d.*

Note.—That the hypothesis of this proposition is false and cannot be conceived save in so far as we have regard for the sole nature of man, or rather for God, not in so far as he is infinite, but in so far alone as he is the cause of man's existence, is obvious from the fourth proposition of this part. And this and the other points seem to have been meant by Moses in his history of the first man. For in that no other power of God is conceived save that by which he created man, that is, a power by which he consulted only the advantage of man; and thus it is related that God prohibited free man from eating of the tree of knowledge of good and evil, and that as soon as he ate of it, at once he began to fear death rather than to desire to live: again, when man found woman, who agreed most perfectly with his own nature, he knew that there could be nothing in nature more useful to him; but that afterwards, when he thought that the brute creation were similar to himself, he began at once to imitate their emotions (see Prop. 27, Part III.) and lost his freedom, which the Patriarchs under the guidance of the spirit of Christ, that is, the idea of God, afterwards recovered: on this idea alone it depends that man should be free, and that he should desire for other men the good which he desires for himself, as we showed above (Prop. 37, Part IV.).

PROP. LXIX. The virtue of a free man appears equally great in refusing to face difficulties as in overcoming them.

Proof.—An emotion cannot be hindered or taken away save by a contrary emotion and one that is stronger (Prop. 7, Part IV.). But blind daring and fear are emotions which can be conceived equally great (Prop. 5 and 3, Part IV.). Therefore an equally great virtue or fortitude (see def., Note, Prop. 59, Part III.) of mind is required to restrain daring as to restrain fear, that is (Def. Emo. 40 and 41), a free man declines dangers with the same mental virtue as that with which he attempts to overcome them. *Q.e.d.*

Corollary.—Therefore a free man is led by the same fortitude of mind to take flight in time as to fight; or a free man chooses from the same courage or presence of mind to fight or to take flight.

Note.—What is courage or magnanimity, or what I understand by it, I have explained in the Note on Prop. 59, Part III. But I understand by danger all that which can be the cause of any evil, namely, pain, hatred, disagreement, etc.

PROP. LXX. A free man, who lives among ignorant people, tries as much as he can to refuse their benefits.

Proof.—Every one judges according to his own disposition what is good (see Note, Prop. 39, Part III.). Therefore an ignorant man who has conferred a benefit on any one will estimate it according to his own disposition, and if he sees it to be estimated less by him to whom he gave it, he will be pained (Prop. 42, Part II.). But the free man desires to join other men to him in friendship (Prop. 37, Part IV.), and not to repay men with similar gifts according to their emotion towards him: he tries to lead himself and others according to the free judgment of reason, and to do those things only

The Strength of the Emotions 189

which he knows to be of primary importance. Therefore a free man, lest he should become hateful to the ignorant, and lest he should be governed by their desire or appetite, instead of by reason alone, endeavours as far as possible to refuse their benefits. *Q.e.d.*

Note.—I say " as far as possible," for although men are ignorant, they are nevertheless men and can confer human aid, greater than which there is none, in time of necessity. And it often happens that it is necessary to receive benefits from them, and consequently to repay them in kind. To which must be added that even in refusing benefits caution must be used lest we seem to despise or to refuse them for fear of having to repay them in kind, and thus, while we are trying to avoid their hatred, incur their offence. Wherefore in refusing benefits we must have regard for use and honour.

PROP. LXXI. Only free men are truly grateful one to the other.

Proof.—Only free men are truly useful one to the other, and are united by the closest bond of friendship (Prop. 35, and its first Coroll.), and endeavour to benefit each other with an equal impulse of love (Prop. 37, Part IV.). And therefore (Def. Emo. 34) only free men are truly grateful one to the other. *Q.e.d.*

Note.—The gratitude which men who are led by blind desire have one to the other is usually rather trading or bribery than gratitude. Moreover, ingratitude is not an emotion. But ingratitude is nevertheless base, inasmuch as it indicates that man is affected with too great hatred, anger, pride, or avarice. For he that does not repay gifts by reason of foolishness is not ungrateful, and far less is he who is not moved by the gifts of a courtesan to serve her lust, nor of a thief to hide his theft, or any other similar person. But, on the contrary, he shows that he has a constant mind, for he will not allow himself to be bribed by any gifts to work himself or the commonwealth harm.

PROP. LXXII. A free man never acts by fraud, but always with good faith.

Proof.—If a free man were to do something by fraud in so far as he is free, he would act according to the dictate of reason (for thus far only we call him free); and therefore to act fraudulently would be a virtue (Prop. 24, Part IV.), and consequently (same Prop.) it would be most advantageous to each one to act fraudulently, that is (as is self-manifest), it would be most advantageous for men to agree only in what they say, but to be contrary one to the other in what they do, which (Coroll., Prop. 31, Part IV.) is absurd. Therefore a free man, etc. *Q.e.d.*

Note.—If it be asked, " If a man can liberate himself from a present danger of death by deception, would not reason for the sake of his self-preservation persuade him to deceive?" it may be answered in the same manner, "That if reason persuaded him that, it would persuade it to all men, and therefore reason would persuade men not to unite their forces and have laws in common save in deception one to the other, that is, not to have common laws, which is absurd."

Prop. LXXIII. A man who is guided by reason is more free in a state where he lives according to common law than in solitude where he is subject to no law.

Proof.—A man who is guided by reason is not held in subjection by fear (Prop. 63, Part IV.), but in so far as he endeavours to preserve his being according to the dictates of reason, that is (Note, Prop. 66, Part IV.), in so far as he endeavours to live freely, he desires to have regard for common life and advantage (Prop. 37, Part IV.), and consequently (as we showed in Note 2, Prop. 37, Part IV.) he desires to live according to the ordinary decrees of the state. Therefore a man guided by reason desires, so as to live with more freedom, to regard the ordinary laws of the state. *Q.e.d.*

Note.—These and such things which we have shown of the true freedom of man have reference to fortitude, that is (Note, Prop. 59, Part III.), to courage and nobility. Nor do I think it worth while to show here separately all the properties of fortitude, and far less that a strong man hates no one, is enraged with no one, envies no one, is indignant with no one, despises no one, and is in no wise proud. For these points, and all which relate to the true life and religion, are shown with conviction from Prop. 37 and 46, Part IV., namely, that hatred should be overcome by love, and that every one led by reason desires for his fellows the good he desires for himself. To which must be added what we noted in the Note of Prop. 50, Part IV., and in other places, namely, that a strong man considers this above all things, that everything follows from the necessity of divine nature; and accordingly, whatever he thinks to be a nuisance or evil, and whatever, moreover, seems to him impious, horrible, unjust, or disgraceful, arises from the fact that he conceives these things in a disturbed, mutilated, and confused manner: and on this account he endeavours to conceive things as they are in themselves, and to remove obstacles from true knowledge, as, for example, hatred, rage, envy, derision, pride, and the other emotions of this kind which we have noted in the previous propositions: and therefore he endeavours as much as he can, as we said, to act well and rejoice. How far human virtue lends itself to the attainment of this, and what it is capable of, I shall show in the next part.

APPENDIX

What I have said in this part concerning the right manner of life is not so arranged that it can be seen at one glance, but has been proved by me in parts, for then I could easily prove one from another. I have determined, therefore, to collect the parts here and reduce them to their principal headings.

I. All our endeavours or desires follow from the necessity of our nature in such a manner that they can be understood either through this alone, as through their proximate cause, or in so far as we are a part of nature which cannot be adequately conceived through itself without other individuals.

II. Desires which follow from our nature in such a way that they can be understood through it alone are those which have reference to the mind in so far as this is conceived to consist of adequate ideas; the remaining desires have no reference to the mind save in so far as it conceives things inadequately, and their force and increase are not defined by human power, but by power which is outside us. Therefore the first are called actions, while the second, passions. For the former always indicate our power, and the latter, on the contrary, indicate our want of power and our mutilated knowledge.

III. Our actions, that is, those desires which are defined by the power or reason of man, are always good: the others can be both good and bad.

IV. It is therefore extremely useful in life to perfect as much as we can the intellect or reason, and of this alone does the happiness or blessedness of man consist: for blessedness (*beatitudo*) is nothing else than satisfaction of mind which arises from the intuitive knowledge of God. But to perfect the intellect is nothing else than to understand God and his attributes and actions which follow from the necessity of his nature. Wherefore the ultimate aim of a man who is guided by reason, that is, his greatest desire by which he endeavours to moderate all the others, is that which brings him to conceive adequately himself and all things which can come within the scope of his intelligence.

V. Accordingly no rational life is without intelligence, and things are only good in so far as they help man to enjoy intellectual life, which is defined intelligence (*intelligentia*). But those things which prevent a man from perfecting his reason and enjoying a rational life—these things, I say, alone we call evil.

VI. But inasmuch as all things of which man is the effecting cause are necessarily good, therefore nothing evil can happen to man save from external causes, namely, in so far as he is a part of the whole of nature, to whose laws human nature is forced to submit, and to agree with which it is compelled in almost infinite ways.

VII. Nor can it come to pass that man is not a part of nature and not follow its common order of things; but if he be thrown among individuals who agree with him in nature, by that very fact his power of acting is aided and fostered. And if, on the other hand, he be thrown among individuals who agree with him in no wise in nature, he shall scarcely be able to accommodate himself with them without a great change in his nature.

VIII. Whatever is granted in the nature of things which we judge to be evil, or capable of preventing us from existing and enjoying a rational life, we may remove from us in the safest and most certain way possible: and whatever, on the other hand, is granted which we judge to be good or useful for the preserving of our being and the enjoyment of rational life, we may seize and use in whatever way we please. And absolutely every one can do by the sovereign right of nature whatever he thinks will be of advantage to him.

IX. Nothing can agree more with the nature of anything

than the remaining individuals of the same species: and therefore (No. 7) nothing is granted more useful to man for preserving his being and enjoying rational life than man who is led by reason. Again, inasmuch as we know of nothing among individual things which is more excellent than man who is led by reason, therefore every one can show his skill and ingenuity in nothing better than in so educating men that they live according to the command of their own reason.

X. In so far as men are affected one towards the other with envy or any other emotion of hatred they are contrary reciprocally, and consequently they are the more to be feared the more power they have than the other individuals of nature.

XI. Minds are conquered not by arms, but by love and magnanimity.

XII. It is above all things useful to men that they unite their habits of life (*consuetudines*) and bind themselves together with such bonds by which they can most easily make one individual of them all, and to do those things especially which serve for the purpose of confirming friendship.

XIII. But for this skill and vigilance are required. For men are varied (for those are rare who live according to the rules prescribed by reason), and moreover they are generally envious and more prone to revenge than pity. It is a matter, therefore, of considerable force of mind to regard each one according to his disposition and to contain oneself and not imitate the emotions of others. But those who cavil at men and prefer rather to reprobate vices than to inculcate virtues, and who do not solidify but unloosen the minds of men— these, I say, are a nuisance both to themselves and to others. Wherefore many, owing to too great impatience of mind and a false zeal for religion, have preferred to live among beasts rather than among men: just as children or youths who cannot bear with equanimity the reproaches of their parents, run away to enlist and choose the inconveniences of war and the command of a tyrant rather than the conveniences of home and paternal admonition, and who will bear any kind of burden provided they may thereby spite their parents.

XIV. Therefore, although men are as a rule governed in everything by their desire or lust, yet from their common society or association many more advantages than disadvantages arise or follow. Wherefore it is but right to bear the injuries arising therefrom with equanimity, and to be zealous for those things which keep peace and friendship.

XV. The things which give birth to harmony or peace are those which have reference to justice, equity, and honourable dealing. For men are ill pleased not only when a thing is unjust or iniquitous, but also when it is disgraceful or when any one despises the customs received among them. But for attracting love those things are especially necessary which relate to religion and piety. On which points see Notes 1 and 2, Prop. 37, and Note, Prop. 46, and Note, Prop. 73, Part IV.

XVI. Harmony or peace is often born of fear, but then it is not trustworthy. Moreover, fear arises from weakness of the mind, and therefore does not appertain to the use of reason: nor does compassion, although it seems to bear in it a sort of piety.

XVII. Men, moreover, are won over by open-handedness (*largitas*), especially those who have not the wherewithal to purchase what is necessary for sustaining life. However, to give aid to every poor man is far beyond the reach of the wealth and power of every private man. For the riches of a private man are far too little for such a thing. Moreover, the ability and facility of approach of every man are far too limited for him to be able to unite all men to himself in friendship: for which reason the care of the poor is incumbent on society as a whole, and relates to the general advantage only.

XVIII. In accepting benefits and returning thanks our duty must be wholly different: concerning which see Note, Prop. 70, and Note, Prop. 71, Part IV.

XIX. Moreover, meretricious love, that is, the lust of generation, which arises from beauty, and absolutely all love which acknowledges any other cause than freedom of the mind, passes easily into hatred, unless—what is still worse—it be a sort of madness, and then it is fostered more by discord than by harmony (see Coroll., Prop. 31, Part III.).

XX. As for what concerns matrimony, it is certain that it is in concord with reason if the desire of uniting bodies is engendered not from beauty alone, but also from the love of bearing children and wisely educating them: and moreover,

if the love of either of them, that is, of husband or wife, has
for its cause not only beauty, but also freedom of mind.

XXI. Flattery also gives birth to peace or concord, but
only by means of the abhorrent crime of slavery or by means
of perfidy: none are more taken in by flattery than the proud,
who wish to be the first and are not.

XXII. There is in self-despising a false kind of piety and
religion; and although self-despising is contrary to pride,
yet one who despises himself is the nearest to a proud man
(see Note, Prop. 57, Part IV.).

XXIII. Shame also is conducive of concord or peace, but
only in those things which cannot be hidden. Again, as
shame is a sort of pain, it has no relation to the use of reason.

XXIV. The remaining emotions of pain towards men are
opposed to justice, equity, honourable life, piety, and religion,
and although indignation seems to be a species of equity, yet
life would be lawless in many a place where each one could
pass judgment concerning the actions of another and vindi-
cate his own or the right of another.

XXV. Courtesy (*modestia*), that is, the desire of pleasing
men which is determined by reason, has reference (as we said
in the Note of Prop. 37, Part IV.) to piety. But if it arises
from emotion, then it is ambition, or a desire whereby men,
under the false guise of piety, excite discords and seditions.
For he who desires to aid the others either by word or deed
so that they may enjoy the greatest good—he, I say, will
strive above all to win over their love to himself, and not
bring them to a state of wonderment so that this system may
receive his name or to give any cause absolutely for envy.
Moreover, in his common speech he will take care not to make
reference to vice and to speak very sparingly of human want
of power: but not at all so of human virtue or power, and in
what way it may be completely brought about that man
endeavours to live not from fear or aversion, but moved only
by an emotion of pleasure according to the dictate of reason,
as far as in them lies.

XXVI. Save men we do not know any individual thing in
nature in whose mind we may rejoice or which we may join
to us in bonds of friendship or any other kind of habit: and
therefore whatever exists in nature besides man, reason does
not postulate that we should preserve for our advantage, but
teaches us that we should preserve or destroy it according to

our various need, or adapt it in any manner we please to suit ourselves.

XXVII. The advantage we reap from things which are outside us, together with experience and knowledge which we acquire from the fact that we observe them and change them from one form to another, is the principal preservation of the body: and in this manner those things are especially useful which can so feed and nourish the body that all its parts can rightly perform their office. For the more the body is apt to be affected in many modes or to affect external bodies in many modes, the more apt is the mind for thinking (see Prop. 38 and 39, Part IV.). But there seem to be very few things of this kind in nature. Wherefore for the nourishment of the body as it is required it is necessary to use many foods of different nature: for the human body is composed of many parts of different nature which need continuous and varied nourishment so that the whole body may be equally fit to discharge all the duties which can follow from its nature, and consequently that the mind may be equally fit for the conception of many things.

XXVIII. But for preparing these things the force or strength of one man would scarcely suffice if men did not indulge in mutual exchange and aid. This exchange is now carried on by means of money. Whence it has come to pass that the image of money occupies the principal place in the mind of the vulgar, for they can scarcely imagine any kind of pleasure unless it be accompanied with the idea of money as the cause.

XXIX. Now this vice is only theirs who seek to acquire money, not from need nor by reason of necessity, but because they have learned the arts of gain wherewith to raise themselves to a splendid estate. They feed their bodies of course according to custom, but sparingly, for they think they lose as much of their goods as they spend on the nourishment of their body. But those who know the true use of money and moderate their desire of money to their requirements alone are content with very little.

XXX. Since, therefore, those things are good which aid the parts of the body to fulfil their duties, and since pleasure consists in the fact that man's power in so far as it consists of the mind or body is aided or increased—those things then which bring pleasure are good. But since things do not act with the end in view of giving us pleasure, and since their power of acting is not tempered according to our need, and moreover, since pleasure as a rule has reference to one part of the body rather than the rest, the most of our emotions (unless we have regard for reason and keep watch over them) and our desires also are excessive. To which must be added that we hold that first according to emotion which is pleasant in the present, nor can we estimate a future thing with the same emotion of mind (see Note, Prop. 44, and Note, Prop. 60, Part IV.).

XXXI. But superstition, on the contrary, seems to call that good which is brought on by pain and that bad which pleasure brings on. But as we have already said (see Note, Prop. 45, Part IV.), no one save an envious person takes pleasure in my want of power and inconvenience. For the greater emotion of pleasure we are affected with, the greater perfection we pass to, and consequently the more we partake of the divine nature: nor can pleasure ever be evil which is moderated by a true regard for our advantage. But he, on the other hand, who is led by fear and does what is good in order to avoid what is evil, is not led by reason (see Prop. 63, Part IV.).

XXXII. But human power is considerably limited and infinitely surpassed by the power of external causes, and therefore we have not absolute power of adapting things which are outside us for our usage. But we shall bear with equanimity those things which happen to us contrary to that which a regard for our advantage postulates, if we are conscious that we have performed our duty and cannot extend the power we have to such an extent as to avoid those things, and moreover, that we are a part of nature as a whole, whose order we follow. If we understand this clearly and distinctly, that part of us which is called our understanding, or rather intelligence, that is, the best part in us, will acquiesce in this entirely, and will endeavour to persist in that acquiescence. For in so far as we understand, we can desire nothing save that which is necessary, nor can we absolutely acquiesce in anything save what is true: and therefore in so far as we understand this rightly, the endeavour of the best part of us agrees with the order of the whole of nature.

FIFTH PART

CONCERNING THE POWER OF THE INTELLECT OR HUMAN FREEDOM

Preface

I PASS on at last to that part of the Ethics which concerns the manner or way which leads to liberty (*de modo sive via quæ ad libertatem ducit*). In this part then, concerning the power of reason, I shall endeavour to show what power reason has over the emotions, and moreover, what is mental liberty or blessedness (*mentis libertas seu beatitudo*): from which we shall see how far a wise man excels an ignorant. But in what manner or by what means the intellect must be perfected, and again, by what art the body must be completely cured so that it may perform its functions correctly, does not appertain to this part: for the latter relates to medicine and the former to logic. Here, therefore, I shall show, as I said, the power of the mind or reason, and above all things how great and of what kind is its power over the emotions to restrain and moderate them. For we have not complete command over our emotions, as we have already shown. The Stoics, however, were of opinion that the emotions depend absolutely on our free will, and that we have absolute command over them. But they were compelled by the outcry of experience, not by their principles, to confess that not little practice and zeal were required to restrain and moderate them. This some one has endeavoured to point out by the example (if I remember rightly) of two dogs, one a domestic dog and the other hunting: namely, that it can at length be brought about that the domestic dog hunts and the hunting dog refrains from hunting and chasing the hares. This opinion is not a little favoured by Descartes, for he held that the soul or mind was particularly united to a certain part of the brain, called the pineal gland, by means of which it feels all the movements that take place in the body and external objects, and which the mind by the very fact that it wishes can move in various ways. He held that this gland is suspended in the middle of the brain in such a way that it can be moved by the least motion of the animal spirits. He held, moreover, that this gland is suspended in the middle of the brain in as many ways as the animal spirits impinge on it, and moreover, that there are impressed on that gland as many marks as there were varied external objects propelling the animal spirits towards it: whence it comes about that if the gland is afterwards suspended by the will of the mind moving it in various ways, in this or that way in which it was at one time suspended by spirits driven in this or that way, then the gland drives away and determines the animal spirits in the same way as they were repulsed before by a similar suspension of the gland. He held, moreover, that every wish or will of the mind is united to a certain motion of the gland, *e.g.*, if any one has the wish to see a distant object, this will bring it about that the pupil is extended; but if he thought only of the dilatation of the pupil alone, it would profit him nothing to have the wish to see that thing, inasmuch as the motion of the gland which serves to impel the animal spirits towards the optic nerve in a convenient way for contracting or dilating the pupil, is not joined in nature to the wish to contract or dilate it, but with the wish to see objects near or far. He held, finally, that although each motion of this gland seems to be connected by nature to a certain one of our thoughts at the beginning of our lives, yet it could be joined through habit to others: this he endeavours to prove in the *Passions de l'Ame*, Part I., Art. 50.[1] Hereby he concludes that there is no mind so weak that it cannot, if well directed, acquire absolute power of its passions. For these as defined by him are perceptions or feelings or disturbances of the mind which have reference to it as species, and which are produced, preserved, and strengthened by some movement of the spirits (see Descartes' *Passions de l'Ame*, Part I., Art. 27). But since we can join each motion of the gland, and consequently of the spirits, to any will, the determination of the will depends

---

[1] *Passions de l'Ame*, by Renate Descartes, written by him in French, but now rendered in Latin for the benefit of other nations, in the city of Amsterdam, by H. D. M., 1656. Part I. On the passions in general, and as occasion demands on the whole nature of man. Part II. On the number and order of the passions, and an explanation of the six primary ones. Part III. On individual passions.

on our power alone. If, therefore, we determine our will by certain fixed decisions according to which we wish to direct the actions of our life, and unite the movements of the passions which we wish to have to these decisions, we shall acquire absolute dominion over our passions. This is the opinion of that illustrious man (as I gather it from his own words), which I would scarcely have believed to have been put forward by so great a man, were it less acute. I cannot sufficiently wonder that a philosophic man, who clearly stated that he would deduce nothing save from self-evident bases of argument, and that he would assert nothing save what he perceived clearly and distinctly—one, moreover, who so many times reproved the Schoolmen for wishing to explain obscure things by means of occult qualities, should take an hypothesis far more occult than all the occult qualities. What does he understand, I ask, by the union of mind and body? What clear and distinct conception, I say, has he of thought closely united with a certain particle of quantity or extension? Truly I should like him to explain this union through its proximate cause. But he conceived the mind so distinct from the body that he could not assign a cause for this union nor for the mind itself, but he had perforce to recur to the cause of the whole universe, that is, to God. Again, I should like to know what degree of motion can the mind impart to this pineal gland, and with what force can it hold it suspended? For I know not whether this gland can be acted upon more quickly or slowly by the mind than by the animal spirits, and whether the movements of the passions which we unite securely to certain firm decisions cannot be disjoined from them by causes appertaining to the body: from which it would follow that although the mind fixedly proposed to go out against dangers and had joined to this decision the motions of daring, yet at the sight of the peril the gland would be so suspended that the mind would only be able to think of flight. And clearly as there is no relation between will and motion, so also there can be no comparison between the power or strength of the mind and body; and consequently the strength of one cannot be determined by the strength of the other. Add to this that this gland is not found thus situated in the middle of the brain, which has such easy action all around and in such a number of ways, and that the nerves are not all extended to the cavities of the brain. Finally, I omit everything he asserts concerning the will and its liberty, since I have more than sufficiently shown that it is false. Therefore, inasmuch as the mind's power, as I showed above, is defined by intelligence alone, the remedies for the emotions, which I think every one experiences, but does not accurately observe nor distinctly see, we shall determine from mere knowledge of the mind and deduce therefrom all things which relate to its blessedness.

AXIOMS

I. If in the same subject two contrary actions are excited, a change must take place in both or in one of them until they cease to be contrary.

II. The power of the effect is defined by the power of its cause in so far as its essence is explained or defined through the essence of its cause. This axiom is clear from Prop. 7, Part III.

PROPOSITIONS

PROP. I. Just as thoughts and the ideas of things are arranged and connected in the mind, so the modifications of the body, or the images of things, are exactly arranged and connected in the body.

Proof.—The order and connection of ideas is the same as the order and connection of things (Prop. 7, Part II.), and *vice versâ*, the order and connection of things is the same (Coroll., Prop. 6 and 7, Part II.) as the order and connection of ideas. Wherefore just as the order and connection of ideas in the mind is made according to the order and connection of the modifications of the body (Prop. 18, Part II.), so *vice versâ* (Prop. 2, Part III.), the order and connection of the modifications of the body is made according as thoughts and the ideas of things are arranged and connected in the mind. *Q.e.d.*

PROP. II. If we remove disturbance of the mind or emotion from the thought of an external cause and unite it to other thoughts, then love or hatred towards the external cause, as well as waverings of the mind which arise from these emotions, are destroyed.

Proof.—Now that which constitutes the form of love or hatred is pleasure or pain accompanied by the idea of an external cause (Def. Emo. 6 and 7). When this then is removed, the form of love or hatred is also removed: and therefore these emotions and those which arise from them are destroyed. *Q.e.d.*

PROP. III. An emotion which is a passion ceases to be a passion as soon as we form a clear and distinct idea of it.

Proof.—An emotion which is a passion is a confused idea (Gen. Def. Emo.). If, therefore, we form a clear and distinct idea of this emotion, this idea will be distinguished from the emotion in so far as it has reference to the mind alone by reason alone (Prop. 21, Part II., with its Note): and therefore (Prop. 3, Part III.) the emotion will cease to be a passion. *Q.e.d.*

Corollary.—Therefore the more an emotion becomes known to us, the more it is within our power and the less the mind is passive to it.

PROP. IV. There is no modification of the body of which we cannot form some clear and distinct conception.

Proof.—Things which are common to all can only be adequately conceived (Prop. 38, Part II.): and therefore (Prop. 12, and Lemma 2, which is to be found after Prop. 13, Part II.) there is no modification of the body of which we cannot form some clear and distinct conception. *Q.e.d.*

Corollary.—Hence it follows that there is no emotion of which we cannot form some clear and distinct conception. For an emotion is the idea of a modification of the body (Gen. Def. Emo.), which on that account (prev. Prop.) must involve some clear and distinct conception.

Note.—Since there is nothing from which some effect does not follow (Prop. 36, Part I.), and whatever follows from an idea which is adequate in us we understand clearly and distinctly (Prop. 40, Part II.), it follows that every one has power of understanding himself and his emotions, if not absolutely at least in part clearly and distinctly, and consequently of bringing it about that he is less passive to them. For this purpose care must be taken especially that we understand clearly and distinctly each emotion as far as this may be possible, so that the mind may be determined by the emotion to think those things which it clearly and distinctly perceives and in which it acquiesces entirely: and thus the emotion is separated from the thought of an external cause and united to true thoughts. From which would happen not only that love, hatred, etc., would be destroyed (Prop. 2, Part V.), but also that appetites and desires which are wont to arise from such emotion could have no excess (Prop. 61, Part IV.). For it must be noted above all that it is one and the same appetite through which a man is said to be active and passive. E.g., we have shown that human nature is so disposed that each one desires that others should live according to his idea of life (see Note, Prop. 31, Part III.): and this desire in a man who is not guided by reason is a passion which is called ambition, and which differs very little from pride; and, on the contrary, in a man who is guided by reason it is an action or virtue which is called piety (see Note 1, Prop. 37, Part IV., and the second proof of that Prop.). And in this manner all appetites or desires are only passions in so far as they arise from inadequate ideas, and they are accredited to virtue when they are excited or generated by adequate ideas. For all desires by which we are determined to do anything can arise both from adequate and inadequate ideas (see Prop. 59, Part IV.). And this remedy for emotions (to return from my digression), which consists in a true knowledge of them, is excelled by nothing in our power we can think of, since no other power of the mind is granted than that of thinking and forming adequate ideas, as we showed above (Prop. 3, Part III.).

PROP. V. Emotion towards a thing which we imagine simply and not as necessary nor possible nor contingent, is, *cæteris paribus*, the greatest of all.

Proof.—Emotion towards a thing which we imagine to be free is greater than that towards one which is necessary (Prop. 49, Part III.), and consequently still greater than that towards a thing which we imagine as possible or contingent (Prop. 11, Part IV.). But to imagine a thing as free is nothing else than that we imagined it simply while we were ignorant of the causes by which it was determined for acting (from what we have shown in the Note of Prop. 35, Part II.). Therefore emotion towards a thing which we imagine simply is greater, *cæteris paribus*, than towards a thing necessary, possible, or contingent, and consequently the greatest. *Q.e.d.*

PROP. VI. In so far as the mind understands all things as necessary it has more power over the emotions or is less passive to them.

Proof.—The mind understands all things as necessary (Prop. 29, Part I.), and to be determined for existing and acting by the infinite connection of causes (Prop. 28, Part I.): and therefore (prev. Prop.) it brings it about that it is less passive to the emotions which arise from them and (Prop. 48, Part III.) it will be affected less towards them. *Q.e.d.*

Note.—The more this knowledge, namely, that things are necessary, is applied to individual things which we imagine more distinctly and vividly, the greater is this power of the mind over the emotions, which is borne witness to by experience. For we see the pain caused by the loss of some good to be lessened or mitigated as soon as he who lost it considers that it could have been preserved in no manner. Thus also we see that no one pities an infant for that it cannot talk, walk, reason, or lastly, that it lives so many years almost unconscious of self. But if most were born full grown and only one now and then an infant, then we should pity each infant: for then we should regard infancy not as a thing natural and necessary, but as a flaw or mishap in nature. And we could note many other examples of this kind.

PROP. VII. Emotions which arise or are excited by reason, if we regard time, are greater than those which are referred to individual things which we regard as absent.

Proof.—We do not regard a thing as absent by reason of the emotion with which we imagine it, but by reason of the fact that the body is affected by another emotion which cuts off the existence of that thing (Prop. 17, Part II.). Wherefore an emotion which is referred to a thing which we regard as absent is not of such a nature that surpasses and overcomes the other actions and power of man (concerning which see Prop. 6, Part IV.), but contrariwise is of such a nature that it can be hindered in some manner by those modifications which cut off the existence of its external cause (Prop. 9, Part IV.). But emotion which arises from reason has reference necessarily to the common properties of things (see def. reason in Note 2, Prop. 40, Part II.) which we always regard as present (for there can be nothing to cut off their present existence), and which we always imagine in the same manner (Prop. 38, Part II.). Wherefore such an emotion remains the same always, and consequently (Ax. 1, Part V.) emotions which are contrary to it, and which are not aided by their external causes, must more and more accommodate themselves with it until they are no longer contrary, and thus far emotion which arises from reason is the stronger. *Q.e.d.*

Prop. VIII. The more an emotion is excited by many causes concurring at the same time, the greater it will be.

Proof.—Many causes can do more at the same time than if they were fewer (Prop. 7, Part III.). And therefore (Prop. 5, Part IV.) the more an emotion is excited by many causes at the same time, the stronger it is. *Q.e.d.*

Note.—This proposition is clear also from Ax. 2 of this part.

Prop. IX. Emotion which has reference to many different causes which the mind regards at the same time as the emotion itself is less harmful, and we are less passive to it and less affected toward each cause than another emotion equally great which has reference to one alone or fewer causes.

Proof.—An emotion is bad or harmful only in so far as the mind is prevented by it from thinking as much as before (Prop. 26 and 27, Part IV.). And therefore that emotion by which the mind is determined for regarding many objects at the same time is less harmful than another equally great which detains the mind in the contemplation of one alone or fewer objects in such a manner that it cannot think of the others: which was the first point. Again, inasmuch as the essence of the mind, that is (Prop. 7, Part III.), its power, consists of thought alone (Prop. 11, Part III.), therefore the mind is less passive to an emotion by which it is determined for the regarding of many things than to an emotion equally great which holds the mind occupied in regarding one alone or fewer objects: which is the second point. Finally, this emotion (Prop. 48, Part III.), in so far as it has reference to many external causes, is less towards each one of them. *Q.e.d.*

Prop. X. As long as we are not assailed by emotions which are contrary to our nature we are able to arrange and connect the modifications of the body according to their intellectual order.

Proof.—The emotions which are contrary to our nature, that is (Prop. 30, Part IV.), which are evil, are evil in so far as they prevent the mind from understanding (Prop. 27, Part IV.). As long, then, as we are not assailed by emotions which are contrary to our nature, so long the mind's power by which it endeavours to understand things is not hindered; and therefore so long it has the power of forming clear and distinct ideas and of deducing certain ones from others (see Note 2, Prop. 40, and Note, Prop. 47, Part II.): and consequently so long (Prop. 1, Part V.) we have the power of arranging and connecting the modifications of the body according to their intellectual order. *Q.e.d.*

Note.—By this power of rightly arranging and connecting the modifications we can bring it to pass that we are not easily affected by evil emotions. For (Prop. 7, Part V.) greater force will be required to hinder emotions arranged and connected according to their intellectual order than if they were vague and uncertain. The best thing then we can bring to pass, as long as we have no perfect knowledge of our emotions, is to conceive some manner of living aright or certain rules of life, to commit them to memory, and to apply them continuously to the individual things which come in our way frequently in life, so that our imagination may be deeply affected with them and they may be always ready for us. *E.g.*, we placed among the rules of life (Prop. 46, Part IV., with its Note) that hatred must be overcome by love or nobleness, not requited by reciprocated hatred. But in order that this rule may be always ready for us when we need it, we must often think and meditate on the common injuries done to men, and in what manner and according to what method they may best be avoided by nobility of character. For thus we unite the image of the injury to the image of this rule, and it will always be ready for us (Prop. 18, Part II.) when an injury is done to us. If we always have in mind a regard for our true advantage and the good which follows from mutual friendship and common intercourse, and moreover, if we remember complete mental satisfaction (*animi acquiescentia*) arises from the right way of life (Prop. 52, Part IV.), and that men, like other things, act according to the necessity of nature—

then the injuries or hatred which are wont to arise from them would occupy a lesser part of the mind and would be easily overcome; or if rage which arises from the greatest injuries is not easily overcome, it will nevertheless be overcome, although not without much wavering of the mind, in a far less space of time than if we had not meditated on these things, as is clear from Prop. 6, 7, and 8 of this part. We must think of courage in the same manner in order to lay aside fear, that is, we must enumerate and imagine the common perils of life and in what manner they may best be avoided and overcome by courage. But let it be noted that we must always pay attention in the ordering of our thoughts and images (Coroll. Prop. 63, Part IV., and Prop. 59, Part III.) to those things which are good in each thing, so that we may be determined always for action by an emotion of pleasure. *E.g.*, if any one sees that he seeks honour too eagerly, let him think of the right use of it, to what end it should be sought, and by what means it may be acquired: and not of its abuse and vanity and the inconstancy of men, or of other things of this kind, of which no one ever thinks save from an unhealthy mind. For ambitious men assail themselves with such thoughts when they despair of attaining the honour which they long for, and while they utter forth their rage they appear wise. Wherefore it is certain that those are most desirous of honour or glory who cry out the loudest of its abuse and the vanity of the world. And this is not proper to the ambitious, but to all to whom fortune is unfavourable and who are powerless in mind. For a poor man who is greedy will not cease to talk of the abuse of money and the evils of riches: by which he does nothing else than show not only his own poverty, but also that he cannot bear to see others rich. Thus those who are badly received by their sweethearts think of nothing save the fickleness, deception, and the other often related faults of womankind, all of which, however, they immediately forget as soon as they are received again. He therefore who moderates his emotions and desires from a love of freedom—he, I say, endeavours as much as possible to obtain a knowledge of the virtues and their causes, and to fill his mind with that joy which arises from a true knowledge of them, and by no means to regard the vices of men, to disparage his fellows and rejoice in a false species of liberty. And he that has diligently observed what is said here (for it is not difficult) and makes use of it, will be able in a short space of time to direct his actions for the most part according to the direction of reason.

PROP. XI. The more any image has reference to many things, the more frequent it is, the more often it flourishes, and the more it occupies the mind.

Proof.—The more an image or emotion has reference to many things, the more causes there are by which it can be excited and cherished, all of which the mind (hypothesis) regards at the same time with the emotion. And therefore the emotion is more frequent or more often flourishes, and (Prop. 8, Part V.) it occupies the mind more. *Q.e.d.*

PROP. XII. The images of things are more easily joined to images which have reference to things which we understand clearly and distinctly than to others.

Proof.—Things which we clearly and distinctly understand are either the common properties of things or what we deduce from them (see def. reason in Note 2, Prop 40., Part II.), and consequently they are more often excited in us (prev. Prop.). And therefore it can more easily happen that we should regard things at the same time with these than with other things, and consequently (Prop. 18, Part II.) that they are associated with these more easily than with other things. *Q.e.d.*

PROP. XIII. The more an image is associated with many other things, the more often it flourishes.

Proof.—The more an image is associated with many other things, the more causes there are by which it can be excited. *Q.e.d.*

PROP. XIV. The mind can bring it to pass that all the modifications of the body or images of things have reference to the idea of God.

Proof.—There is no modification of the body of which the mind cannot form a clear and distinct conception (Prop. 4, Part V.). And therefore it can bring it to pass (Prop. 15, Part I.) that all the images have reference to the idea of God. *Q.e.d.*

PROP. XV. He who understands himself and his emotions

loves God, and the more so the more he understands himself
and his emotions.

Proof.—He who clearly and distinctly understands himself
and his emotions, rejoices (Prop. 53, Part III.) accompanied
with the idea of God (prev. Prop.).   And therefore (Def.
Emo. 6.) he loves God, and (by the same argument) the
more so the more he understands himself and his emotions.
Q.e.d.

Prop. XVI. This love towards God must occupy the mind
chiefly.

Proof.—This love is associated with all the modifications
of the body (Prop. 14, Part V.), by all of which it is cherished
(Prop. 15, Part V.).   And therefore (Prop. 11, Part V.) it
must chiefly occupy the mind.   *Q.e.d.*

Prop. XVII. God is free from passions, nor is he affected
with any emotion of pleasure or pain.

Proof.—All ideas, in so far as they have reference to God, are
true (Prop. 32, Part II.), that is (Def. 4, Part II.), they are
adequate: and therefore (Gen. Def. Emo.) God is without
passions.   Again, God cannot pass to a higher or a lower
perfection (Coroll. 2, Prop. 20, Part I.): and therefore (Def.
Emo. 2 and 3) he is affected with no emotion of pleasure or
pain.   *Q.e.d.*

Corollary.—God, to speak strictly, loves no one nor hates
any one.   For God (prev. Prop.) is affected with no emotion
of pleasure or pain, and consequently (Def. Emo. 6 and 7)
loves no one nor hates any one.

Prop. XVIII. No one can hate God.

Proof.—The idea of God in us is adequate and perfect
(Prop. 46 and 47, Part II.).   And therefore in so far as we
regard God we are active (Prop. 3, Part III.), and consequently (Prop. 59, Part III.) there can be no pain accompanied by the idea of God, that is (Def. Emo. 7), none can
hate God.   *Q.e.d.*

Corollary.—Love towards God cannot be changed into
hatred.

Note.—But it may be raised in objection to this, that while
we understand God as the cause of all things, by that very
fact we look to him as the cause of pain.   But to this I make
answer, that in so far as we understand the causes of pain

it ceases to be a passion (Prop. 3, Part V.), that is (Prop. 59, Part III.), thus far it ceases to be pain: and therefore in so far as we understand God to be the cause of pain we rejoice.

PROP. XIX. He who loves God cannot endeavour to bring it about that God should love him in return.

Proof.—If man desired this, he would therefore desire (Coroll., Prop. 17, Part V.) that the God whom he loves should not be God, and consequently (Prop. 19, Part III.) he would desire to be pained, which (Prop. 28, Part III.) is absurd. Therefore he who loves God, etc. *Q.e.d.*

PROP. XX. This love towards God cannot be polluted by an emotion either of envy or jealousy, but it is cherished the more, the more we imagine men to be bound to God by this bond of love.

Proof.—This love towards God is the greatest good which we can desire according to the dictate of reason (Prop. 28, Part IV.), and it is common to all men (Prop. 36, Part IV.), and we desire that all should enjoy it (Prop. 37, Part IV.). And therefore (Def. Emo. 26) it cannot be stained by the emotion of envy, nor again by the emotion of jealousy (Prop. 18, Part V., and the def. jealousy, which see in Note, Prop. 35, Part III.); but, on the other hand (Prop. 31, Part III.), it must be cherished the more, the more men we imagine to enjoy it. *Q.e.d.*

Note.—We can then show in the same manner that there is no emotion which is directly contrary to this love by which this love can be destroyed: and therefore we can conclude that this love towards God is the most constant of all emotions, nor can it be destroyed in so far as it has reference to the body, save with the body itself. But of what nature it may be, in so far as it has reference to the mind alone, we shall see later. In these propositions I have comprehended all the remedies for the emotions, or everything which the mind considered in itself can do to restrain the emotions. From which it is apparent that the mind's power over the emotions consists: 1st. In the knowledge of the emotions (see Note, Prop. 4, Part V.). 2nd. In the fact that the emotions are separated from the thought of the external cause which we imagine confusedly (see Prop. 2, with its Note, and Prop. 4, Part V.). 3rd. In time in which the emotions which have reference to things which we understand surpass those which have reference to things which we conceive confusedly and in a mutilated manner (see Prop. 7, Part V.). 4th. In a multitude of causes by which the emotions which have reference to the common properties of things or to God are fostered (see Prop. 9 and 11, Part V.). 5th. Finally, in the order in which the mind can arrange and connect one to the other its emotions (see Note, Prop. 10, and Prop. 12, 13, and 14, Part V.).

But in order that this power of the mind over the emotions may be better understood, it must first be noted that emotions are called great by us when we compare the emotion of one man with that of another, and when we see one man to be more assailed by an emotion than another man, or when we compare one with the other the emotions of one and the same man, and find him to be affected or moved more by one emotion than by another. For (Prop. 5, Part IV.) the force of any emotion is defined by the power of an external cause compared with our own. But the mind's power is defined by knowledge alone: its weakness or passion is estimated by privation of knowledge, that is, by that whereby ideas are said to be inadequate. From which it follows that that mind is most passive whose greatest part is constituted by inadequate ideas, so that it is characterised by passivity rather than activity: and that, on the other hand, is most active which is constituted for the most part of adequate ideas in such a way that although there are as many inadequate ideas in this as in the former, yet it is characterised rather through those which have reference to human virtue than through those which show human weakness. Again, it is to be noted that these unhealthy states of mind and misfortunes owe their origin for the most part to excessive love for a thing that is liable to many variations, and of which we may never seize the mastery. For no one is anxious or cares about anything that he does not love, nor do injuries, suspicions, enmities arise from anything else than love towards a thing of which no one is truly master. From this we can easily conceive what a clear and distinct knowledge, and principally that third kind of knowledge (concerning which see Note, Prop. 47, Part II.), whose basis is the knowledge of God, can do with the emotions, namely, that if it does not remove them entirely in so far as they are passions (Prop. 3, with Note, Prop. 4,

Part V.), at least it brings it about that they constitute the least possible part of the mind (see Prop. 14, Part V.). Moreover, it gives rise to a love towards a thing immutable and eternal (Prop. 15, Part V.), and of which we are in truth masters (Prop. 45, Part II.), and which cannot be polluted by any evils which are in common love, but which can become more and more powerful (Prop. 15, Part V.) and occupy the greatest part of the mind (Prop. 16, Part V.) and deeply affect it. And thus I have done with all that regards this present life. For what I said in the beginning of this note, that I comprehended in these few words the remedies against the emotions, every one can easily see who pays any attention to what we have said in this note, and at the same time to the definitions of the mind and its emotions, and finally to Prop. 1 and 3, Part III. For it is already time that I should pass to those points which appertain to the duration of the mind without relation to the body.

PROP. XXI. The mind can imagine nothing nor recollect past things save while in the body.

Proof.—The mind does not express the actual existence of its body nor conceives the modifications of the body to be actual save while in the body (Coroll., Prop. 8, Part II.), and consequently (Prop. 26, Part II.) it conceives no body as actually existing save while its own body exists. And thus it can imagine nothing (see def. imagination in Note, Prop. 17, Part II.) nor recollect past things save while in the body (see def. memory in Note, Prop. 18, Part II.). *Q.e.d.*

PROP. XXII. In God, however, there is necessarily granted the idea which expresses the essence of this or that human body under the species of eternity.

Proof.—God is not only the cause of this or that human body's existence, but also their essence (Prop. 25, Part I.), which therefore must necessarily be conceived through the essence of God (Ax. 4, Part I.), and that under a certain eternal necessity (Prop. 16, Part I.): and this conception must necessarily be granted in God (Prop. 3, Part II.). *Q.e.d.*

PROP. XXIII. The human mind cannot be absolutely destroyed with the human body, but there is some part of it that remains eternal.

Proof.—There is necessarily in God the conception or idea

which expresses the essence of the human body (prev. Prop.),
which therefore is something necessarily which appertains to
the essence of the human mind (Prop. 13, Part II.).   But we
attribute to the human mind no duration which can be defined
by time, save in so far as it expresses the actual essence of
the human body, which is explained by means of duration
and is defined by time, that is (Coroll., Prop. 8, Part II.), we
do not attribute duration save as long as the body lasts.
But as there is nevertheless something else which is conceived
under a certain eternal necessity through the essence of God,
this something will be necessarily the eternal part which
appertains to the essence of the mind.   *Q.e.d.*

Note.—This idea, as we have said, which expresses under
a certain species of eternity the essence of the body, is a
certain mode of thought which appertains to the essence of
the mind, and which is necessarily eternal.   It cannot happen,
however, that we can remember that we existed before our
bodies, since there are no traces of it in the body, neither
can eternity be defined by time nor have any relation to time.
But nevertheless we feel and know that we are eternal.   For
the mind no less feels those things which it conceives in understanding than those which it has in memory.   For the eyes
of the mind by which it sees things and observes them are
proofs.   Although, therefore, we do not remember that we
existed before, we feel nevertheless that our mind in so far
as it involves the essence of the body under the species of
eternity is eternal, and its existence cannot be defined by
time or explained by duration.   Our mind therefore can only
be said to last, and its existence can be defined by a certain
time only in so far as it involves the actual existence of the
body, and thus far only it has the power of determining the
existence of things by time and of conceiving them under
the attribute of duration.

PROP. XXIV. The more we understand individual things,
the more we understand God.

Proof.—This is clear from Prop. 25, Part I.

PROP. XXV. The greatest endeavour of the mind and its
greatest virtue is to understand things by the third class of
knowledge.

Proof.—The third class of knowledge proceeds from the
adequate idea of certain attributes of God to the adequate

knowledge of the essence of things (see its def. in Note 2, Prop. 40, Part II.), and the more we understand things in this manner, the more (prev. Prop.) we understand God. And therefore (Prop. 28, Part IV.) the greatest virtue of the mind, that is (Def. 8, Part IV.), the mind's power or nature, or (Prop. 7, Part III.) its greatest endeavour, is to understand things according to the third class of knowledge.   *Q.e.d.*

PROP. XXVI. The more apt the mind is to understand things by the third class of knowledge, the more it desires to understand things by this class of knowledge.

Proof.—This is clear. For in so far as we conceive the mind to be apt to understand things by this kind of knowledge, thus far we conceive it as determined to understand things by the same kind of knowledge, and consequently (Def. Emo. 1) the more apt the mind is for this, the more it desires it.   *Q.e.d.*

PROP. XXVII. From this third class of knowledge the greatest possible mental satisfaction arises.

Proof.—The greatest virtue of the mind is to know God (Prop. 28, Part IV.), or to understand according to the third class of knowledge (Prop. 25, Part V.): and this virtue is the greater according as the mind knows more things by this class of knowledge (Prop. 24, Part V.). And therefore he who knows things according to this class of knowledge, passes to the greatest state of perfection, and consequently (Def. Emo. 2) he is affected with the greatest pleasure, and that (Prop. 43, Part II.) accompanied by the idea of himself and his virtue: and therefore (Def. Emo. 25) from this kind of knowledge the greatest satisfaction possible arises.   *Q.e.d.*

PROP. XXVIII. The endeavour or desire of knowing things according to the third class of knowledge cannot arise from the first but the second class of knowledge.

Proof.—This proposition is self-evident. For whatever we understand clearly and distinctly, we understand either through itself or through something else that is conceived through itself: that is, the ideas which are distinct and clear in us, or which have reference to the third class of knowledge (Note 2, Prop. 40, Part II.), cannot follow from ideas mutilated and confused which (same Note) have reference to the first class of knowledge, but from adequate ideas or (same Note) from the second and third class of knowledge. And therefore (Def. Emo. 1) the desire of knowing things by the third class of knowledge cannot arise from knowledge of the first class, but only of the second. *Q.e.d.*

Prop. XXIX. Whatever the mind understands under the species of eternity, it does not understand owing to the fact that it conceives the actual present existence of the body, but owing to the fact that it conceives the essence of the body under the species of eternity.

Proof.—In so far as the mind conceives the present existence of its body, thus far it conceives duration which can be determined by time, and thus far only it has the power of conceiving things with relation to time (Prop. 21, Part V., and Prop. 26, Part II.). But eternity cannot be explained through time (Def. 8, Part I., and its explanation). Therefore the mind thus far has not the power of conceiving things under the species of eternity, but inasmuch as it is the nature of reason to conceive things under the species of eternity (Coroll. 2, Prop. 44, Part II.), and it appertains to the nature of the mind to conceive the essence of the body under the species of eternity (Prop. 23, Part V.), and save these two nothing else appertains to the essence of the mind (Prop. 13, Part II.). Therefore this power of conceiving things under the species of eternity does not appertain to the mind save in so far as it conceives the essence of the body under the species of eternity. *Q.e.d.*

Note.—Things are conceived as actual in two ways by us, either in so far as we conceive them to exist with relation to certain time and space, or in so far as we conceive them to be contained in God and to follow from the necessity of divine nature. But those which are conceived in this second manner as true or real we conceive under a certain species of eternity, and their ideas involve the eternal and infinite essence of God, as we showed in Prop. 45, Part II.: see also its Note.

Prop. XXX. The human mind in so far as it knows itself and its body under the species of eternity, thus far it necessarily has knowledge of God, and knows that it exists in God and is conceived through God.

Proof.—Eternity is the essence of God in so far as this necessarily involves existence (Def. 8, Part I.). Therefore

to conceive things under the species of eternity is to conceive
them in so far as they are conceived through the essence of
God as real entities, or in so far as they involve existence
through the essence of God. And therefore our mind, in so
far as it conceives itself and its body under a species of
eternity, has thus far necessarily a knowledge of God, and
knows, etc. *Q.e.d.*

PROP. XXXI. The third kind of knowledge depends on
the mind as its formal cause in so far as the mind is eternal.

Proof.—The mind conceives nothing under the species of
eternity save in so far as it conceives the essence of its body
under the species of eternity (Prop. 29, Part V.), that is
(Prop. 21 and 23, Part V.), save in so far as it is eternal.
And therefore (prev. Prop.) in so far as it is eternal it has
knowledge of God, and this is necessarily adequate (Prop. 46,
Part II.): and therefore the mind, in so far as it is eternal, is
apt for understanding all those things which can follow from
a given knowledge of God (Prop. 40, Part II.), that is, for
understanding things by the third class of knowledge (see its
def. in Note 2, Prop. 40, Part II.): and therefore the mind
(Def. 1, Part III.), in so far as it is eternal, is the adequate
or formal cause of this. *Q.e.d.*

Note.—The more advanced then every one is in this class
of knowledge, the more conscious he is of himself and God,
that is, the more perfect or blessed he is, which shall be quite
clear from the following propositions. But it must be noted
here that although we are certain that the mind is eternal in
so far as it conceives things under the species of eternity,
we shall consider it in order that what we wish to show may be
explained the more easily and better understood, as if it had
just begun to exist and just begun to understand things under
the species of eternity, as thus far we have done: which we
may do without any danger of error, if we take care to conclude nothing save from premises that are quite obvious.

PROP. XXXII. Whatever we understand according to the
third class of knowledge we are pleased with, and that accompanied with the idea of God as the cause.

Proof.—From this knowledge follows the greatest possible
satisfaction of mind, that is (Def. Emo. 25), pleasure arises,
and that accompanied by the idea of the mind (Prop. 27,

Part IV.), and consequently (Prop. 30, Part V.) accompanied also by the idea of God as the cause. *Q.e.d.*

Corollary.—From the third kind of knowledge arises necessarily the intellectual love of God. For from this kind of knowledge arises (prev. Prop.) pleasure accompanied by the idea of God as the cause, that is (Def. Emo. 6), the love of God, not in so far as we imagine him present (Prop. 29, Part V.), but in so far as we understand God to be eternal: this is what I call intellectual love towards God.

PROP. XXXIII. The intellectual love towards God which arises from the third kind of knowledge is eternal.

Proof.—The third kind of knowledge (Prop. 31, Part V. and Ax. 3, Part I.) is eternal: and therefore (same Ax., Part I.) love which arises from it is also necessarily eternal. *Q.e.d.*

Note.—Although this love towards God has no beginning (prev. Prop.), it has nevertheless all the perfections of love, just as if it had arisen as in the corollary of the previous proposition I supposed. Nor is there any difference here, save that the mind has had from eternity those same perfections which we have now supposed to accrue to it, and that accompanied by the idea of God as the eternal cause. For if pleasure consist in the transition to a greater state of perfection, blessedness clearly consists in the fact that the mind is endowed with that perfection.

PROP. XXXIV. The mind is only liable to emotions which are referred to passions while the body lasts.

Proof.—Imagination is the idea with which the mind regards anything as present (see its def. in Note, Prop. 17, Part II.), which nevertheless indicates rather the present disposition of the human body than the nature of the external body (Coroll. 2, Prop. 16, Part II.). Therefore emotion is imagination (Gen. Def. Emo.) in so far as it indicates the present disposition of the body: and therefore (Prop. 21, Part V.) the mind is only liable to emotions which are referred to passions while the body lasts. *Q.e.d.*

Corollary.—Hence it follows that no love save intellectual love is eternal.

Note.—If we pay attention to the common opinion of men, we shall see that they are conscious of the eternity of their minds; but they confuse eternity with duration, and attribute it to imagination or memory, which they believe to remain after death.

PROP. XXXV. God loves himself with infinite intellectual love.

Proof.—God is absolutely infinite (Def. 6, Part I.), that is (Def. 6, Part II.), the nature of God enjoys infinite perfection, and that (Prop. 3, Part II.) accompanied by the idea of himself, that is (Prop. 11 and Ax. 1, Part I.), by the idea of his cause, and this is what we said to be intellectual love in Coroll., Prop. 32, Part V.

PROP. XXXVI. The mental intellectual love towards God is the very love of God with which God loves himself, not in so far as he is infinite, but in so far as he can be expressed through the essence of the human mind considered under the species of eternity, that is, mental intellectual love towards God is part of the infinite love with which God loves himself.

Proof.—This mental love must be referred to the actions of the mind (Coroll., Prop. 32, Part V., and Prop. 3, Part III.), which therefore is an action with which the mind regards itself accompanied by the idea of God as a cause (Prop. 32, Part V., and its Note), that is (Coroll., Prop. 25, Part I., and Coroll., Prop. 11, Part II.), an action by which God, in so far as he may be expressed through the human mind, regards himself accompanied by the idea of himself. And therefore (prev. Prop.) this mental love is part of the infinite love with which God loves himself. *Q.e.d.*

Corollary.—Hence it follows that God, in so far as he loves himself, loves men, and consequently that the love of God for men and the mind's intellectual love towards God is one and the same thing.

Note.—From this we clearly understand in what consists our salvation, blessedness, or liberty (*salus nostra seu beatitudo seu libertas*), namely, in the constant and eternal love for God, or in the love of God for men. And this love or blessedness is called in the Scriptures " glory "— not without reason. For whether this love has reference to God or the mind, it can rightly be called mental satisfaction, which in truth cannot be distinguished from glory (Def. Emo. 25 and 30). For in so far as it has reference to God it is (Prop. 35, Part V.) pleasure, if I may use this term, accompanied by the idea of himself, just as it is in so far as it has reference to the mind

(Prop. 27, Part V.).   Again, in as much as the essence of our mind consists of knowledge alone, the beginning and basis of which is God (Prop. 15, Part I., and Note, Prop. 47, Part II.), it is hence quite clear to us in what manner and for what reason our mind follows with regard to essence and existence from divine nature and continually depends on God.   I have thought it worth while to note this in order that I may show by this example how much the knowledge of individual things which I called intuition or knowledge of the third kind (see Note 2, Prop. 40, Part II.) is advanced, and more powerful than knowledge which I called universal or of the second class.   For although I showed in the first part in general that all things (and consequently the human mind) depend on God with regard to essence and existence, that proof, though perfectly legitimate and placed beyond the reach of doubt, does not affect the mind in the same manner as when it is concluded from the essence of any individual thing which we say depends on God.

PROP. XXXVII. There is nothing in nature which is contrary to this intellectual love or which can remove it.

Proof.—This intellectual love follows necessarily from the nature of the mind in so far as it is considered as an eternal truth through the nature of God (Prop. 33 and 29, Part V.). If, therefore, there be anything contrary to this, it must be contrary to what is true, and consequently whatever could remove this love would bring it about that what is true should be made false, which (as is self-evident) is absurd. Therefore there is nothing in nature, etc.   *Q.e.d.*

Note.—The axiom of the fourth part relates to individual things in so far as they are considered with relation to certain time and place, of which I think no one will doubt.

PROP. XXXVIII. The more the mind understands things by the second and third kinds of knowledge, the less it will be passive to emotions which are evil, and the less it will fear death.

Proof.—The essence of the mind consists of knowledge (Prop. 11, Part II.).   The more things then the mind understands by the second and third kinds of knowledge, the greater will be that part of it that remains (Prop. 29 and 23, Part V.), and consequently (prev. Prop.) the greater will be the part of it that is not touched by emotions which are contrary to

our nature, that is (Prop. 30, Part IV.), which are evil. The
more then the mind understands things by the second and
third kinds of knowledge, the greater will be that part of it
which remains unhurt, and consequently it will be less subject to emotions, etc. *Q.e.d.*

Note.—Hence we understand what I touched on in Note,
Prop. 39, Part IV., and which I promised to explain in this
part, namely, that death is the less harmful the more the
mind's knowledge is clear and distinct, and consequently the
more the mind loves God. Again, inasmuch as (Prop. 27,
Part V.) from the third kind of knowledge arises the greatest
possible satisfaction, it follows that the human mind may
be of such a nature that that part of it which we showed to
perish with the body may be of no moment to it in respect
to what remains. But I shall deal with that more fully soon.

PROP. XXXIX. He who has a body capable of many
things, has a mind of which the greater part is eternal.

Proof.—He who has a body apt for doing many things is
less assailed by emotions which are evil (Prop. 38, Part IV.),
that is (Prop. 30, Part IV.), by emotions which are contrary
to our nature. And therefore (Prop. 10, Part V.) it has the
power of arranging and connecting the modifications of the
body according to intellectual order, and consequently of
bringing it to pass (Prop. 14, Part V.) that all the modifications of the body have reference to the idea of God, from
which it follows (Prop. 15, Part V.) that he is affected with
love towards God, and this love must occupy or constitute
the greatest part of his mind (Prop. 16, Part V.): and therefore (Prop. 33, Part V.) he has a mind of which the greatest
part is eternal. *Q.e.d.*

Note.—Inasmuch as human bodies are capable of many
things, there is no doubt but that they may be of such a
nature that they may be referred to minds which have a great
knowledge of themselves and God, and of which the greatest
or principal part is eternal, and therefore that they should
scarcely fear death. But in order that these points may be
more clearly understood, it must be remarked here that we
live subject to continual variation, and according as we
change into a better or worse state we are called happy
(*felices*) or unhappy (*infelices*). For he who passes from
being an infant or child into being a corpse, is said to be un-

happy, while, on the other hand, he is said to be happy who is enabled to live through the whole period of life with a healthy mind in a healthy body. And in truth, he who has a body, as, for example, an infant or child capable of the least number of things and mostly dependent on external causes, has a mind which, considered in itself, is conscious scarcely of itself, of God, or things: whereas he who has a body capable of many things has a mind which, considered in itself, is very conscious of itself, of God, and things. In this life then we principally endeavour to change the body of an infant, in so far as its nature allows and is conducive thereto, so that it is capable of many things, and so that it is referred to a mind which is most conscious of God, itself, and other things: or so that all that which has reference to its memory or imagination should be scarcely of any moment whatever with respect to its intellect, as I said in the Note, prev. Prop.

PROP. XL. The more perfection anything has, the more active and the less passive it is; and contrariwise, the more active it is, the more perfect it becomes.

Proof.—The more perfect anything is, the more reality it has (Def. 6, Part II.), and consequently (Prop. 3, Part III., with its Note) it is more active and less passive: which proof can proceed in an inverted order; from which it may follow that a thing is more perfect the more active it is. *Q.e.d.*

Corollary.—Hence it follows that the part of the mind which remains, of whatever size it is, is more perfect than the rest. For the eternal part of the mind (Prop. 23 and 29, Part V.) is the intellect through which alone we are said to act (Prop. 3, Part III.); but that part which we see to perish is the imagination (Prop. 21, Part V.), through which alone we are said to be passive (Prop. 3, Part III., and Gen. Def. Emo.). And therefore (prev. Prop.) the first part, of whatever size it may be, is more perfect than the other. *Q.e.d.*

Note.—This is what I had determined to show concerning the mind in so far as it is considered without relation to the existence of the body. From this and from Prop. 21, Part I., and other propositions, it is apparent that our mind, in so far as it understands, is an eternal mode of thinking, which is determined by another eternal mode of thinking, and this one again by another, and so on to infinity: so that they all constitute at the same time the eternal and infinite intellect of God.

PROP. XLI. Although we did not know that our mind is eternal, we would hold before all things piety and religion, and absolutely all things which we have shown in Part IV., to have reference to courage and nobility.

Proof.—The first and only basis of virtue or a system of right living is (Coroll., Prop. 22 and 24, Part IV.) the seeking of what is useful to oneself. But to determine these things which reason dictates to be useful to us, we had no regard for the eternity of the mind, which we have only considered in this fifth part. Therefore, although we were ignorant at that time that the mind is eternal, yet we held those things first which we showed to have reference to courage and nobleness. And therefore, though we were ignorant of it now, we should hold first these precepts of reason. *Q.e.d.*

Note.—The general notion of the vulgar seems to be quite the contrary. For most seem to think that they are free in so far as they may give themselves up to lust, and that they lose their right in so far as they are obliged to live according to the divine laws. They therefore think that piety, religion, and all things which have reference to fortitude of mind are burdens which after death they will lay aside, and hope to receive a reward for their servitude, that is, their piety and religion. Not by this hope alone, but also, and even principally, by the fear of suffering dreadful punishments after death, are they induced to live, as far as their feebleness and weak-mindedness allows them, according to the divine laws; and if this hope or fear were not in men, but, on the other hand, if they thought that their minds were buried with their bodies, and that there did not remain for the wretches worn out with the burden of piety the hope of longer life, they would return to life according to their own ideas, and would direct everything according to their lust, and obey fortune rather than themselves. This seems no less absurd to me than if a man, when he discovered that he could not keep his body alive for ever with wholesome food, should straightway seek to glut himself with poison and deadly foods; or that a man, when he discovered that his mind was not eternal or immortal, should prefer to live without any mind at all: this all seems so absurd to me that it scarcely deserves to be refuted.

PROP. XLII. Blessedness is not the reward of virtue, but

virtue itself: nor should we rejoice in it for that we restrain our lusts, but, on the contrary, because we rejoice therein we can restrain our lusts.

Proof.—Blessedness consists of love towards God (Prop. 36, Part V., and its Note), and this love arises from the third kind of knowledge (Coroll., Prop. 32, Part V.). And therefore this love (Prop. 59 and 3, Part III.) must be referred to the mind in so far as it is active, and therefore it is virtue itself (Def. 8, Part IV.): which is the first point. Again, the more the mind rejoices in this divine love or blessedness, the more it understands (Prop. 32, Part V.), that is (Coroll., Prop. 3, Part V.), the more power it has over the emotions, and (Prop. 38, Part V.) the less passive it is to emotions which are evil. And therefore, by the very fact that the mind rejoices in this divine love or blessedness, it has the power of restraining lusts, inasmuch as human power to restrain lusts consists of intellect alone. Therefore no one rejoices in blessedness because he restrained lusts, but, on the contrary, the power of restraining lusts arises from blessedness itself. *Q.e.d.*

Note.—Thus I have completed all I wished to show concerning the power of the mind over emotions or the freedom of the mind. From which it is clear how much a wise man is in front of and how stronger he is than an ignorant one, who is guided by lust alone. For an ignorant man, besides being agitated in many ways by external causes, never enjoys one true satisfaction of the mind: he lives, moreover, almost unconscious of himself, God, and things, and as soon as he ceases to be passive, ceases to be. On the contrary, the wise man, in so far as he is considered as such, is scarcely moved in spirit: he is conscious of himself, of God, and things by a certain eternal necessity, he never ceases to be, and always enjoys satisfaction of mind. If the road I have shown to lead to this is very difficult, it can yet be discovered. And clearly it must be very hard when it is so seldom found. For how could it be that it is neglected practically by all, if salvation were close at hand and could be found without difficulty? But all excellent things are as difficult as they are rare.

TREATISE ON THE CORRECTION OF THE UNDERSTANDING

(tractatus de intellectus emendatione)

AND ON THE WAY IN WHICH IT MAY BE DIRECTED TOWARDS A TRUE KNOW-LEDGE OF THINGS

TREATISE ON THE CORRECTION OF THE UNDERSTANDING

(*tractatus de intellectus emendatione*)

AND ON THE WAY IN WHICH IT MAY BE DIRECTED TOWARDS A TRUE KNOWLEDGE OF THINGS

I. On the Good Things which Men desire for the most Part

1. After experience had taught me that all things which frequently take place in ordinary life are vain and futile; when I saw that all the things I feared and which feared me had nothing good or bad in them save in so far as the mind was affected by them, I determined at last to inquire whether there might be anything which might be truly good and able to communicate its goodness, and by which the mind might be affected to the exclusion of all other things: I determined, I say, to inquire whether I might discover and acquire the faculty of enjoying throughout eternity continual supreme happiness. 2. I say " I determined at last, " for at the first sight it seemed ill advised to lose what was certain in the hope of attaining what was uncertain. I could see the many advantages acquired from honour and riches, and that I should be debarred from acquiring these things if I wished seriously to investigate a new matter, and if perchance supreme happiness was in one of these I should lose it; if, on the other hand, it were not placed in them and I gave them the whole of my attention, then also I should be wanting in it. 3. I therefore turned over in my mind whether it might be possible to arrive at this new principle, or at least at the certainty of its existence, without changing the order and common plan of my life: a thing which I had often attempted in vain. For the things which most often happen in life and are esteemed as the greatest good of all, as may be gathered from their works, can be reduced to these three

headings: to wit, Riches (*divitiæ*), Fame (*honor*), and Pleasure (*libido*). With these three the mind is so engrossed that it cannot scarcely think of any other good. 4. As for pleasure, the mind is so engrossed in it that it remains in a state of quiescence as if it had attained supreme good, and this prevents it from thinking of anything else. But after that enjoyment follows pain, which, if it does not hold the mind suspended, disturbs and dullens it. The pursuit of fame and riches also distracts the mind not a little, more especially when they are sought for their own sake, inasmuch as they are thought to be the greatest good.[1] 5. By fame the mind is far more distracted, for it is supposed to be always good in itself, and as an ultimate aim to which all things must be directed. Again, there is not in these, as there is in pleasure, repentance subsequently, but the more one possesses of either of them, the more the pleasure is increased and consequently the more one is encouraged to increase them; but, on the other hand, if at any time our hope is frustrated, then there arises in us the deepest pain. Fame has also this great drawback, that if we pursue it we must direct our lives in such a way as to please the fancy of men, avoiding what they dislike and seeking what is pleasing to them.

6. When I saw then that all these things stood in the way to prevent me from giving my attention to a search for something new, nay, that they were so opposed to it that one or the other had to be passed by, I was constrained to inquire which would be more useful to me; for as I said, I seemed to wish to lose what was certain for what was uncertain. But after I had considered the matter for some time, I found in the first place that if I directed my attention to the new quest, abandoning the others, I should be abandoning a good uncertain in its nature, as we can easily gather from what has been said, to seek out a good uncertain not in its nature (for I was seeking a fixed good), but only uncertain in the possibility of success. 7. But by continuous consideration I came at last to see that if I could only deliberate on the matter from within I should avoid a certain evil for a certain

---

[1] This might be more fully and distinctly explained by distinguishing riches according as they are sought for their own sake—for the sake of honour, pleasure, health, or the advancement of the arts and sciences. But that must be reserved for its own place, for it is not the place here to inquire into this more accurately.—*Sp.*

good. For I saw myself in the midst of a very great peril and obliged to seek a remedy, however uncertain, with all my energy: like a sick man seized with a deadly disease, who sees death straight before him if he does not find some remedy, is forced to seek it, however uncertain, with all his remaining strength, for in that is all his hope placed. But all those remedies which the vulgar follow not only avail nothing for our preservation, but even prevent it, and are often the cause of the death of those who possess them, and are always the cause of the death of those who are possessed by them.[1]

8. For there are many examples of men who have suffered persecution even unto death for the sake of their riches, and also of men who, in order to amass wealth, have exposed themselves to so many perils that at last they have paid the penalty of death for their stupidity. Nor are the examples less numerous of those who have suffered in the most wretched manner to obtain or defend their honour. Finally, the examples are innumerable of those who have hastened death upon themselves by too great a desire for pleasure. 9. These evils seem to have arisen from the fact that the whole of happiness or unhappiness is dependent on this alone: on the quality of the object to which we are bound by love. For the sake of something which no one loves, strife never arises, there is no pain if it perishes, no envy if it is possessed by some one else, nor fear, nor hatred, and, to put it all briefly, no commotions of the mind at all: for all these are consequences only of the love of those things which are perishable, such as those things of which we have just spoken. 10. But the love towards a thing eternal and infinite alone feeds the mind with pleasure, and it is free from all pain; so it is much to be desired and to be sought out with all our might. For I did not use the words " if I could only deliberate on the matter thoroughly or from within " ill-advisedly; for although I could perceive all this quite clearly in my mind, I could not lay aside at once all greed, pleasure, and honour.

II. On the True and Supreme Good

11. One thing I could see, and that was that as long as the mind was employed with these thoughts, it turned away

[1] This should be more accurately proved.—*Sp.*

from its former subjects of thought and meditated seriously on this new plan: which was a great comfort to me. For I saw that those evils were not of such a state that they could not be cured by remedies. And although at the commencement these intervals were rare and lasted for a very short space of time, yet afterwards the true good became more and more apparent to me, and these intervals more frequent and of longer duration, especially after I saw that the acquisition of money and desire for pleasure and glory are only in the way as long as they were sought for their own sakes and not as means to attain other things. But if they are sought as means they will be limited, and far from being in the way, they will help in the attainment of the end for which they are sought, as we shall show in its proper place.

12. I will at this point only briefly say what I understand by true good, and at the same time what is supreme good. In order that this may rightly be understood, it must be pointed out that good and bad are terms only used respectively: and therefore one and the same thing can be called good or bad according to the various aspects in which we regard it, just as we explained of perfect and imperfect.[1] For nothing regarded in its own nature can be called perfect or imperfect, especially after we know that all things which are made, are made according to the eternal order and the fixed laws of nature. 13. But as human weakness cannot attain that order in its knowledge, and in the meantime man conceives a human nature more firm than his own, and at the same time sees nothing that could prevent him from acquiring such a nature, he is incited to seek means which should lead him to such perfection: and everything that can be a means to enable him to attain it is called a true good. For the greatest good is for him to attain to the enjoyment of such a nature together with other individuals, if this can be. What is that nature I shall show in its proper place, namely, that it is the knowledge of the union which the mind has with the whole of nature.[2] 14. This then is the end to attain which I am striving, namely, to acquire such a nature and to endeavour that many also should acquire it with me. It is then part of my happiness that many others should understand as I do, and that their understanding and desire

<hr />
[1] Cf. Spinoza's *Ethics*, Part IV., Preface.
[2] This will be explained more fully in its place.—*Sp.*

should be entirely in harmony with my understanding and desire; and in order to bring this to pass it is necessary to understand as much of nature as will suffice for the acquiring of such a nature,[1] and moreover to form such a society as is essential for the purpose of enabling most people to acquire this nature with the greatest ease and security. 15. Again, attention must be paid to *Moral Philosophy* and the *Theory for the Education of Children,* and inasmuch as health is not an insignificant means to this end, the whole of the science of *Medicine* must be consulted, and finally, as many things which are difficult are rendered easy by skill and contrivance, and we can thus save a great deal of time and convenience in life, the art of *Mechanics* must in no wise be despised. 16. But above all things, a method must be thought out of healing the understanding and purifying it at the beginning, that it may with the greatest success understand things correctly. From this every one will be able to see that I wish to direct all sciences in one direction or to one end,[2] namely, to attain the greatest possible human perfection: and thus everything in the sciences that does not promote this endeavour must be rejected as useless, that is, in a word, all our endeavours and thoughts must be directed to this one end.

III. Certain Rules of Life

17. But inasmuch as while we endeavour to attain this and give all our attention in order to be able to direct our intellect in the right way it is necessary to live, we are obliged on that account before all things to suppose certain rules of life to be good, namely—

I. To speak in a manner comprehensible to the vulgar, and to do for them all things that do not prevent us from attaining our end. For from the multitude we may reap no little advantage, if we make as many concessions as possible to their understanding. Add to this that we shall thus prepare friendly ears to give us a good hearing when we wish to tell them what is the truth.

[1] Note that here I only take the trouble to enumerate such sciences as are necessary for what we require, and I pay no attention to their order.—*Sp*.

[2] There is but one end for the sciences, to which they all must be directed.—*Sp*

II. To enjoy only such pleasures as are necessary for the preservation of health.

III. Finally, to seek only enough money or anything else as is necessary for the upkeep of our health and life, and to comply with such customs as are not opposed to what we seek.

IV. On the Four Modes of Perception

18. With these rules laid down, I may now direct my attention to what is the most important of all, namely, to the correction of the understanding and the means of rendering it capable of understanding things in such a way as is necessary to the attainment of our end. To bring this about, the natural order we observe exacts that I should recapitulate all the modes of perception which I have used thus far for the indubitable affirmation or negation of anything, so that I may choose the best of all, and at the same time begin to know my strength and nature which I wish to perfect.

19. If I remember rightly, they can all be reduced to four headings, namely—

I. Perception is that which we have *by hearsay* or from some sign which may be called to suit any one's taste.

II. Perception is that which we have *from vague experience*, that is, from experience which is not determined by the intellect, but is only called an idea because it happened by chance and we have no experienced fact to oppose to it, and so it remains unchallenged in our minds.

III. Perception is that *wherein the essence of one thing is concluded from the essence of another*, but not adequately: this happens when we infer a cause from some effect, or when it is concluded from some general proposition that it is accompanied always by some property.[1]

IV. Finally, perception is *that wherein a thing is perceived*

---

[1] When this takes place we understand nothing of the cause, on account of the fact that we consider it in the effect. This is sufficiently manifest from the fact that the cause then is not explained save in most general terms, namely these: therefore something is given; therefore some power is granted, etc; or also from the fact that it expresses negatively: therefore this or that is not, etc. In the second case, something is attributed to the cause by reason of the effect, which will clearly be understood, as we shall soon show in an example; but only a property, never the essence, of any individual thing.—*Sp.*

through its essence alone or through a knowledge of its proximate cause.

20. All these I shall illustrate by an example. *By hearsay* I know my birthday, and that certain people were my parents, and the like: things of which I have never had any doubt. *By vague experience* I know that I shall die: and I assert that inasmuch as I have seen my equals undergo death, although they did not all live for the same space of time, nor died of the same illness. Again, *by vague experience* I know also that oil is good for feeding a flame, that water is good for extinguishing it. I know also that a dog is a barking animal, and man a rational animal: and thus I know nearly all things that are useful in life. 21. We conclude one thing *from another* in the following manner: After we have clearly perceived that we feel a certain body and no other, we thence conclude clearly that a soul or mind is united to that body, and that the union is the cause of that feeling;[1] but what is this feeling and union we cannot absolutely understand from that.[2] Or after I know the nature of vision and that it has such a property that we see a thing smaller when at a great distance than when we look at it close, I can conclude that the sun is larger than it appears, and other similar things. 22. Finally, a thing is said to be perceived *through its essence alone* when from the fact that I know something, I know what it is to know anything, or from the fact that I know the essence of the mind, I know it to be united to the body. By the same knowledge we know that two and three make five, and that if there are two lines parallel to the same line they shall be parallel to each other, etc. But the things which I have been able to know by this knowledge so far have been very few.

[1] From this example it can clearly be seen what I just noted. For we understand by that union nothing save that feeling, the effect, namely, from which we infer the cause of which we understand nothing. —*Sp.*

[2] Such a conclusion, although it is certain, is not safe, save to such as take the greatest precaution; for unless this is done they will fall into error at once. For when they conceive things thus abstractly, and not through their true essence, they are at once confused by their imagination. For that which in itself is one, men imagine to be multiplex. For they give to things which they conceive abstractly, apart, and confusedly, names which are altered from their true signification to apply to other more familiar things: whence it comes about that the latter are imagined in the same manner as the former are wont to be imagined, to which at first the names were given.—*Sp.*

23. In order that all these things may be better understood I shall employ one example, namely, this one: Three numbers are given to find the fourth, which is to the third as the second is to the first. Tradesmen will say at once that they know what is to be done to find the fourth number, inasmuch as they have not yet forgotten the operation, which they learned without proof from their teachers. Others again, from experimenting with small numbers where the fourth number is quite manifest, as with 2, 4, 3, and 6, where it is found that by multiplying the second by the third and dividing the answer by the first number the quotient is six, have made it an axiom, and when they find this number which without that working out they knew to be the proportional, they thence conclude that this process is good invariably for finding the fourth proportional. 24. But mathematicians, by conviction of the proof of Prop. 19, Bk. 7, *Elements* of Euclid, know what numbers are proportionals from the nature and property of proportion, namely, that the first and fourth multiplied together are equal to the product of the second and third. But they do not see the adequate proportionality of the given numbers; or if they do, it is not from that proposition, but intuitively without any process of working.

V. On the Best Mode of Perception

25. In order that from these the best mode of perception may be chosen, we must briefly enumerate what are the necessary means for the attainment of our end, namely, these:

I. To know our nature which we desire to perfect, exactly, and also at the same time as much of the nature of things as is necessary.

II. To gather from these the differences, agreements, and oppositions of things.

III. To conceive rightly to what extent they are passive.

IV. To compare this with the nature and power of man. And from these points the greatest perfection to which man can attain will easily be apparent.

26. From the consideration of these points we shall see what mode of perception we must choose.

As to the first, it is quite clear that from hearsay, besides the fact that our knowledge is very uncertain, we perceive nothing of the essence of the thing, as is obvious from our example; and as when the existence of an individual thing is not known its essence also is not known (as shall soon be clear), we can obviously conclude that all certainty which we have from hearsay is far removed from scientific knowledge. For no one can ever be affected by hearsay, unless the understanding of that person precede it.

27. As for the second mode, it cannot be said to possess the idea of proportion which is sought.[1] Besides the fact that the thing is very uncertain and indefinite, no one can ever perceive anything in things of nature by such a mode save accidental properties which are never clearly understood unless their essences are previously known. Whence we can conclude that this mode also must be laid aside.

28. From the third mode it must be admitted that we obtain an idea of the thing and conclude it without any danger of error; but nevertheless it is not a means in itself whereby we may acquire our perfection.

29. The fourth mode alone comprehends the adequate essence of the thing, and that without any danger of error; and therefore it must be adopted above all others. Therefore in what manner this mode must be obtained so that we may understand unknown things by means of such knowledge, and at the same time as speedily as possible, we shall proceed to explain.

VI. On the Instruments of the Understanding, True Ideas

30. Now that we know what knowledge is necessary to us, we must describe the way and method in which we must know with this knowledge the things that are to be known. To do this, the first thing to be considered is that this inquiry must not be one stretching back to infinity: I mean to say that in order to find the best method of investigating what is true, we must not stand in need of another method to investigate this method of investigating, nor in need of a third one to investigate the second, and so on to infinity. For by such a method we can never arrive at a knowledge of what is true, nor at any knowledge whatever. For it is

[1] Here I shall treat somewhat more in detail of experience, and shall examine the method of proceeding of the empirics and recent philosophers.—*Sp.*

the same thing as with artificial instruments, of which we might argue in the same manner. For in order to work iron a hammer is needed, and in order to have a hammer it must be made, for which another hammer and other instruments are needed, for the making of which others again are needed, and so on to infinity; and in this manner any one might vainly endeavour to prove that men have no power of working iron. 31. But in the same way as men in the beginning were able with great labour and imperfection to make the most simple things from the instruments already supplied by nature, and when these were completed with their aid, made harder and more complex things with more facility and perfection, and thus gradually proceeding from the most simple works to instruments, and from instruments to other harder pieces of work, they at last succeeded in constructing and perfecting so many and such difficult instruments with very little labour, so also the understanding by its native strength (*vis sua nativa*)[1] makes for itself its intellectual instruments wherewith it acquires further strength for other intellectual works,[2] and with these makes others again and the power of investigating still further, and so gradually proceeds until it attains the summit of wisdom. 32. That this is the case with the understanding can easily be seen as soon as it is understood what is the method of investigating the truth, and what are those natural instruments which are so needed for the construction of other instruments from them, in order to proceed further. To show this I shall go on in this fashion.[3]

33. A true idea (for we have a true idea) is something different from its ideal (*ideatum*). For a circle is one thing, and the idea of one another; for the idea of a circle is not something having a circumference and a centre, as is a circle, nor is the idea of a body the body itself. And as it is something different from its ideal, it must also be something intelligible in itself, that is, the idea as regards its formal essence can be the object of another objective

[1] By native strength I understand that which is not caused in us by external causes, and which I shall afterwards explain in my philosophy.—*Sp.*

[2] I have called them works here: what they are I shall explain in my philosophy.—*Sp.*

[3] Note that here I shall take the trouble to show not only what I have just said, but also that thus far we have rightly proceeded, and other things most necessary to be known.—*Sp.*

essence; and again, this second objective essence will also be, when regarded in itself, something real and intelligible, and so on indefinitely. 34. For example, Peter is something real; but the true idea of Peter is the objective essence of Peter and something real in itself and altogether different from Peter. Since, therefore, the idea of Peter is something real having its peculiar essence, it will also be something intelligible, that is, the object of another idea, and this idea will have in itself objectively all that the idea of Peter has in itself formally (*formaliter*); and again, the idea which is that of the idea of Peter has in its turn its essence, which can be the object of another idea, and so on indefinitely. This every one can find out for himself when he sees that he knows what is Peter, and also knows that he knows, and also knows that he knows that he knows, etc. Whence it is certain that in order to understand the essence of Peter it is not necessary to know the idea itself of Peter, and far less the idea of the idea of Peter: which is the same thing as if I said that it is not necessary to know that I know, in order to know, far less to know that I know that I know, no more than in order to understand the essence of a triangle it is necessary to understand the essence of a circle.[1] But in these ideas the contrary is required. For in order to know that I know, I must necessarily first know. 35. Hence it is clear that certainty is nothing else than the objective essence, that is, the mode in which we feel formal essence is certainty itself. Whence it is also clear that for the certainty of truth no other sign is needed than to have a true idea; for as we have shown, it is not necessary in order to know, to know that I know. From which also it is again clear that no one can know what is the greatest certainty, unless he have an adequate idea or the objective essence of anything, that is, certainty is the same thing as objective essence.

VII. ON THE RIGHT METHOD OF KNOWING

36. As, then, the truth needs no sign, but it suffices to have the objective essences of things, or what is the same thing,

[1] Note that we are not here inquiring in what manner this first objective essence is innate in us, for that appertains to the investigation of nature where these things are more fully explained, and where it is shown at the same time that without an idea there can be no affirmation nor negation nor any wish.—*Sp.*

ideas, in order to remove all doubt, it follows that the true
method is not to seek a sign of the truth after the acquisition
of ideas, but that the true method is the way in which truth
itself, or the objective essences or ideas of things (for truth
and the objective essences and ideas have the same signification), must be sought in their proper order.¹   37. Again, the
method must necessarily have something to say of reasoning
and understanding, that is, the method is not reasoning for
the purpose of understanding the causes of things, and far
less is it the understanding the causes of things; but it is to
understand what is a true idea by distinguishing it from
other perceptions and investigating its nature, in order that
we may thence have knowledge of our power of understanding, and so accustom our mind that it may understand by that
one standard all things that are to be understood, setting out
for ourselves as aids certain rules, and taking care that the
mind is not overburdened with useless facts.   38. Whence
it may be gathered that method is nothing else than reflective
knowledge (*cognitio reflexiva*) or the idea of an idea: and
inasmuch as the idea of an idea cannot be granted unless the
idea itself be granted first, therefore the method will not be
granted unless the idea be first granted.   Whence we infer that
that will be the good method which shows in what manner the
mind must be directed according to the standard of a given
true idea.   Again, since the ratio between two ideas is the
same as the ratio between the formal essences of those ideas,
it follows that reflective knowledge of an idea of a being most
perfect will be more excellent than reflective knowledge of
other ideas: that is, that method will be the most perfect
which shows, according to the standard of the given idea of
the most perfect being, in what manner the mind must be
directed.   39. From these points it can be easily understood
in what manner the mind by understanding many things
may acquire more instruments whereby to proceed with its
understanding more easily.   For as we may gather from
what has been said, there ought to exist in us before all
things a true idea as the innate instrument, and with the
understanding of this true idea there comes also the understanding of the difference between this perception and all
others.   Of this consists one part of the method.   And since

¹ What searching in the mind (*quærere in anima*) is, is explained in
my philosophy.—*Sp.*

it is quite obvious that the mind understands itself the more, the more it understands things of nature, it is certain that this part of the method will be more perfect according as the mind understands more things, and will then become most perfect of all when it has regard for and reflects on the knowledge of a most perfect being. 40. Again, the more the mind knows, the better it understands its forces and the order of nature; the more it understands its forces or strength, the better it will be able to direct itself and lay down rules for itself; and the more it understands the order of nature, the more easily it shall be able to liberate itself from useless things: of this, as we have said, consists the whole method. 41. Add to this that the idea objectively is under the same conditions as its ideal is in reality. If, therefore, anything were granted in nature having no relation or dealings with other things, then if its objective essence be granted also, which must agree in all respects with its formal essence, it will also have no relation or dealings with other ideas,[1] that is, we could conclude nothing concerning it; and, on the other hand, those things that have relation or dealings with other things, as all things that exist in nature, are understood, and their objective essences have the same relation or dealings, that is, other ideas are deduced from them, which again have relation or dealings with others, and the instruments for proceeding with our quest are increased. This is what we were endeavouring to prove. 42. Again, from this last point we mentioned, namely, that an idea must agree in all respects with its formal essence, it is clear that in order that our mind may represent a true example of nature, it must produce all its ideas from the idea which represents the origin and source of all nature, so that it may become the source of other ideas.

43. Perhaps some one may be surprised that when we say that the good method was that one which showed in what manner the mind must be directed according to the standard of a given true idea, we prove this by argument; for this seems to show that it is not self-evident, and therefore it may be asked if we have argued well and correctly. If we argue well, we must begin from a given idea, and when to

[1] To have relation or dealings with other things (*commercium habere cum aliis rebus*), is to be produced by other things or to produce them.—*Sp.*

begin from a given idea needs a proof, we must thus prove our argument, and then again another, and so on to infinity. 44. But to this I make answer, that if any one by some chance had thus proceeded in his investigation of nature, namely, by acquiring other ideas according to the standard of a given true idea in due order, he would never have doubted his truth,[1] by the fact that truth, as we have shown, makes itself evident, and thus all things would flow spontaneously towards him. But since this never or rarely happens, I was thus forced to lay down these points in order that we might acquire by forethought what we cannot acquire by chance, and at the same time in order that it may be clear that for proving the truth and good argument we never lack good instruments nor truth itself and good argument. For I have proved good argument by good arguing, and thus I still endeavour to do. 45. Moreover, this is what men are accustomed to in their inward meditations. But the reason why it rarely happens in our inquiries into nature that this thing is investigated in its due order is owing to prejudices, the cause of which we shall explain later on in our philosophy; again, it is owing to the fact that there is need of considerable and accurate distinction, as I shall afterwards show (which is most laborious); and finally, owing to the state of human things, which, as has already been shown, is exceedingly changeable. Besides these there are other reasons which we shall not investigate.

46. If perchance any one should ask why I at the commencement did not show before all things these truths of nature in this order (for the truth makes itself manifest), I reply to him and warn him not to reject here as false whatever things occur, for that they are paradoxes, but first to be good enough to consider the order in which we have proved them, and then he will go away assured that we have been following the truth. This is why I premised these remarks.

47. If after this there is still some sceptic who remains doubtful of this first truth and all the things which we have deduced according to its standard, then surely he must be speaking contrary to his real opinion, or we must confess that there are men purblind as regards the mind, either owing to their birth or some prejudices, that is, some external

---

[1] Thus also we do not doubt our own truth.—*Sp*.

cause; for they are not conscious of themselves. If they affirm or doubt anything, they know not that they affirm or doubt it: they say that they know nothing, and say that they are ignorant of the fact that they know nothing; nor do they say this with certainty, for they fear to confess that they exist as long as they know nothing, to such an extent that they ought to remain silent, lest perchance they might suppose something which has the savour of truth. 48. Again, we cannot speak to them of the sciences; for as for that which relates to life and the habits of society, necessity compels them to suppose themselves to exist, and to seek what is useful to themselves, and to affirm and deny many things by oath. For if anything is proved to them, they do not know whether the argumentation is proved or is wanting in some particular. If they deny, oppose, or grant, they do not know that they deny, grant, or oppose; and therefore they must be regarded as machines which lack any mind at all.

49. But let us now resume our proposition. Thus far we have in the first place the end towards which we shall endeavour to direct all our thoughts. We know in the second place what is the best perception by whose means we can arrive at our perfection. We know in the third place what is the first way in which the mind should strive to go, in order to begin well: this is that it should proceed with the standard of a given true idea in its inquiries according to certain rules. In order that this should turn out well, this method must afford, in the first place, the distinguishing of a true idea from all other perceptions, and the keeping the mind from these perceptions; secondly, to draw up rules that unknown things may be perceived according to a certain standard; thirdly, to make some order lest the mind be overburdened with useless details. As soon as we had knowledge of this method, we saw, fourthly, that it would be perfect when we had the idea of a perfect being. This should be observed in the beginning, in order that we may more rapidly arrive at the knowledge of such a being.

VIII. First Part of the Method—On Fictitious Ideas

50. Let us then begin with the first part of our method, which is, as I said, to distinguish and separate the true idea

from other perceptions and to restrain the mind lest it confuse false, feigned, and doubtful ideas with true ones. This I intend to explain in great detail in this place, in order to retain the readers in the thought of a thing so necessary, and because there are many who have doubts concerning what is true, owing to the fact that they do not pay attention to the distinction that exists between true perception and all others, in such a way that they are like men who, while they are awake, have no doubt that they are awake, but afterwards, at some time in their sleep, as often happens, they think they are certainly awake, and afterwards when they find that this is false, doubt also that they are awake: this happens because they never distinguish between sleeping and waking.

51. Meanwhile I give warning that I shall not explain here the essence of each perception through its proximate cause, for that appertains to philosophy; but shall only deal with that which method postulates, that is, what concerns fictitious, false, and doubtful perception, and in what manner we may be delivered from them. Let our first inquiry then be made concerning a fictitious idea.

52. Since every perception is of a thing considered as existing, or of its essence alone, and fictions most frequently happen concerning things considered as existing, I shall speak first of this point, namely, when existence alone is feigned, and the thing which is feigned in such an action is understood or supposed to be understood. *E.g.*, I feign that Peter, whom I know to have gone home, is gone to see me, and suchlike.[1] Here I ask what does this idea concern? I see that it concerns possible things, not things either necessary or impossible. 53. I call a thing *impossible* whose nature implies a contradiction if it exists; *necessary*, whose nature implies a contradiction if it does not exist; *possible*, whose existence, that is, its nature, does not imply a contradiction whether it exists or does not, but the necessity or impossibility of whose existence depends on causes unknown to us, while we feign its existence: and therefore if its necessity or impossibility, which depends on external causes, were known to us, we could feign nothing concerning it. 54. Whence it follows that of any God or anything omniscient

---

[1] See further on what we shall say of hypotheses which are clearly understood by us: the fiction consists of the fact that we say that they exist in heavenly bodies—*Sp.*

we can surely feign nothing. For as for what appertains to us, once I know that I exist, I cannot feign that I exist or not,[1] any more than I can feign that an elephant can go through the eye of a needle; nor can I, once I know the nature of God, feign that God exists or does not.[2] The same must be understood of a chimera, for I cannot feign one whose nature implies existence. From which is clear what I said, namely, that the fiction of which we are speaking here does not concern eternal truths.[3] 55. But before I proceed any further, this must be noted by the way, that the difference there is between the essence of one thing and that of another is the same as there exists between the reality or existence of that thing and the reality (*actualitas*) and existence of the other; therefore if we wish to conceive the existence, *e.g.*, of Adam through existence in general, it will be the same as if in order to conceive his essence we should have regard to the nature of being, in order to define Adam as a being; therefore the more generally existence is conceived, the more confusedly it is conceived, and the more easily it can be ascribed to anything; and contrariwise, the more in detail a thing is conceived, the more clearly it is understood, and the more difficult it is to ascribe it, through want of attention to the order of nature, to any other thing than itself. This is worthy of note.

56. We now arrive at the place to consider those things which are usually called fictitious, although we clearly understand that the thing is not as we feign it. *E.g.*, although I know that the earth is round, nothing prevents me from telling any one that it is a hemisphere, and that it is like half an apple moulded on a salver, or that the sun moves round the earth, and such-like things. If we pay attention to these points we shall see nothing which does not agree with what has

---

[1] As a thing, once it is understood, makes itself evident, we need only an example without any other proof. In the same way, the contradiction has only to be brought before us, to appear false, as will soon be evident when we speak of fiction concerning essence.—*Sp*.

[2] Note that although many say they doubt whether God exists, they have nothing in their minds save a mere name, or they feign something they call God, which is not in harmony with the nature of God, as I shall afterwards show in its proper place.—*Sp*.

[3] I shall soon show that no fiction concerns eternal truths. For by eternal truth I understand one that is affirmative and never negative. Thus the first and eternal truth is " God is; " but it is not an eternal truth that " Adam thinks." " A chimera exists not " is an eternal truth, but not " Adam thinks not."—*Sp*.

been said, if we only notice that we may have at some time
made an error and now may be conscious of it; again, that
we can feign, or at least think, that other men may fall into
the same error or in one in which we fell before. We can
thus feign, I say, as long as we see no impossibility. Therefore when I say to any one that the earth is not round, etc.,
I do nothing else than to recall to memory an error which
perhaps I had, or in which, perhaps, I might have slipped,
and then feign or think that he to whom I am speaking is in
such a state that he can fall into that error. I feign this,
I say, as long as I see no impossibility and no necessity: if I
truly understood them, I should be able to feign no longer,
and could only say that I attempted to do it.

57. It remains for us to note those things that are supposed
in problems, for it sometimes happens that they concern
impossibilities. *E.g.*, when we say, let us suppose that this
burning candle is not burning, or let us suppose that it burns
in some imaginary space where there are no bodies. These
and similar suppositions can be made at random, although
this last one is clearly understood to be impossible. But
although this takes place, nothing is feigned. For in the
first place, I did nothing else than recall to memory another
candle not burning [1] (or this same one unlighted), and what
I think of this latter candle I understand of the former one,
having no regard for the flame. In the second place, nothing
else happens than to withdraw the thoughts from circum-
jacent bodies so that the mind may give itself up to the
contemplation of the candle regarded in itself alone; and
thus afterwards I may conclude that the candle has no
cause for its own destruction, so that if there were no circum-
jacent bodies, the candle and also its flame would remain
just the same, and such-like. There is therefore no fiction
here, but merely true assertions. [2]

[1] When I speak afterwards of fiction which concerns essences, it will
be clearly apparent that fiction never makes anything new, or affords
anything to the mind, but that only such things as are in the brain or
imagination are recalled to the memory, and that the mind regards
them all at the same time confusedly. For example, speech and tree
are recalled to the memory, and when the mind confusedly attends
to both without distinction, it thinks of a tree speaking. The same is
understood of existence, especially, as we said, when it is conceived
generally as a being, for then it is easily applied to all things which
occur in the memory at the same time. This is very worthy of
notice.—*Sp.*

[2] The same must be understood of hypotheses which are made to

58. Let us now pass on to fictions which concern essences alone, or with some reality or existence at the same time. Concerning these the principal point to be considered is that the less the mind understands and nevertheless perceives more, the greater will be its power of feigning, and the more it understands, the lesser will be its power. *E.g.*, in the same manner in which we saw above that we cannot feign while we think that we think or do not think, thus also, as soon as we know the nature of body we cannot feign an infinite fly, or as soon as we know the nature of the mind [1] we cannot feign that it is square, although anything may be expressed in words. But as we said, the less men know of nature, the more easily they can feign things; just as that trees speak, that men are turned in a moment into stones, that ghosts appear in mirrors, that of nothing something is made, that the Gods themselves are changed into men and beasts, and infinite other things of this kind.

59. Perhaps some one will think that fiction limits fiction, but that understanding does not, that is, after I have feigned something, and by my own free will have asserted that this thing exists in the nature of things, I am prevented from thinking of this under any other form. *E.g.*, as soon as I have feigned (to speak as one of them) the nature of body to be of such a kind, and persuaded myself of my own free will that it really exists, I can no longer feign, *e.g.*, that a fly is infinite, and that after I have feigned the essence of the soul, I cannot feign it square, etc. 60. But this must be looked into. In the first place, they either deny or grant that we can understand anything. If they grant that we can, then necessarily that which is said of fiction must be said of understanding. But if they deny this, let us who know that we know something see what they mean. They say this: that the mind can feel and perceive in many modes

explain certain movements which are in harmony with heavenly phenomena, save that if these are applied to celestial movements, we conclude from them the nature of the heavens, which, however, can be quite different, especially as for the explanation of such movements many other causes can be conceived.—*Sp*.

[1] It often happens that man recalls this word " mind " to memory, and forms at the same time some corporeal image. When these two are represented at the same time, he easily thinks that he imagines and feigns a corporeal mind, because he does not distinguish the name from the thing. I beg, therefore, that the readers be not too precipitate to refute this: which I hope they will not do, if they attend to the examples as accurately as possible, and also to what follows.—*Sp*.

not itself, nor the things which exist, but only those things which neither in themselves nor anywhere exist, that is, that the mind can create of its own force sensations or ideas which do not belong to anything; and therefore they regard the mind partially as God. Again, they say that we or our mind have such liberty that we can restrain ourselves, or our mind or its liberty. For after our mind has feigned anything and affixed its assent to it, it cannot think or feign it in any other way, but it is constrained by that first fiction to think in such a manner as will not be opposed to it. They are thus forced to admit all the absurdities which I have enumerated, by reason of their fiction, to overthrow which I shall not take the trouble with any proofs.[1] 61. But leaving them in their mistakes, we shall take care to draw from what speech we had with them some truth that may be of service to what we are dealing with, namely this: The mind when it pays attention to a fictitious thing and one false to its nature, so as to turn it over in its mind and understand it, and to deduce in proper order from it such things as are to be deduced, will easily make manifest its falsity; and if the fictitious thing be true to its nature when the mind pays attention to it in order to understand it, and begins to make deductions from it in proper order, it proceeds happily without interruption, just as we saw that from a false fiction the mind was soon driven to show its absurdity and make other deductions for itself.

62. In no wise, therefore, must we fear to feign anything, provided that we only perceive the thing clearly and distinctly. For if perchance we say that men are changed in a moment into beasts, that is said very generally, to such an extent indeed that there would be no conception, that is, no idea or coherence of subject and predicate in the mind; if there were such a conception, we should see the means and causes how and why such a thing took place. Again, no attention has been paid to the nature of subject and predicate. 63. Further, if the first idea is not feigned, and

---

[1] Although I seem to conclude this from experience (and who will say that is nothing?), yet inasmuch as a proof has been wanting, he that requires it may find it here. As there can be nothing in nature that opposes its laws, but as all things are made according to certain laws of nature, so that certain things produce their effects according to certain laws with irrefragable connection, it hence follows that the mind, when it conceives a thing truly, proceeds to form its effects objectively. See further on where I speak of a false idea.—*Sp.*

if all the other ideas are deduced from it, gradually the hurry to feign will vanish. Again, as a fictitious idea cannot be clear and distinct, but only confused, and as all confusion proceeds from the fact that the mind knows a thing that is entire or composed of many parts only in part, and does not distinguish what is known from the unknown, on account of the fact that it regards simultaneously and without any distinction many things that are contained in one thing: hence it follows that if the idea be of a thing very simple, it cannot but be clear and distinct, for such a thing cannot be known in part, but either as a whole or not at all. 64. It follows, in the second place, that if a thing that is composed of many parts is divided in thought into its simplest parts, and each part is regarded in itself, all confusion will vanish. It follows, in the third place, that fiction cannot be simple, but that it is made from the combination of different confused ideas, which are those of different things and actions existing in nature, or better, from simultaneous attention to, without mental assent to these different ideas.[1] For if it were simple it would be clear and distinct, and consequently true. If it were made from the combination of distinct ideas, their composition would also be clear and distinct, and consequently true. *E.g.*, as soon as we know the nature of a circle and the nature of a square, it is impossible for us to combine these two and make a square circle or a square mind, or such-like. 65. Let us conclude again briefly, and see how it need in no wise be feared that fiction will be confused with true ideas. As for the first fiction of which we have spoken, where the thing is clearly conceived we see that if that thing which is clearly conceived, and also its existence, be in itself an eternal truth, we can feign nothing concerning such a thing; but if the existence of the thing conceived be not an eternal truth, we must only take care that its existence be compared with its essence, and that attention is paid at the same time to the order of nature. As for the second fiction, which we said to be simultaneous attention without the mind's assent to different confused ideas of things and actions existing in

[1] N.B.—Fiction regarded in itself does not differ much from dreaming, save that in dreams there are no causes offered which are offered to the waking through their senses: from which it is gathered that these representations which take place during that time are not drawn from things external to us. But error, as I shall soon show, is a waking man's dream, and if it become too prominent it is called delirium.—*Sp.*

nature, we have seen also that a very simple thing cannot be feigned but understood, and that a compound thing cannot either, if we have regard for the simple parts from which it is composed; and that from these things we cannot even feign any actions which are not true, for we shall be at the same time obliged to consider in what manner and why such a thing was made.

IX. On the False Idea

66. Now that these points are understood, let us pass to the inquiry as to a false idea, in order that we may see what it concerns, and how we may take precautions lest we fall into false perceptions. Both of these things will not be so difficult to us now that we have made the inquiry into the fictitious idea, for there is no difference between them save that the latter presupposes the mind's assent, that is (as we have already pointed out), that there are no causes presented with the representations from which, as in fiction, the mind can gather that these representations have not arisen from things without, and which is practically nothing else than dreaming with one's eyes open or while one is awake. Therefore this false idea concerns or (to speak in better terms) is referred to the existence of the thing whose essence is known, or the essence, in the same way as the fictitious idea. 67. What has reference to existence, is corrected in the same way as a fictitious idea. What has reference to essence is corrected in the same manner as fiction. For if the nature of a thing known supposes necessary existence, it is impossible that we should be deceived concerning the existence of that thing; but if the existence of that thing be not an eternal truth, as is its essence, but, on the other hand, the necessity or impossibility of existing depend on external causes, then all things must be regarded in the way we spoke of when dealing with fiction, for it is corrected in the same manner. 68. As for the other false idea which is referred to essences or also to actions, such perceptions are always necessarily confused, composed of different confused perceptions of things existing in nature, as when men are persuaded that there are deities in woods, in images, in brutes, and other things; that there are bodies from whose composition alone the understanding is made; that dead bodies reason, walk,

speak; that God is deceived, and such-like things. But ideas which are clear and distinct can never be false. For the ideas of things which are conceived clearly and distinctly are either very simple or composed of simple ideas, that is, deduced from simple ideas. That a very simple idea cannot be false every one can see, provided he know what is the truth or understanding and what is falsity.

69. As for what relates to that which constitutes the form of truth, it is certain that true thought is distinguished from false not only by extrinsic marks, but principally by intrinsic ones. For if some workman conceive a building properly, although this building has never existed, nor ever will exist, the thought will be true and will be the same whether the building exists or not; and contrariwise, if any one should say that Peter, for example, exists, and yet did not know whether Peter existed, that thought, with respect to the former, is false, or if you wish, not true, although Peter really exists. Nor is this statement, " Peter exists," true, save in respect to him who certainly knows that Peter exists. 70. Whence it follows that there is something real in ideas wherewith the true are distinguished from the false; and this must be inquired into in order that we may have the best standard of truth (for we said that our thoughts must be determined according to the given standard of a true idea, and that the method is reflective knowledge) and may know the properties of the understanding; nor can it be said that this difference arises from the fact that true thought is to know things through their primary causes, in which it differs considerably from false thought, as I have just explained it. For thought is said to be true when it involves objectively the essence of some principle which has no cause, and is known through itself and in itself. 71. Wherefore the form of true thought must be placed in that thought itself, without relation to others; nor does it acknowledge the object as its cause, but must depend on the power and nature of the intellect. For if we suppose that the understanding has perceived some new being which has never existed, as some conceive the intellect of God before he created things (which perception clearly could have arisen from no object), and from this perception to have deduced correctly other perceptions, all those thoughts would be true, and determined by no external object, but would depend on the power and

nature of the intellect alone. Wherefore that which constitutes the form of true thought is to be sought in thought itself, and to be deduced from the nature of the intellect. 72. In order that this may be investigated, let us place before our eyes some *true* idea, whose object we know with the greatest certainty to depend on our power of thinking, and to have no object in nature; for in such an idea, as is clear from what has been said, we shall be more easily able to investigate what we wish. *E.g.*, to form the conception of a sphere, I feign a cause at my pleasure, namely, a semicircle revolving round its centre, and thus causing, so to speak, a sphere by its rotation. This clearly is a true idea, and although we know that no sphere in nature was ever caused in that manner, this is nevertheless a true perception and a very easy manner of forming a conception of a sphere. It must now be noted that this perception affirms that a semicircle revolves, which affirmation would be false if it were not joined to the conception of a sphere, or of a cause determining a motion such as this, or absolutely if this affirmation were isolated. For then the mind would tend alone to the affirmation of the motion of a semicircle, which is not contained in the conception of a semicircle, nor arises from the conception of a cause determining the motion. Wherefore *falsity* consists in this alone, that something is affirmed of some other thing which is not contained in the conception of that of which we have formed—as motion or rest from a semicircle. Whence it follows that simple thoughts cannot but be *true*—as the simple idea of a semicircle, motion, quantity, etc. Whatever these affirmations contain is equal to their conception, and does not extend further. Wherefore we may at our own free will form simple ideas without any danger of error. 73. It now remains only to inquire by what power our mind can form them and how far that power extends; for when that is found we shall easily see the supreme knowledge to which we may attain. For it is certain that this power does not extend itself to infinity. For when we affirm anything of anything else which is not contained in the conception we form of it, it indicates a defect in our perception, or that we have mutilated or hacked ideas and thoughts. For we see that the motion of a semicircle is false when it is isolated in the mind, but it is true when it is associated with the conception of a sphere or the conception of any cause determining such a movement. For if it is the nature of a thinking being that at first sight it forms true or adequate ideas, it is certain that inadequate ideas arise in us, owing to the mere fact that we are part of some thinking being of whom certain thoughts some as a whole, some in part alone constitute our mind.

74. But here there is another point to be considered, which was not worth while raising with regard to fiction—one which gives rise to the greatest deception: it is that it happens that certain ideas which are in the imagination are also in the understanding, that is, they are clearly and distinctly conceived; then as long as we do not distinguish between the true and the false, certainty, that is, a true idea, is mixed with indistinct ideas. *E.g.*, certain Stoics heard perhaps the word " soul," and also that it is immortal, but yet only imagined this confusedly; they imagined also and understood at the same time that very subtle bodies penetrate all things and are penetrated by none. When all these things were imagined simultaneously, accompanied by the certainty of this axiom, they were made certain at once that the mind was formed of these very subtle bodies, and that they could not be divided, etc. 75. But we are delivered from this also when we endeavour to examine all our perceptions according to the standard of a given true idea. Care must be taken, as we said at the beginning, with those perceptions which we have from hearsay and vague experience. Add to this that such deception arises from the fact that things are conceived too abstractly, for it is self-evident enough that I cannot apply what I conceive in its true object to another object. It arises finally from the fact that we do not understand the primary elements of the whole of nature; whence, proceeding without order and confusing nature with abstract things which may yet be axioms, we confuse ourselves and pervert the order of nature. But we who proceed with the least abstraction and begin with the primary elements, that is, with the source and origin of nature as far back as possible —we, I say, if we do this, need have no fear of such deception. 76. But as for the knowledge of the origin of nature, there is no fear that we should confuse it with abstract ideas, for when anything abstract is conceived, as all general things, they are more fully comprehended in the understanding than the particular things corresponding to them can exist truly

in nature. Again, when there are many things in nature whose difference is so small that it almost escapes the understanding, then it can easily happen (if they are abstractly conceived) that they are confused. But as the origin of nature, as we shall see afterwards, cannot be conceived either abstractly or generally, nor can be further extended in the understanding than it really is, and has no similarity with changeable things, there is no fear of confusion to be entertained as regards its idea, provided we have the standard of truth (as we have already shown). This is, then, a being unique, infinite,[1] that is, all being, and that beyond which nothing can be granted.[2]

X. On the Doubtful Idea

77. Thus far we have dealt with the false idea. It remains for us to inquire into the doubtful idea, that is, inquire what are those things which lead us into doubt, and at the same time in what manner this doubt may be removed. I speak of true doubt in the mind, and not of that which we see to take place when any one says he doubts in so many words, whereas there is no doubt in his mind. It is not the province of this method to correct this, but it pertains rather to an inquiry into obstinacy and its correction. 78. Doubt, therefore, is never induced in the mind by the thing doubted, that is, if there be only one idea in the mind, whether it be false or true, there would be no doubt or certainty, but only a certain sensation. For it is in itself nothing else than a certain sensation; but it is there by reason of another idea, which is not clear and distinct enough for us to be able to conclude from it anything certain concerning the thing of which we doubt, that is, the idea which causes us to doubt is not clear and distinct. E.g., if some one has never thought of the deception of the senses, either from experience or anything else, he will never doubt whether the sun is greater or smaller than it appears. Whence countrymen often wonder when they hear that the sun is larger than the

---

[1] Those things are not attributes of God which show forth his essence, as I shall show in my philosophy.—*Sp.*

[2] This has been shown above already. For if such a being does not exist, it could never be produced: and therefore the mind could understand more than nature could furnish, which has been shown above to consist of falsity.—*Sp.*

earth. But doubt generally arises from thinking of the deception of the senses,[1] and if any one, after doubting, acquire a true knowledge of the senses, and in what manner, through their instrumentality, things are represented at a distance, then all doubt is removed. 79. Whence it follows that we cannot call true ideas into doubt, owing to the fact that perchance some deceiving God exists who deceives us in things which are most certain, as long as we have a clear and distinct idea, that is, if we pay attention to the knowledge we have of the origin of all things, and find nothing to teach us that he is not a deceiver in that knowledge by which, if we regard the nature of a triangle, we find its three angles to be equal to two right angles. But if we have such knowledge of God as we have of a triangle, then all doubt is removed. And in the same manner in which we can arrive at the knowledge of a triangle, although we do not know for certain whether some arch deceiver deceives us—in that manner, I say, we can arrive at the knowledge of God, although we do not know for certain whether there be any arch deceiver; and when we have it, it will suffice to remove, as I said, all doubt which we can have of clear and distinct ideas. 80. Again, if any one rightly proceeds by investigating what is to be investigated, without any interruption in the connection of things, and knows in what manner problems must be determined, before we attain to the knowledge of them, he will never have any but very certain ideas, that is, clear and distinct ones. For *doubtfulness* is nothing else than suspension of the mind concerning some affirmation or negation which we would affirm or deny if something did not appear, which being unknown, our knowledge of that thing must necessarily be imperfect. Whence it may be gathered that doubt always arises from the fact that things are inquired into without order.

XI. On Memory and Forgetfulness—Conclusion

81. These are the points on which I promised to treat in the first part of the method. But in order that I may not omit anything in them that may conduce to a knowledge of

---

[1] That is, it is known that the senses sometimes deceive us. But it is only confusedly known, for we do not know in what manner they deceive us.—*Sp.*

the understanding and its powers, I shall treat briefly on
memory and forgetfulness. Of these the principal point to
consider is that memory is strengthened both with and
without the aid of the understanding; for in the first case,
the more intelligible a thing is, the more easily it is retained
in the memory, and contrariwise, the less intelligible it is,
the more easily we forget it. *E.g.*, if I pronounce a number
of loose unconnected words, it is far harder to remember them
than if I pronounce them in the form of a story. 82. It is
strengthened, moreover, without the aid of the understanding, namely, by the force with which the imagination or that
sense (called common) is affected by some individual corporeal
thing. I say *individual*, for the imagination is only affected
by individual things. For if any one should read, say one
love story alone, he will remember it the better as long as
he does not read others of the same kind, for then it will
flourish alone in the imagination. But if there are many of the
same kind, we shall imagine all at the same time and confuse
them. I say also *corporeal*, for the imagination is affected
alone by bodies. As, therefore, the mind is strengthened by
the understanding and also without it, it is thence to be
concluded that it is something different from the understanding, and that neither memory nor forgetfulness concerns
the understanding considered in itself. 83. What, then, is
memory? It is nothing else than sensation of impressions
on the brain accompanied with the thought to determine the
duration of the sensation;[1] this reminiscence also shows
For then the mind thinks of that sensation, but not under
continuous duration; and thus the idea of this sensation is
not the duration of sensation, that is, memory. But whether
ideas themselves are open to corruption we shall see in our
philosophy. And if this seems very absurd to any one, it
will suffice to our purpose if he reflects that the more singular
a thing is, the more easily it is remembered, as is clear from
the example of the comedy just given. Again, the more
intelligible a thing is, the more easily it is remembered; and

[1] But if the duration be undetermined, the memory of that thing
is imperfect: this every one seems to have learned from nature. For
often in order that we may believe better some one in what he says, we
ask when and where a thing happened. Although ideas themselves
have their duration in the mind, yet as we are accustomed to determine
duration by the aid of some measure of motion, which also is made
with the aid of the imagination, we preserve no memory which appertains to the mind alone.—*Sp.*

therefore we cannot but remember a thing that is very singular and sufficiently intelligible. 84. Thus, then, we have distinguished between a true idea and other perceptions, and have shown that fictitious ideas, false ideas, and other ones have their origin from the *imagination*, that is, from certain fortuitous and unconnected sensations (so to speak) which do not arise from the power of the mind, but from external causes, according as the body, sleeping or waking, receives various motions. Or if one wishes, he may take whatever he likes for imagination, provided he admits it is something different from the understanding and that the soul has a passive relation with it. Then let it be what you will, once we know that it is something vague and to which the soul is passive, and know at the same time in what manner, by the aid of the understanding, we are freed from it. Wherefore also let none be surprised that I, before having proved that there are bodies and other necessary things, speak of the imagination, of the body and its composition. For as I have said, I may take it as I will, provided I know it is something vague, etc.

85. But we have shown that a true idea is simple or composed of simple ideas, and that it shows how and why anything is or is made, and that its objective effects proceed in harmony with the formality (*formalitas*) of its object: which is the same thing as the ancients said, that true science proceeds from cause to effect, save that they never, as far as I know, conceived what we have here, namely, that the soul acts according to certain laws and resembles a spiritual automaton. 86. Hence, as far as it is permitted in the beginning, we have acquired a knowledge of our understanding and that standard of a true idea, so that we fear no longer that we shall confuse the true with the false and fictitious; nor shall we be surprised any longer why we understand certain things which do not fall under the imagination, and that other things are in the imagination which are strongly opposed to the understanding; finally, others that are in harmony with it, since we know that the operations by which imaginations are produced are made according to laws far different to the laws of the intellect, and that the soul with regard to the imagination is passive. 87. From this also it is certain how easily those may fall into error who do not accurately distinguish between intellect and imagination. These are the errors into

which they usually fall: that extension must be local; that
it must be finite; that its parts are distinguished one from
the other in reality; that it is the primary and only foundation
of all things, and occupies at one time more space than at
another, and many other such things, all of which are directly
opposed to the truth, as we shall show in its proper place.

88. Again, as words are a part of imagination, that is,
according as they are composed in vague order in the memory
owing to condition of the body, we can feign many conceptions, therefore it must not be doubted but that words,
just as the imagination, can be the cause of many great
errors, unless we take the greatest precautions with them.
89. Moreover, they are arranged to suit the speaker's pleasure
and the comprehension of the vulgar, so that they are only
the signs of things according as they are in the imagination,
but not according as they are in the understanding; which
is clearly apparent from the fact that on all those which are
only in the intellect and not in the imagination, negative
names are often bestowed, such as incorporeal, infinite, etc.;
and also many things which are really affirmative are expressed negatively, and contrariwise, as uncreated, inde-
pendent, infinite, immortal, etc., because their contraries
are much more easily imagined, and therefore occurred first
to men and usurped positive names. We affirm and deny
many things because the nature of words allows us to affirm
and deny, but not the nature of things; and therefore when
this is not known we can easily take the false for the
true.

90. Let us avoid, moreover, another great cause of confusion which prevents the understanding from reflecting on
itself. It is that as we do not make a distinction between
imagination and understanding, we think that those things
which we easily imagine are clearer to us, and that which
we imagine we think we understand. So that those things
which should be put last we put first, and thus the true order
of progress is perverted and nothing may legitimately be
concluded.

XII. SECOND PART OF THE METHOD—ON DOUBLE PERCEPTION

91. Now in order to pass on to the second part of this

method,[1] I shall propound first the aim to which we endeavour to arrive in this method, and then the means for the attainment of that end. The aim is to have clear and distinct ideas, namely, such as arise from the mind alone, and not from fortuitous movements of the body. Then again, in order that all ideas may be reduced to one, we shall endeavour to connect and arrange them in such a manner that our mind as far as possible may reflect objectively the formality (*formalitas*) of nature, both as a whole and as parts.

92. As for the first point, as we have already said, it is required for our final end that a thing must be conceived either through *its essence alone* or *through its proximate cause*. Namely, if a thing be in itself, or, as it is commonly termed, its own cause, then it must be understood through its essence alone; but if a thing be not in itself, but requires a cause to exist, then it must be understood through its proximate cause. For in truth knowledge of effect is nothing else than to acquire a more perfect knowledge of cause.[2] 93. Whence we shall never be allowed, while we deal with the inquiry into things, to conclude anything from abstractions, and we must take the greatest care not to confuse those things which are only in the understanding with those which are in the thing itself. But the best conclusion must be drawn from some particular affirmative essence, or from a true and legitimate definition. For the understanding cannot descend from universal axioms to individual things, since axioms are extended to infinity, and do not determine the understanding for the regarding of one individual thing more than another. 94. Wherefore the correct way of discovering this is to form thoughts according to some given definition; and this will proceed more happily and more easily the better we define the thing. And therefore the cardinal point of all this second part of the method concerns this alone, namely, the knowledge of the conditions of good definition, and again, in the manner of finding them. Firstly, then, I shall treat on the *conditions of definition*.

[1] The principal rule of this part, as follows from the first part, is to regard closely all ideas which we find in us through pure understanding, so that we may distinguish them from those which we imagine: this distinction may be discovered through the properties of each, namely, those of the imagination and intellect.—*Sp.*

[2] Note that it appears from this that we cannot understand anything in nature without thus increasing at the same time our knowledge of the primary cause, or God.—*Sp.*

XIII. On the Conditions of Definition

95. In order that a *definition* may be called *perfect,* it must explain the inmost essence of a thing, and we must take care in forming this not to allow any of its properties to usurp its place. In order to explain this, and omitting any examples in which I might seem to wish to expose the errors of other people, I will give the example of some abstract thing of which it is indifferent to us how we define it, namely, a circle, which if it is defined as a figure of which lines drawn from the centre to the circumference are equal, no one there is but can see that this definition does not explain the essence of a circle, but only a property of it. And although, as I said, this is of small moment when it concerns figures and other entities of reasoning, yet when it concerns physical and real entities it is of the utmost importance, for the properties of things are not understood as long as their essences are unknown; if then we omit these, we shall necessarily pervert the connection of the understanding which must reflect the connection of nature, and we shall wander far away from what we are aiming at. 96. In order that we may be delivered from this fault, *these things must be observed* in definition.

I. If the thing is created, the definition must, as I said, comprehend its proximate cause. *E.g.,* a circle according to this rule must be defined thus: to be a figure which is described by any line of which one extremity is fixed and the other movable; for this definition clearly comprehends its proximate cause.

II. The conception or definition of a thing is required to be such that all the properties of that thing, regarded in itself and not conjoined with others, can be concluded from it, as can be seen in this definition of a circle. For from that it is clearly concluded that all lines from the centre to the circumference are equal; and that this is a necessary requirement of a definition is so clear to any one who pays attention to it, that there seems to be no need to waste time in proving it, nor even to show that from this second requirement it follows that all definition must be affirmative. I speak of intellectual affirmation, having no regard for verbal affirmation, which on account of want of words may often express something negatively although it be understood affirmatively.

97. The requirements of the definition of a thing uncreated are these—

I. To exclude all cause, that is, to need no object outside its being for its explanation.

II. When its definition is given there must remain no room for doubt as to whether it exists or not.

III. It must contain, as far as the mind is concerned, no substantives which can be turned into adjectives, that is, it must not be explained through abstractions.

IV. And finally (although it is not very necessary to note this), it is required that all its properties be concluded from its definition. All of these things will be manifest to any one accurately attending to this.

98. I said also that the best conclusion would be drawn from the affirmative essence of a particular thing. For the more specialised an idea is, the more distinct it is, and therefore the more clear. Whence the knowledge of particular things must be sought mostly by us.

XIV. OF THE MEANS BY WHICH ETERNAL THINGS ARE KNOWN

99. It is required with regard to order, and that all our perceptions may be arranged and connected, that as soon as is possible and consonant with reason we should inquire whether there be a certain being, and at the same time of what nature is he, who is the cause of all things: this we should do in order that his objective essence may be the cause of all our ideas, and then our minds, as I said, will reflect as much as possible nature; for then it will have objectively nature's essence, order, and union. Whence we can see that it is above all things necessary to us that we should deduce all our ideas from physical things or from real entities, proceeding, as far as possible, according to the series of causes from one real entity to another, and in such a manner that we never pass over to generalities and abstractions, either in order to conclude anything real from them or to conclude them from anything real; for either of these interrupt the true progress of the intellect. 100. But it must be noted that I do not understand here by series of causes and real entities a series of individual mutable things, but on the series of fixed and eternal things. For it would

be impossible for human weakness to follow up the series of individual mutable things, both on account of their number surpassing all count, and on account of the many circumstances in one and the same thing of which each one may be the cause that it exists or does not. For indeed their existence has no connection with their essence, or (as I have said) it is not an eternal truth. 101. However, there is no need that we should understand their series, for the essences of individual mutable things are not to be drawn from their series or order of existence, which would afford us nothing save their extrinsic denominations, relations, or at the most their circumstances, which are far removed from the inmost essence of things. But this is only to be sought from fixed and eternal things, and from the laws inscribed in those things as in their true codes, according to which all individual things are made and arranged: nay, these individual and mutable things depend so intimately and essentially (so to speak) on these fixed ones that without them they can neither exist nor be conceived. Whence these fixed and eternal things, although they are individual, yet on account of their presence everywhere and their widespread power, will be to us like generalities or kinds of definitions of individual mutable things, and the proximate causes of all things.

102. But although this be so, there seems to be no small difficulty to surmount in order that we may arrive at the knowledge of the individual things, for to conceive all things simultaneously is a thing far beyond the power of human understanding. But the order, so that one thing may be understood before another, as we said, must not be sought from their series of existence, nor even from eternal things; for with these things all are simultaneous in nature. Whence other aids must necessarily be sought beside those which we employed to understand eternal things and their laws: however, this is not the place to treat of them, nor is it necessary until we have acquired a sufficient knowledge of eternal things and their infallible laws, and until the nature of our senses has become known to us.

103. Before we proceed to inquire into the knowledge of individual things, there will be time for us to treat on those aids all of which tend to enable us to know how to use our senses, and to make experiments under certain rules and in

a certain order which suffice for the determination of the thing into which we are inquiring, so that we may determine from them according to what laws of eternal things that thing was made, and so that its inmost nature may become known to us, as I shall show in its place. Here, to return to my purpose, I shall endeavour only to treat of those things which seem necessary to enable us to attain to knowledge of eternal things, and form definitions of them according to the conditions above mentioned.

104. To do this it must be recalled to mind what we said above, namely, that when the mind pays attention to any thought in order to examine it, and deduces in good order from it whatever is to be deduced, if it is false, it detects the falsity; but if it is true, then it proceeds happily without any interruption to deduce true things from it—this, I say, is required for what we want, for from a want of basis our thoughts may be brought to a close. 105. If, therefore, we wish to investigate the first thing of all, there must necessarily be some basis which directs our thoughts towards it. Again, inasmuch as method is reflective knowledge, this basis which must direct our thoughts can be nothing else than the knowledge of that which constitutes the form of truth and the knowledge of the understanding and its properties and forces. When this is acquired we shall have a basis from which we may deduce our thoughts and the way in which the understanding, according to its capacity, can arrive at a knowledge of eternal things, having regard by the way for the power of the understanding.

XV. On the Power of the Understanding and its Properties

106. If, as I showed in the first part, it appertains to the nature of thought to form ideas, it must now be inquired what we understand by the forces and power of the understanding. For as the principal part of our method is to understand best the forces and nature of the understanding, we are necessarily obliged (by that which I dealt with in the second part of the method) to deduce these things from the definition of thought and the understanding. 107. But thus far we have no rules for finding definitions, and as we cannot state these without a knowledge of nature or a

definition of the understanding and its power, hence it follows either that the definition of the understanding must be clear of itself or that we cannot understand anything. But this is not clear of itself. However, inasmuch as its properties, like all things we have from the understanding, cannot be clearly and distinctly understood unless its nature is previously known, the definition of the understanding becomes clear if we regard its properties which we understand clearly and distinctly. Let us therefore enumerate the properties of the understanding and append them, and begin to discuss the instruments innate in us.[1]

108. The *properties of the understanding* which I have principally noted and which I clearly understand are these—

I. That it involves certainty, that is, that it knows things to exist formally just as they are contained in it objectively.

II. That it perceives certain things or forms certain ideas absolutely, and certain ones from others. Namely, it forms absolutely an idea of quantity, and has no regard for other thoughts; but it only forms ideas of motion after having considered the idea of quantity.

III. The ideas it forms absolutely express infinity; but determinate ideas are formed from others. For the idea of quantity, if the understanding perceives it by means of a cause, then it determines the quantity, as when it perceives a body to be formed from the motion of a plane, a plane from the motion of a line, a line from the motion of a point: these perceptions do not serve for the understanding but only for the determination of a quantity. This is clear from the fact that we conceive them to be formed, so to speak, from motion, yet this motion is not perceived unless quantity is perceived; and we can prolong the motion in order to form a line of infinite length, which we could do in no wise if we did not have the idea of infinite quantity.

IV. It forms positive ideas rather than negative ones.

V. It perceives things not so much under the form of duration as under a certain species of eternity, or rather in order to perceive things it regards neither their number nor duration; but when it imagines things it perceives them determined in a certain number and in duration and quantity.

VI. Ideas which we form clear and distinct seem to follow from the mere necessity of our nature in such a manner that

[1] See above, § 29, etc.

they seem to depend absolutely on our power; but the contrary is the case with confused ideas. They are often formed in us against our will.

VII. The ideas of things which the intellect forms from their ideas can be determined in many modes by the mind: as for determining, *e.g.*, the plane of an ellipse it feigns a pencil fixed to a cord to be moved around two centres, or it conceives an infinite number of points always having the same relation to a given straight line, or a cone cut in an oblique plane so that the angle of inclination is greater than the angle at the vertex of the cone, or in infinite other ways.

VIII. The more perfection of any object ideas express, the more perfect they are. For we do not admire the architect who planned a chapel so much as the architect who planned some great temple.

109. The remaining things which are referred to thought, such as love, pleasure, etc., I shall not stop to consider, for they have nothing to do with what we are now dealing with, nor can they be perceived unless the understanding is also perceived. For when perception is removed, all these vanish with it.

110. False or fictitious ideas have nothing positive (as we have abundantly shown) through which they may be called false or fictitious; but only from the want of knowledge are they so called. Therefore false and fictitious ideas, in so far as they are such, can teach us nothing of the essence of thought; but this must be sought from the positive properties just mentioned, that is, we must choose something common from which these properties necessarily follow, or which when granted, infers these properties, and which when removed, removes also these properties.

The remainder of this Treatise is wanting

INDEX

The letters after the figures denote the four quarters of the page, a the first, b the second, etc. ; the foot is indicated by e.

Ambition, 138c.
Anger, definition of, 137b.
Attribute, 3c, d.

Benefits, caution in refusing, 188d–189.
Benevolence, definition of, 137b.
Bible, imperfections of, ixe–x.
Blessedness, 217c, 218c, 219e ; nature of, 223e–224.
Body, the human, 52b–53.

Cause, 2d ; definition of, 84c ; final causes denied, 31a–33. See God, the only free cause.
Christ's teaching, universality of, xb ; C. the wisdom of God, xib.
Compassion, definition of, 133c.
Concord, things that promote, 195a ; need for c., 193e.
Consternation, definition of, 138a.
Contempt, 120a ; definition of, 130a.
Contingent, definition of, 26c ; things, 71e–72, 144c.
Conventions, relativity of, viiia.
Courage, species of, 126d.
Cowardice, definition of, 137d.
Creation, mode of, could not have been otherwise, 26a–29. See God the cause of all things.
Cruelty, definition of, 137c.

Daring, definition of, 137d.
Death, fear of, how overcome, 220d–221 ; f. of d. does not influence the wise, 187b ; nature of d., 170c ; d. an alien thing, 92d.
Definition, conditions of, 258a–259.
Dejection, 178e–179 ; related to envy, 180a.
Denunciation of others, causes of, 208a ; d. of sin deprecated, 193–4.
Derision, definition of, 131b.
Descartes, 200e–202.
Desire arising from reason, 183d, 185b, 186a ; d. for what seems good, 156b ; nature of d. or appetite, 128a ; species of d., 136–139.

Desires, conflict of, 152e–154 ; nature of the d., 123d–124 ; when d. become passions, 204a.
Despair, definition of, 131e ; nature of d., 131e–132.
Disparagement, nature of, 133a.
Divine purpose, no, 30c.
Doubt, nature of, 252d–253.
Dreams, 247 note 1.
Duration, definition of, 38a.

Emotion, definition of, 84e–85 ; 139e–140.
Emotions from many causes, 206b ; accord with the individual disposition or essence, 124d–125 ; how evil e. are overcome, 207b–209 ; harmful e., 206c–207 ; origin and nature of e., 83–140 ; e. and passions, 203a, 218c ; power of mind over e., 205a, 211d–212 ; e. arising from reason, 205c ; strength of the e., 141–197 ; understanding the e., 203e–2, 204, 205a, 207a.
Emulation, definition of, 136d.
Envy, 101c ; definition of, 133b ; e. natural to man, 121d ; nature of e., 122c.
Essence, definition of, 37c.
Eternal things, xviiib.
"Eternitatis, sub specie". See Eternity, under species of.
Eternity, definition of, 2b ; "under species of e.," 213d, 216c, d,e. See Time.
Evil, knowledge of, inadequate, 185d–186.
Excommunication (Jewish), viiie–ix.

Falsity, nature of, 145d–146.
Fame, love of, 228b.
Family training, influence of, 134b.
Fatalism, xviib.
Fate, God and, 29b.
Fear, accidental causes of, 117b ; f. arises from weakness of mind, 194b, 197c ; definition of f., 131c ; f. of men, 193b ; doing good under compulsion of, 184e–185.
Fiction. See Ideas, fictitious.
Flattery, 195a.
Force, where powerless, 193b.
Free man in society, the, 190c.
Free will denied, 74e–75, 78c, 88d–90.

Freedom, human (or mental), 199–224; false idea of, 223b, 224c; f. is life according to dictates of reason, 187b, c; moral freedom, xviid.

Glory, love of, 138c.
God, 1–36; acts according to His own laws, 15d–18; does not act with evil in view, 30c; attributes of G. eternal, 18c–20; attributes and modes of, 41b; things for which G. cannot be blamed, xiiie–xiv; G. cause of all things, 17d–18c, 21b–29; G. the only free cause, 16a; G. not corporeal, 11d; decrees of G., 27c–28; definition of G., 1e; all things dependent on G., 220b; G. the essence of all things, 213d–214; essence of G. infinite and eternal, 72e–74; existence of G. proved from nature of thought, 252a and note 2; ex. of G. self-evident, 243a and notes 2 and 3; G. necessarily existent, 4a, 7e–10; no G. but G., 11b; nothing exists without G., 11c; immanence of G., 18b; G. immutable, 19b, 27a–29; impassibility of G., 210b; intellect of G., 16b–18; knowledge of G., 214d–215d, 217b; k. of G. the greatest good, 159d–160; k. of G. necessary to man, 192a (See Mind, essence of); love of G. (subj. gen.) 219c; love of G. (obj. gen.), 209e–211, 221c; intellectual 1. of G., 217e–218, 219a–220; G. loves Himself, 219a; G. and the human mind, 85c–86; mind of G., xc; G. equivalent to Nature, viic, xc; G. non-moral, xixb; omnipotence of G., 16d–17, 29c, 39d–40; G. perfect, 27a–29; G. a thinking being, 40d; thought an attribute of G., 38e–39; will of God, xixd–xx; w. of G. not free, 27b–28; w. of G. not like human will, 17b.
Good agrees with our nature, 161a; desire of future g., 186c; f. g. neglected because of present pleasure, 184c; the greatest g. common to all, 165b; the greatest g. is knowledge of God, 159d–160, 165b; nature of the supreme g., 230b; search for the s. g., 227b–231.
Good and bad, nature of, 169d–170, 171a; g. and b. relative, 143c–144, 160b, d, 230b.
Good and evil, knowledge of, 149c, 152c; relativity of g. and e., xiiic, xvb, 111b.
Gratitude, 176c; definition of, 137b; nature of g., 189c.
Grief, 172b.

Happiness, ixb (Spinoza); definition of, xvd; h. as reward, xvic; no right to h., xivc; search for h., 227–228.
Hatred, 100d–101, 110d–111, 111e–113, 114a; cause of h., 162c–163; h. conquered by love, 174c; definition of h., 130d; h. never good, 173b. See Love and hatred.

Health, relation of, to pleasure, 183a.
Hell, fear of, no true motive for virtue, 223c.
Hope, accidental causes of, 117b; definition of h., 131c.
Humility, 134e–135; definition of h., 133d; excessive h., 135c; when h. is not a virtue, 177d.

Idea, definition of, 37d–38; the doubtful i., 252–3; the false i., 248–252.
Ideas, 40c–44, 63c–66; adequate i., 85c–86, 90a; fictitious i., 241e–248; formation of i., 262b–263; i, and images, 77a; true i., 235d–237; i. true and false, 69e–71, 76c–77.
Images, mental, 67b–68, 97d–99.
Imagination, inferior part played by, 222d, 244 note 1, 245 note 1, 254b, 255a; i, and intellect, difference between, 255d–256; nature of i., 150a; power of i., 149e–152.
Immortality, xviie–xviii; hope of i. not necessary to virtue, 223a; i. of the mind, 220d–223. See Mind, essence of, eternal.
Indignation, definition of, 132d.
Intellect, nature of the, 24c–25; necessity of perfecting the i., 192a; power of the i., 199–224.
Intelligible, necessity of the, 231a.
Intolerance, xii note 1.

Jealousy, 108d–109.
Judgments, divine, 31a–32.

Knowing, right method of, 237e–241.
Knowledge, means of, 259c–261; nature of k., 68c–69; "he who increaseth k. increaseth sorrow," 154a. See Perception, Understanding.

Laughter, 174d.
Love, excessive, 172c; passing into hatred, 194d; 1. and hated, 95a–118.

Man, essence of, 44c–46; m. part of nature, 107c; 147b–148; natural rights of m., 167d–169; m. a social animal, 164c–165.
"Many men, many minds," 35a–d.
Matrimony, when in harmony with reason, 194e–195.
Memory, 55e–56; definition of m., 254d; m. and forgetfulness, 253e–256.
Mental images, 149e–150; sources of mental satisfaction, 215c, 217e–218, 219d.
Merriment and melancholy contrasted, 171c.

Index

Mind and body, 47b–48, 53e–63, 86d–89 ; 93d–95 ; interactions of, 148d–149, 202c, 221d–222 ; m. dependent on body, 196a, 213c ; how to remove disturbances of m., 202e–203 ; essence of m. is knowledge of God, 166a ; eternal essence of m., 213e–214, 218e, 220a–223 ; e.e. of m. consists of knowledge, 220d–221d ; human m. acts and suffers, 85c–86 ; h.m. part of intellect of God, 46b ; nature and origin of m., 37–81 ; perturbations of m., xiic ; how to avoid p. of m., 229c ; weakness of m., 175a, 178e–179.

Mode, definition of, 1d ; modes infinite, 21c–22.

Money, desire for, 196d, 208d ; when permissible, 230a, 232a.

Natural science, xxd–xxl.

Nature, laws of, xiiia, man part of n., 192c.

Ovid, 154a.

Pain, definition of, 128e–129.

Pantheism, viic–viii, xixc, 11a, c, 18b. See God.

Partiality, 175d ; definition of, 133a.

Passion, force of, 148b ; passions and actions compared, 191d ; control of the p. 124c ; nature of the p., 123b. See Emotions.

Passivity, nature of, 146d.

Perception, modes of, 232d–235.

Perfect and imperfect, meaning of, 141–144.

Perfection, 222b.

Philosophy of Spinoza, vii–xxii.

Pineal gland, 199e–201.

Pity, 100b, 103a ; definition of, 132c ; p. opposed to reason, 175e–176 ; p. may be useless, 175e–176.

Pleasure, definition of, 128e ; p. good, 171b ; p. and pain, 93b, 95d–127 ; pursuit of p., 227e–229 ; varying views of, 196e–197.

Pleasures and pains, imaginary, 118d–119.

Politeness, definition of, 138c.

Poverty, relief of, duty of society, 194c.

Praise, 120e–121.

Pride, 102b, 103c, 178e–179 ; definition of, 134c ; p. and envy related, 179e–180 ; p., how fostered, 175d ; nature of pride, 134c–135, 179c–180.

Punishment from sense of duty, 177a.

Querulousness, 208b.

Reason, dictates of, 154d–156 ; functions of r., xvc ; guidance of r. leads to choice of greater good, 186a ; following the g. of r., 163c–165, 165d, 175b, 175e–176 ; living according to r., 158b, e–159, 193a, c ; mind under the guidance of r., 184a, 185b.

Regret, definition of, 136b.

Repentance, definition of, 133e–134 ; when not a virtue, 178b.

Reward of virtue, xvc.

Riches, pursuit of, 229b.

Sadness, definition of, 128e–129.

Salvation difficult, 224d.

Schadenfreude, 100d–101.

Self-complacency, 177b ; definition of, 133d.

Self-control. See Emotions, power of mind over.

Self-depreciation, 195b.

Self-preservation, xive–xiv, 91a–92 ; desire of s., 157b, 158c.

Shame, definition of, 135e ; nature of s., 136a, 181b.

Silence, benefit of, 88c.

Society (or State), foundations of, 168b.

Society of others, effects of, 192c–193, 193e–194.

" Sub specie eternitatis," 72c.

Substance, 3–15 ; s. with attributes, 7c, 10b ; definition of s., 1c ; God the only s., 11a ; s. indivisible, 10d ; s. i..finite, 4d–5.

Suicide, external causes of, 156e–157.

Sympathy, 99d–100, 102c–103.

Teleology. See Causes, final.

Time and eternity, 214b, 216b, 217b, 218e.

Timidity, definition of, 137d.

Titillation, 171e.

Toleration recommended, xiia.

Understanding, on the correction of the, 227–263 ; desire to understand, 158e–159 ; instruments of u., 235d–237 ; power of the u., 261d–263. See Ideas, Images, Intellect, Knowing, Knowledge, Mental, Mind.

Universe, man's place in the, viiic ; u. infinite, xxid.

Useful, definition of the, 169c.

Vainglory, 180d–181.

Veneration, nature of, 122e–123.

Vengeance, definition of, 137c.

Vices, 138e–139.

Virtue, nature of, 156c.

Weakness, moral, 167a.

Will, nature of, 25b–26 ; w. and intellect identified, 76b, 77d–81 ; freedom of w. denied, 64c. See Free will.

Wonder, definition of ,129c.

EVERYMAN'S LIBRARY

A Selected List, arranged under Authors

Anthologies, composite works, etc., are given at the end of the list.

Addison's Spectator, 164–7
Aeschylus' Plays, 62
Aesop's and Other Fables, 657
Ainsworth's Tower of London, 400
   ,,   Old St Paul's, 522
   ,,   Windsor Castle, 709
   ,,   Rookwood, 870
À Kempis's Imitation of Christ, 484
Alcott's Little Women, and Good Wives, 248
   ,,   Little Men, 512
Andersen's Fairy Tales, 4
Anglo-Saxon Chronicle, 624
Aquinas's (Thomas), Selected Writings, 953
Aristophanes' Acharnians, etc., 344
   ,,   Frogs, etc., 516
Aristotle's Ethics, 547
   ,,   Politics, 605
   ,,   Poetics, and Demetrius on Style, etc., 901
   ,,   Metaphysics, 1000
Arnold's (Matthew) Essays, 115
   ,,   Poems, 334
Augustine's (St) Confessions, 200
   ,,   City of God, 982–3
Austen's (Jane) Sense and Sensibility, 21
   ,,   Pride and Prejudice, 22
   ,,   Mansfield Park, 23
   ,,   Emma, 24
   ,,   Northanger Abbey, and Persuasion, 25

Bacon's Essays, 10
   ,,   Advancement of Learning, 719
Bagehot's Literary Studies, 520–1
Balzac's Wild Ass's Skin, 26
   ,,   Eugénie Grandet, 169
   ,,   Old Goriot, 170
   ,,   Cat and Racket, etc., 349
   ,,   Ursule Mirouët, 733
Barbusse's Under Fire, 798
Baxter's Autobiography, 868
Beaumont and Fletcher's Plays, 506
Bede's Ecclesiastical History, 479
Belloc's Stories, Essays, and Poems, 948
Berkeley's (Bishop) New Theory of Vision, 483
Blackmore's Lorna Doone, 304
Blake's Poems and Prophecies, 792
Bligh's A Book of the 'Bounty,' 950
Boccaccio's Decameron, 845–6
Borrow's Wild Wales, 49
   ,,   Lavengro, 119
   ,,   Romany Rye, 120
   ,,   Bible in Spain, 151
Boswell's Life of Johnson, 1–2
   ,,   Tour to the Hebrides, 387
Boyle's The Sceptical Chymist, 559
Brontë's (A.) Tenant of Wildfell Hall, 685
Brontë's (C.) Jane Eyre, 287
   ,,   Shirley, 288
   ,,   Villette, 351
   ,,   The Professor, 417
Brontë's (E.) Wuthering Heights, 243

Browne's (Frances) Granny's Wonderful Chair, 112
Browne's (Thos.) Religio Medici, etc., 92
Browning's Poems, 1833–44, 41–2
   ,,   1871–90, 964
Bulfinch's The Age of Fable, 472
Bunyan's Pilgrim's Progress, 204
   ,,   Grace Abounding, and Mr Badman, 815
Burke's American Speeches, etc., 340
   ,,   Reflections on the French Revolution, etc., 460
Burney's Evelina. 352
Burns's Poems and Songs, 94
Butler's (Samuel) Erewhon and Erewhon Revisited, 881
   ,,   The Way of All Flesh, 895
Byron's Complete Poetical and Dramatic Works, 486–8
   ,,   Letters, 931

Caesar's War Commentaries, 702
Canton's Child's Book of Saints, 61
   ,,   Invisible Playmate, etc., 566
Carlyle's French Revolution, 31–2
   ,,   Sartor Resartus, 278
   ,,   Past and Present, 608
   ,,   Essays, 703–4
   ,,   Reminiscences, 875
Carroll's (Lewis) Alice in Wonderland, etc., 836
Castiglione's The Courtier, 807
Cellini's Autobiography, 51
Cervantes's Don Quixote, 385–6
Chaucer's Canterbury Tales, 307
   ,,   Troilus and Criseyde, 992
Chesterfield's Letters to his Son, 823
Chesterton's (C.) A History of the United States, 965
Chrétien de Troyes's Arthurian Romances, 698
Cicero's Offiens, Essays, and Letters, 345
Cobbett's Rural Rides, 638–9
Coleridge's Biographia Literaria, 11
   ,,   Golden Book of Poetry, 43
   ,,   Lectures on Shakespeare, 162
Collins's Woman in White, 464
   ,,   The Moonstone, 979
Collodi's Pinocchio, 538
Converse's Long Will, 328
   ,,   House of Prayer, 923
Cook's (Captain) Voyages, 99
Cooper's Last of the Mohicans, 79
   ,,   The Prairie, 172
Cowper's Letters, 774
   ,,   Poems, 872
Crèvecœur's Letters from an American Farmer, 640

Dante's Divine Comedy, 308
Darwin's Origin of Species, 811
   ,,   Voyage of the 'Beagle,' 104
Dasent's Story of Burnt Njal, 558

1

Defoe's Robinson Crusoe, 59
   ,,   Captain Singleton, 74
   ,,   Journal of Plague, 289
   ,,   Moll Flanders, 837
De Joinville's Memoirs of the Crusades, 333
De Quincey's Opium-Eater, 223
De Rojas's Celestina, 100
Demosthenes' Crown and other orations, 546
Descartes' Discourse on Method, 570
Dickens's Barnaby Rudge, 76
   ,,   Tale of Two Cities, 102
   ,,   Old Curiosity Shop, 173
   ,,   Oliver Twist, 233
   ,,   Great Expectations, 234
   ,,   Pickwick Papers, 235
   ,,   Bleak House, 236
   ,,   Nicholas Nickleby, 238
   ,,   Christmas Books, 239
   ,,   Dombey and Son, 240
   ,,   Martin Chuzzlewit, 241
   ,,   David Copperfield, 242
   ,,   Hard Times, 292
   ,,   Little Dorrit, 293
   ,,   Our Mutual Friend, 294
Disraeli's Coningsby, 535
Donne's Poems, 867
Dostoevsky's Crime and Punishment, 501
   ,,   Letters from the Underworld, 654
   ,,   The Idiot, 682
   ,,   Poor Folk, and The Gambler, 711
   ,,   The Brothers Karamazov, 802-3
   ,,   The Possessed, 861-2
Dryden's Dramatic Essays, 568
   ,,   Poems, 910
Dumas's The Three Musketeers, 81
   ,,   The Black Tulip, 174
   ,,   Marguerite de Valois, 326
   ,,   Count of Monte Cristo, 393-4
Du Maurier's Trilby, 863

Eckermann's Conversations with Goethe, 851
Edgeworth's Castle Rackrent, etc., 410
Eliot's Adam Bede, 27
   ,,   Silas Marner, 121
   ,,   Romola, 231
   ,,   Mill on the Floss, 325
   ,,   Middlemarch, 854-5
Emerson's Essays, 12
   ,,   Representative Men, 279
Epictetus' Moral Discourses, 404
Euclid's Elements, 891
Euripides' Plays, 63, 271
Everyman and Medieval Miracle Plays, 381

Faraday's Experimental Researches in Electricity, 576
Fielding's Tom Jones, 355-6
   ,,   Joseph Andrews, 467
   ,,   Amelia, 852-3
   ,,   Jonathan Wild, and the Journal of a Voyage to Lisbon, 877
Flaubert's Madame Bovary, 808
   ,,   Salammbô, 869
   ,,   Sentimental Education, 969
Fletcher's (Beaumont and) Selected Plays, 506
Forster's Life of Dickens, 781-2
Fox's (Charles James) Selected Speeches, 759
Fox's (George) Journal, 754

Francis' (St) The Little Flowers, etc., 485
Franklin's (B.) Autobiography, 316

Gaskell's Cranford, 83
   ,,   Life of Charlotte Brontë, 318
Gibbon's Roman Empire, 434-6, 474-6
Gilchrist's Life of Blake, 971
Gilfillan's Literary Portraits, 348
Gleig's Life of Wellington, 341
Gogol's Dead Souls, 726
   ,,   Taras Bulba, 740
Goldsmith's Vicar of Wakefield, 295
   ,,   Poems and Plays, 415
Goncharov's Oblomov, 878
Gorky's Through Russia, 741
Gray's Poems and Letters, 628
Green's Short History of the English People, 727-8
Grimms' Fairy Tales, 56
Grossmith's Diary of a Nobody, 963

Hamilton's The Federalist, 519
Harvey's Circulation of Blood, 262
Hawthorne's Wonder Book, 5
   ,,   The Scarlet Letter, 122
   ,,   House of Seven Gables, 176
Hazlitt's Characters of Shakespear's Plays, 65
   ,,   Table Talk, 321
   ,,   Lectures, 411
   ,,   Spirit of the Age, etc., 459
Heimskringla: The Norse King Sagas, 847
Heine's Prose and Poetry, 911
Herodotus, 405-6
Hobbes's Leviathan, 691
Holinshed's Chronicle, 800
Holmes's (O. W.) Autocrat, 66
Homer's Iliad, 453
   ,,   Odyssey, 454
Horace's Complete Poetical Works, 515
Houghton's Life and Letters of Keats, 801
Howard's (E.) Rattlin the Reefer, 857
Howard's (John) State of the Prisons, 835
Hudson's (W. H.) Far Away and Long Ago, 956
Hughes's (Thomas) Tom Brown's School-days, 58
Hugo's (Victor) Les Misérables, 363-4
   ,,   Notre Dame, 422
   ,,   Toilers of the Sea, 509
Hume's Treatise of Human Nature, etc., 548-9
Hunt's (Leigh) Selected Essays, 829

Ibsen's The Doll's House, etc., 494
   ,,   Enemy of the People, Ghosts, etc., 552
   ,,   Pretenders, Pillars of Society, Rosmersholm, 659
   ,,   Peer Gynt, 747
Irving's Life of Mahomet, 513

James (Wm) Selections from, 739
Jefferies's (Richard) After London, and Amaryllis at the Fair, 951
   ,,   Bevis, 850
Jerome's (Jerome K.) Three Men in a Boat, 118
Johnson's (Dr) Lives of the Poets, 770-1
   ,,   The Rambler, 994
Jonson's (Ben) Plays, 489-90

Kant's Critique of Pure Reason, 909
Keats's Poems, 101

Kinglake's Eothen, 337
Kingsley's (Chas.) Westward Ho!, 20
       ,,   Water Babies, and Glaucus, 277
       ,,   Hereward the Wake, 296
       ,,   Poems, 793
Koran, 380

La Fontaine's Fables, 991
Lamb's Tales from Shakespeare, 8
  ,, Essays of Elia, 14
  ,, Letters, 342–3
Landor's Imaginary Conversations and Poems, 890
Langland's Piers Plowman, 571
Law's Serious Call, 91
Lear's (Edward) A Book of Nonsense, 806
Leibniz's Philosophical Writings, 905
Lessing's Laocoön, etc., 843
Lewes's Life of Goethe, 269
Lincoln's Speeches, etc., 206
Locke's Civil Government, 751
Lockhart's Life of Napoleon, 3
Longfellow's Poems, 382
Lönnrott's Kalevala, 259–60
Loti's Iceland Fisherman, 920
Lover's Handy Andy, 178
Lucretius' On the Nature of Things, 750
Lützow's History of Bohemia, 432
Lynd's Essays on Life and Literature, 990
Lytton's Last Days of Pompeii, 80

Macaulay's England, 34–7
  ,, Essays, 225–6
Machiavelli's Prince, 280
Maine's Ancient Law, 734
Malory's Le Morte D'Arthur, 45–6
Malthus on the Principle of Population, 692–3
Marie de France, Lays of, 557
Marlowe's Plays and Poems, 383
Marryat's Mr Midshipman Easy, 82
  ,, Masterman Ready, 160
  ,, Children of New Forest, 247
Marx's Capital, 848–9
Maupassant's Short Stories, 907
Melville's Moby Dick, 179
  ,, Typee, 180
Mickiewicz's Pan Tadeusz, 842
Mill's Utilitarianism, Liberty, Representative Government, 482
  ,, Subjection of Women, 825
Milton's Poems, 384
  ,, Prose Writings, 795
Mitford's Our Village, 927
Molière's Comedies, 830–1
Montaigne's Essays, 440–2
More's Utopia, and Dialogue of Comfort against Tribulation, 461
Motley's Dutch Republic, 86–8
Mulock's John Halifax, 123

Napoleon's Letters, 995
Newman's Apologia Pro Vita Sua, 636
  ,, On the Scope and Nature of University Education, etc., 723
Nietzsche's Thus Spake Zarathustra, 892

Ovid: Selected Works, 955
Owen's (Robert) A New View of Society, etc., 799

Paine's Rights of Man, 718

Palgrave's Golden Treasury, 96
Pascal's Pensées, 874
Paston Letters, 752–3
Pater's Marius the Epicurean, 903
Pearson's The Grammar of Science, 939
Pepys's Diary, 53–5
Plato's Republic, 64
  ,, Dialogues, 456
Plutarch's Lives, 407–9
Poe's Tales of Mystery and Imagination, 336
  ,, Poems and Essays, 791
Polo's (Marco) Travels, 306
Pope's Collected Poems, 760
Prescott's Conquest of Mexico, 397–8

Quiller-Couch's Hetty Wesley, 864
  ,, Cambridge Lectures, 974

Rabelais's Gargantua and Pantagruel, 826–827
Radcliffe's (Mrs Ann) The Mysteries of Udolpho, 865–6
Ramayana and Mahabharata, 403
Reade's The Cloister and the Hearth, 29
Renan's Life of Jesus, 805
Ricardo's Principles of Political Economy and Taxation, 590
Richardson's Pamela, 683–4
  ,, Clarissa, 882–5
Robinson's (Wade) Sermons, 637
Rossetti's Poems, 627
Rousseau's Émile, 518
  ,, Social Contract and other Essays, 660
  ,, Confessions, 859–60
Ruskin's Seven Lamps of Architecture, 207
  ,, Sesame and Lilies, 219

Scott's (Sir W.) Ivanhoe, 16
  ,, Bride of Lammermoor, 129
  ,, Guy Mannering, 133
  ,, Heart of Midlothian, 134
  ,, Kenilworth, 135
  ,, Old Mortality, 137
  ,, Quentin Durward, 140
  ,, Redgauntlet, 141
  ,, Rob Roy, 142
  ,, The Talisman, 144
Sévigné's Selected Letters, 98
Sewell's (Anna) Black Beauty, 748
Shakespeare's Comedies, 153
  ,, Histories, etc., 154
  ,, Tragedies, 155
Shchedrin's Golovlyov Family, 908
Shelley's Poetical Works, 257–8
Shelley's (Mrs) Frankenstein, 616
Sheridan's Plays, 95
Sienkiewicz's Tales, 871
  ,, Quo Vadis?, 970
Smith's Wealth of Nations, 412–13
Smollett's Roderick Random, 790
  ,, The Expedition of Humphry Clinker, 975
Snorre Sturlason's Heimskringla: The Norse King Sagas, 847
Somerville and Ross: Experiences of an Irish R.M., 978
Sophocles' Dramas, 114
Southey's Life of Nelson, 52
Spencer's (Herbert), Essays on Education, 504
Spenser's Faerie Queene, 443–4
  ,, The Shepherd's Calendar, 879

Spinoza's Ethics, etc., 481
Spyri's Heidi, 431
Steele's The Spectator, 164–7
  ,,   The Tatler, 993
Stendhal's Scarlet and Black, 945–6
Sterne's Tristram Shandy, 617
  ,,   Sentimental Journey, and Journal to Eliza, 796
Stevenson's Treasure Island, and Kidnapped, 763
  ,,   Master of Ballantrae, and Weir of Hermiston, 763
  ,,   Virginibus Puerisque, and Familiar Studies of Men and Books, 765
  ,,   An Inland Voyage, Travels with a Donkey, and Silverado Squatters, 766
  ,,   Dr Jekyll and Mr Hyde, The Merry Men, etc., 767
  ,,   Poems, 768
Stow's Survey of London, 589
Stowe's Uncle Tom's Cabin, 371
Swedenborg's The True Christian Religion, 893
Swift's Gulliver's Travels, Unabridged Edition, 60
  ,,   Tale of a Tub, etc., 347
  ,,   Journal to Stella, 757
Swinburne's (A. C.), Poems and Prose, 961
Synge's Plays, 968

Tchekhov's Plays and Stories, 941
Tennyson's Poems, 44, 626
Thackeray's Esmond, 73
  ,,   Vanity Fair, 298
  ,,   Pendennis, 425–6
  ,,   Newcomes, 465–6
  ,,   The Virginians, 507–8
  ,,   English Humorists, and The Four Georges, 610
Thoreau's Walden, 281
Thucydides' Peloponnesian War, 455
Tolstoy's Master and Man, Other Parables and Tales, 469
  ,,   War and Peace, 525–7
  ,,   Anna Karenina, 612–13
Trench's On the Study of Words, and English Past and Present, 788
Trollope's Barchester Towers, 30
  ,,   Framley Parsonage, 181
  ,,   The Warden, 182
  ,,   Dr Throne, 360
  ,,   Small House at Allington, 361
  ,,   Last Chronicles of Barset, 391–2
Trotter's The Bayard of India, 396
Turgenev's Virgin Soil, 528
  ,,   Liza, 677
  ,,   Fathers and Sons, 742
  ,,   Smoke, 988
Twain's (Mark) Tom Sawyer, and Huckleberry Finn, 976
Tytler's Principles of Translation, 168

Verne's (Jules) Twenty Thousand Leagues under the Sea, 319
  ,,   Five Weeks in a Balloon and Around the World in 80 Days, 779
Virgil's Aeneid, 161
  ,,   Eclogues and Georgics, 222
Voltaire's Age of Louis XIV, 780
  ,,   Candide and Other Tales, 936

Wakefield's Letter from Sydney, etc., 828
Walpole's Letters, 775
Walton's Complete Angler, 70
Waterton's Wanderings in South America, 772
Webster and Ford's Selected Plays, 899
Wells's (H. G.) Wheels of Chance, and The Time Machine, 915
White's Selborne, 48
Whitman's Leaves of Grass, 573
Wilde's Plays, Prose Writings, and Poems, 858
Wollstonecraft's Rights of Woman, 825
Woolf's (Virginia) To the Lighthouse, 949
Woolman's Journal, etc., 402
Wordsworth's Poems, 203, 311, 998

Zola's Germinal, 897

Anthologies, Composite Volumes, etc.

A Book of British Ballads, 572
A Century of Essays, an Anthology, 653
A Century of Humorous Verse, 813
American Short Stories of the Nineteenth Century, 840
An Anthology of English Prose: From Bede to Stevenson, 675
Anglo-Saxon Poetry, 794
Chinese Philosophy in Classical Times, 973
English Galaxy of Shorter Poems, 959
English Short Stories, 743
Golden Treasury of Longer Poems, 746
Hindu Scriptures, 944
International Modern Plays, 989
Koran, The, 380
Mabinogion, The, 97
Minor Elizabethan Drama, 491–2
Minor Poets of the 18th Century, 844
Minor Poets of the 17th Century, 873
Mother Goose, 473
New Golden Treasury, 695
New Testament, The, 93
Portuguese Voyages, 986
Prayer Books of King Edward VI, 448
Prelude to Poetry, 789
Restoration Plays, 604
Russian Short Stories, 758
Selections from St Thomas Aquinas, 953
Shorter Novels: Elizabethan, 824
  ,,   Jacobean and Restoration, 841
  ,,   Eighteenth Century, 856
Silver Poets of the 16th Century, 985
Table Talk, 906